The United States in the
Contemporary World, 1945-1962

SOURCES IN AMERICAN HISTORY

GENERAL EDITOR: *George H. Knoles*

Professor of History and Director of
the Institute of American History,
Stanford University

1. PROVINCIAL AMERICA, 1600-1763
   BRADLEY CHAPIN, *University of Buffalo*

2. THE REVOLUTIONARY GENERATION, 1763-1789

3. THE YOUNG REPUBLIC, 1789-1815
   JOHN C. MILLER, *Stanford University*

4. EXPANSION AND REFORM, 1815-1850
   CHARLES M. WILTSE,
   Chief Historian, United States Army Medical History Unit

5. THE UNION IN CRISIS, 1850-1877
   ROBERT W. JOHANNSEN, *University of Illinois*

6. THE NATIONALIZING OF AMERICAN LIFE, 1877-1900
   RAY GINGER, *Brandeis University*

7. THE RESPONSIBILITIES OF POWER, 1900-1929
   GEORGE H. KNOLES, *Stanford University*

8. THE NEW DEAL AT HOME AND ABROAD, 1929-1945
   CLARKE A. CHAMBERS, *University of Minnesota*

9. THE UNITED STATES IN THE CONTEMPORARY WORLD,
   1945-1962
   RICHARD L. WATSON, JR., *Duke University*

The United States in the Contemporary World, 1945-1962

Edited by Richard L. Watson, Jr.

Duke University

$\boxed{Fp}$

The Free Press, New York
Collier-Macmillan Limited, London

Preface

THE FREE PRESS SOURCES IN AMERICAN HISTORY
series reviews the history of the United States from
its beginnings in the seventeenth century to the present. Each of
the nine volumes consists of from 15 to 35 carefully chosen contemporary documents illustrating the major themes—political, economic, social, and cultural—of American history and civilization.
The volume editors, selected for their specialized knowledge of
the periods into which the series is divided, have drawn upon
the rich resources of the American past for the materials to be
included in their respective books. They have ranged over the
principal geographical areas of the United States and have exploited a wide variety of genres—governmental and political
party documents, descriptive and analytical accounts, theoretical
writings, and literary products. History is a seamless web and
one learns about himself and his past by exploring the multi-
various experiences of his forbears and their reflections upon
those experiences.

The editors have kept the student in mind while selecting
the items to be reprinted in each volume. They have not only
chosen significant documents, but they have respected the intentions of the original writers to the extent that the materials are
offered substantially as the authors produced them with a minimum of cutting and editing. We have, therefore, put together
a set of volumes containing a limited number of major documents reproduced *in extenso* rather than a series containing
hundreds of snippets which can suggest, at best, only an impressionistic view of history. To promote thoughtful reading and
discussion of these materials we have introduced each selection
with headnotes containing biographical and bibliographical data.
Moreover, we have included in each headnote three or four suggestions indicating what students should look for in reading the
documents; these do not tell the reader what is in the material,

but they are very useful in directing his attention to the salient points covered. Finally, the editors have added to each note two or three titles of books that might be consulted for further study of the author of the document or of the problem or episode dealt with in the selection.

Each volume contains an extended introductory essay, an interpretive narrative written by the volume editor, which treats the period as a whole and relates the documents to the history under consideration. These essays incorporate both factual and conceptual information obtained from recent historical research; they reflect the new findings of contemporary scholarship.

Professor Richard L. Watson, Jr., in *The United States in the Contemporary World, 1945-1962,* has provided us with a very useful guide to the study of the history of our own day. The historian dealing with contemporary history faces a number of disabilities. For one thing, he is generally too close to the events he describes to be able accurately to sift the important from the insignificant; the old adage that there is nothing so stale as yesterday's headlines carries a sharp lesson for one who essays to write the history of the recent past. For another thing, there is, paradoxically, too much material and not enough material available to the researcher. There is, on the one hand, a veritable mountain of data—newspapers, magazines, radio and TV interviews, pamphlets, news releases, and other matter—that seems to accumulate at a geometrical ratio. Moreover, a spate of memoirs, autobiographies, and journalistic accounts of the shifting scene pours forth, deluging the reading public; the faithful researcher can be swamped by the flood of words. On the other hand, despite this superabundance of information, usually the inside story—often the true story—is confined to letters, reports, and memoranda that do not become available to the historian for years, sometimes decades, after the events transpired. Finally, although one tries to submerge his own predilections and biases, frequently the passions engendered by political campaigns and party battles, as well as basic ideological commitments, prevent the scholar from viewing the contemporary world with unprejudiced eyes.

To be sure, he who studies the present has some advantages over the student who investigates the remote past. He faces no such paucity of materials as confronts the researcher of antiquity. There is, moreover, the sense of immediacy which need not be lost—the "feel" of the situation possessed by the man who was there and saw the events with his own eyes or who talks with the man who was there. Then there are opportunities through interviews to learn what the participants did and what motivated their actions.

Professor Watson has brought the skills of the trained historian to the task of selecting and presenting this volume of documents dealing with recent American history. He has achieved a wise balance in his collection between domestic and foreign affairs, as well as finding room for items that throw light upon our culture as it enters a new age of science and technology. Although he has discussed a wide variety of topics in his introductory essay and has presented an equally varied collection of materials, he has not lost sight of the direction that our national life has taken since 1945; he has guided our steps along that path.

Stanford University   GEORGE HARMON KNOLES

Contents

Preface by George H. Knoles   v

Introduction: Response to the Challenges of the 1950s—
Development of National Power   1

1. The Atomic Bomb and the End of the War   27
   Official Government Reports on the Bombing
   of Hiroshima

2. Philosophical Basis of the Policy of Containment   46
   George F. Kennan's "The Sources of Soviet Conduct"

3. The Marshall Plan for European Recovery   65
   Secretary Marshall's Report to the Senate Committee
   on Foreign Affairs

4. The Principle of Collective Action   81
   NATO as an Instrument of International Peace
   A. The Vandenberg Resolution
   B. From the Text of the North Atlantic Treaty

5. Military Capitalism and Prestige Politics   88
   C. Wright Mills's *The Power Elite*

6. Strategic Controversy over Korea   108
   A. General Douglas MacArthur: "Don't Scuttle the Pacific—
   Communism a Global Enemy"
   B. Testimony of General of the Army Omar N. Bradley,
   Chairman of the Joint Chiefs of Staff

7. Communists in the Army: "No Sense of Decency"   133
   Excerpt from the Army-McCarthy Hearing

8. The Fair Deal at Home and Abroad   144
   Harry S. Truman's State of the Union Message, 1948

9. Opposition from a Conservative Republican   160
   Robert A. Taft's Reply to Truman

10. **Lower Taxes and Reduced Government Spending** 171
Dwight D. Eisenhower's Budget Message of 1954

11. **Spokesman for the Negro Revolution** 181
James Baldwin's "Stranger in the Village"

12. **The Supreme Court Rules on Segregation** 195
Brown v. Board of Education [of Topeka]

13. **United States Prestige Abroad** 205
The U.S. Information Agency Report,
August 29, 1960

14. **Poisoning the World with Pesticides** 216
Rachel L. Carson's *Silent Spring*

15. **Computers and Automation as a Way of Life** 227
Donald N. Michael's *Cybernation: The Silent
Conquest*

16. **The New Frontier** 249
A. John F. Kennedy's Inaugural Address
B. John F. Kennedy's Budget Message of 1962

17. **Ten-Year Prospect in Space Exploration** 270
Staff Report of the Select Committee on Astronautics
and Space Exploration, 1959

18. **The Cuban Missile Crisis and its Resolution** 289
Khrushchev v. Kennedy in the Nuclear Age
A. Statement by Premier Khrushchev
B. The Answer by President Kennedy
C. Text of Address by President to U. S. Editors
D. Text of Kennedy's Address Outlining Cuban Missiles
Situation
E. Stevenson Address

Introduction:
Response to the Challenges of the 1950s
—Development of National Power

"THIS NEW YEAR OF 1945 CAN BE THE GREATEST year of achievement in human history. Nineteen-forty-five can see the final ending of the Nazi-Fascist reign of terror in Europe. Nineteen-hundred-and-forty-five can see the closing in of the forces of retribution about the center of the malignant power of imperialistic Japan. Most important of all— 1945 can and must see the substantial beginning of the organization of world peace." So spoke Franklin Delano Roosevelt in his Annual Message to Congress of January 1945 while German armies were making a final massive effort in the Battle of the Bulge, Russian armies were driving the Germans back along the Eastern Front; American amphibious forces were landing in Luzon and preparing for an attack on Iwo Jima; and B-29s based on Guam were launching increasingly heavy bombardment attacks on the Japanese home islands. Roosevelt himself was preparing, apparently with considerable optimism, for the Yalta conference; and scientists at Los Alamos were almost ready to begin assembling the first atomic bomb.

The overwhelming triumphs of the Allied military forces in 1945 bred a sense of optimism as to the future as preparations were made for the war's end. Experiences drawn from the aftermath of World War I undoubtedly gave the historically minded some grounds for confidence that the same mistakes would not be made twice. At the same time, the historically minded must also have realized that a peace settlement after six years of unlimited warfare on a global scale would involve problems that might prove overwhelming.

1]

Would the people of the United States support a world organization endowed with sufficient powers to preserve the peace? How could wartime devastation be repaired? Would the armed forces be allowed to disband as had been the case following World War I? Could the scientific and technical discoveries of the wartime period be converted to peacetime uses? Could the full employment of the war years be maintained in peacetime? Would the domestic reforms of the New Deal be extended? What would be the effect of the war on the United States as a civilization? Could the wartime alliances be preserved in making the peace? All these questions and others faced the United States in January 1945, but perhaps the most immediate question was how soon would the war be over?

Few probably realized that the United States would in fact remain at war for decades after the Axis was defeated. Few probably sensed the scope of the changes in American society, attitudes, and foreign and domestic policy which would take place in the 1950s. And it was the war that was primarily responsible for the speed and in many instances the characteristics of the transformation. The war made it impossible to divide American policy into neat compartments, one devoted to domestic affairs, another to foreign affairs, and a third to matters of defense. The experiences of the 1950s have demonstrated the unreality of any analysis which tries to keep such activities separate. Military security has from the beginning of the United States been a key factor in determining the ways in which the nation would develop. In the 1950s military insecurity became the decisive factor.

Already there were indications that new techniques of warfare might in the future make the United States a battlefield. The Germans had introduced self-propelling ballistic missiles in May 1944. Jet fighters were making the fastest planes of World War II look slow, and immediately after Franklin D. Roosevelt's death on April 12, 1945, Secretary of War Stimson informed the new president, Harry S. Truman, of the development of the atomic bomb. The rapidly moving events as the war came to a close compelled Truman to make decisions without taking the time carefully to study the situation. At least three of these were to have momentous consequences for the future: whether to throw the prestige of the United States behind a new world organization; whether to use the atomic bomb in the war against Japan; and how to react to the Soviet Union's unwillingness to implement the terms of the Yalta agreements.

Truman's decisive reaction to these difficult questions was to characterize his decision-making throughout his presidency. One of his first presidential acts to give assurances that the San Francisco Conference, planned to organize the United Nations, would meet as scheduled. Equally promptly after he had learned that an atomic bomb had been successfully detonated, be ordered that another be dropped on a military target in Japan [1].* Finally in spite of his admitted goodwill toward Joseph Stalin, he decided to be "tough" in his negotiations with the Soviet Union on the grounds that "Force is the only thing the Russians understand."[1]

These three decisions form the base for the development of American defense policy after World War II. The conversion from isolationism during the war of Arthur H. Vandenberg and his subsequent brilliant championship of the UN symbolized what appears to have been overwhelming support in the United States for a world organization. Between 1946 and 1962 the United Nations was both theoretically and usually in fact an essential ingredient of American policy. At the same time, the UN lacked any visible means of preventing aggression at a time when hostility was rapidly developing between the power blocs revolving around the United States and the Soviet Union, and crises soon arose which seemed to call for more than moral suasion. In 1947, for example, Great Britain's economic weakness forced her to withdraw from the Middle East. Fearful lest the Soviet Union would move into the vacuum left there, Truman announced his "doctrine" which would place the resources of the United States in support of Greece and Turkey. Before the doctrine received senatorial approval, however, Senator Vandenberg saw to it that the relationship between American policy and the UN was made clear, even authorizing "the Security Council or the General Assembly to terminate the American program."[2]

---

*Numerals within square brackets denote the number of the selection cited in this book.

1. Harry S. Truman, *Memoirs: I. Year of Decisions* (Garden City, N.Y.: Doubleday, 1955), p. 412.

2. Arthur H. Vandenberg, Jr., (ed.), *The Private Papers of Senator Vandenberg* (Boston: Houghton, 1952), p. 346.

Making the United Nations an essential feature of foreign policy, however, became only one of the revolutionary steps taken by the United States within a few years after the war. Equally important were steps taken as a result of the reaction of idea men in the State Department to practical situations. In 1946 and 1947, when Russian pressure in the Middle East and against Greece and Turkey led to the Truman Doctrine, George Kennan, one of the leading authorities on Soviet Russia in the Foreign Service, was formulating the philosophical basis for a "policy of containment" in an article entitled "Sources of Soviet Conduct" [2]. At the same time Western Europe faced economic collapse; its governments were tottering, and local Communist parties were preparing to pick up the pieces. By March 1947 the United States had already contributed some $11 billion in UNRRA aid, but these contributions had been primarily for relief rather than permanent reconstruction, and obviously were not preventing increasingly rapid deterioration. On June 5, 1947, Secretary of State Marshall, reflecting the ideas of Dean Acheson, George Kennan, and other members of the State Department's Policy Planning Staff, called for collaborative effort between the United States and European governments for the reconstruction of Europe [3].

Marshall's call for action launched the numerous programs which were designed to promote economic reconstruction and at the same time to prevent the expansion of Communism. Unlike the period of the 1920s when private American dollars were haphazardly used in Europe and elsewhere, the period from 1945 to June 1961 saw three different presidents—two Democrats and one Republican—supported by a bipartisan majority in both Houses of Congress pour almost $85 billion of public funds into all types of foreign aid. Of this sum, more than $64 billion were outright grants. The European Recovery Program, or Marshall plan, financed European recovery through 1951. At this point, and particularly during the Eisenhower administration, the emphasis shifted to "mutual security," a program designed to strengthen the military defenses of friendly nations against aggression from Soviet Russia and her associates. Finally, in a message to Congress in March 1961, President Kennedy called for a shift back to a principal emphasis on long-term economic and social development, especially in "underdeveloped" areas, without, however, discarding military aid.

While American public finance was undergoing a revolutionary change as a result of its foreign aid programs, the implementation of the containment policy from 1947 to 1962 proved equally revolutionary. Following World War I, the United States had become a party to the treaties of the Washington Conference and the Kellogg-Briand Pact. None of these committed the United States to anything if the treaties were broken. After 1947 came a whole series of pacts and treaties: The Truman Doctrine (1947), the North Atlantic Treaty (ratified in 1949), the United States-Japanese Security Treaty and the Tripartite Security Treaty (United States, Australia, and New Zealand) of 1951, the Bogotá Conference (1948) which codified all previous agreements with Latin American countries and set up the Organization of American States, and the Baghdad Pact (1955) involving Iran, Iraq, Turkey, Pakistan. All of these in varying degrees called for some sort of positive action by the United States if parties to the pacts were attacked. Particularly in the North Atlantic Pact, the United States repudiated its historic principle of independent action and bound itself to use its own armed forces if necessary to protect any one of the others against attack. At the same time those responsible for showing up the defense structure againt Communist aggression saw to it that at least in theory the new pacts were in accord with Article 51 of the UN charter which authorized regional pacts for defense purposes [4].

The division of the world into two hostile coalitions, the revolution in both the nature and means of delivery of new weapons, and the responsibilities assumed in the regional pacts led to another major change in American defense policy which in turn had profound effects upon both society and the economy. This change was the transformation of the United States from a nation predominantly concerned with peacetime pursuits, where a uniform was rarely seen except in parades, to one where civilian needs were subordinated to defense, where the profession of a soldier had become respectable, and where it was a rare family that did not have at least one member in uniform.

President Truman took cognizance of the new demands of world policy when he appointed a distinguished advisory commission with Karl Compton of the Massachusetts Institute of Technology as chairman to study problems of national security. Compton reported in June 1947, almost simultaneously with the appearance of Kennan's "Sources of Soviet Conduct," and the trial balloons for the Marshall plan. The Commission pointed out that the essential ingredient in any national security program was a strong, healthy, educated population; that the experiences of the prewar and war years demonstrated the need for a coordinated national intelligence service; that the requirements of national security called for scientific research and development directed by a national science foundation together with a program for industrial mobilization and stockpiling; that the armed forces should consist of a front-line strategic bombing command backed by army, navy, marine, and air forces all reorganized within the framework of a unified command; and that manpower for these forces should be provided by a universal military training program compulsory for all young men at the age of eighteen or upon completion of high school.

These comprehensive recommendations led to continual and sometimes bitter congressional and interservice debate for the next ten years. The issues were numerous, but usually the controversy revolved around two broad questions significant not only for defense policy but for society in general. One of these questions was how to provide military manpower. Historically the United States had relied upon a tiny professional army and the militia or national guard supplemented by volunteers for wartime service. The Civil War had seen experiments in the draft, but not until World War I were the principles worked out for selective service and trained reserves. Immediately after World War I, the armed forces reverted to traditional peacetime status. Selective service was abandoned, and weapons, armament, and men were limited by an economically minded Congress and a pacifist people, although the reserve system remained.

With the outbreak of war in Europe in 1939, a new era in military manpower began. In 1940, for the first time in peacetime, Congress passed a conscription act, taking as a model the Selective Service Act of World War I. Immediately after the war the Selective Service Act was allowed to lapse when hope still persisted for the preservation of wartime friendships. With the increased tension in 1947 which led to the Berlin blockade in the following year, selective service was reinstituted and a brisk debate began as to the best way of providing military manpower for the future.

The presidents from Franklin Roosevelt through Eisenhower recommended universal military service. Their recommendations, however, never received sufficient support in Congress, the opponents of UMT arguing that it would not provide manpower for the present emergency, that it was a symbol of "militarism," and that with modern arms, specialists rather than massed armies were needed. Thus the solution to the manpower problem in the 1950s was a combination of periodic renewals of the Selective Service Act, a strengthening of the reserve system climaxed by the Military Reserves Act of 1955, periodic attempts to streamline the National Guard, particularly by Secretary of Defense McNamara in 1962, and continual efforts to make the profession of a soldier attractive.

Equally significant in symbolizing the growing militarization of the United States was the National Security Act of 1947. The background of this enactment was not simply the recommendations of the Compton Committee. The experiences of the war and the immediate prewar period pointed to the need for a greater degree of coordination among the services and between the services and the civilian branches of the government. The rapidity with which weapon systems were changing obviously called for a permanent status to scientific research; and the growing prestige of the Army Air Forces during the war climaxed by the delivery of the atomic bomb indicated that champions of the airplane would be more successful than after World War I in fighting for equal status in the services' hierarchy.

In any case, by 1946 various proposals had been made to provide for the greater national security of the United States. Although the questions involved were comprehensive, the battle that developed revolved largely around the unification of the armed forces. Efficiency, economy, service rivalries, fear of centralized militarism, effective use of weapons—all these questions and others were raised when a single department of defense, a single chief of staff, and a single service were recommended as a substitute for the two services then in existence. Most Navy men opposed radical change. They contended that unified theater commands and the coordination provided by the Joint Chiefs of Staff during the War had provided sufficient unification. Most Army and Army Air Force leaders, including Marshall, Eisenhower, Arnold, and MacArthur, took the opposite position. They insisted that Joint Chiefs had not provided sufficient coordination, and that the Army Air Forces should no longer be subordinate to the other services.

So bitter did the controversy become that some despaired as to whether a solution could be found. President Truman persisted, however, and Secretary of the Navy Forrestal, although opposing extreme unification proposals, quietly worked for a compromise. The result was the National Security Act of 1947, the most important enactment for military policy since the National Defense Act of 1920. The first part of this act, entitled "Coordination for National Security," created three new institutions. The National Securities Resources Board was to coordinate civil and military mobilization.[3] The Central Intelligence Agency, the famous CIA, was designed to coordinate those activities which aimed at gaining knowledge of enemies or potential enemies and to evaluate such intelligence. Of most importance was the National Security Council designed to advise the President on matters having to do with the integration of foreign and defense policies and consisting of the President, Secretary of State, Secretary of Defense, the Secretaries of the Army, Navy, and the Air Force, the Chairman of the National Security Resources Board, and certain others if designated by the President.[4]

The second section of the Act, that devoted to the National Military Establishment, incorporated the essential compromise which made the Act generally acceptable. This section abolished the cabinet positions of War and Navy by creating a single Department of Defense with subordinate secretaries of the Army, Navy, and Air Force. There was no single chief of staff, but the Air Force, as a service, was given equal status with the other two, and each service had its Chief of Staff. The Joint Chiefs of Staff, created informally in 1941 to meet the needs of

3. This institution never realized its potentialities and was replaced by the Office of Defense Mobilization in 1953 and the Office of Civil and Defense Mobilization in 1959.

4. The amendments of 1949 changed this membership to include the President, Vice President, Secretaries of State and Defense, Chairman of the National Security Resources Board, and certain others if designated.

wartime coordination, was established officially to consist of the three chiefs of staff. A Munitions Board to coordinate matériel production and procurement and a Research and Development Board completed the new defense structure.

The new Act was by no means a complete success. Few missed the anomaly of talking in terms of unification and yet substituting three coequal services for two. Rivalries persisted, and bitter arguments over production of aircraft carriers and long-range bombers, the responsibility for employment and production of air defense and long-range missiles, and the legitimacy of officers in the services speaking out against Defense Department policy marred the vision of service accord. Differences developed in the Joint Chiefs of Staff where agreement became so difficult that perhaps the most important section in an Amendment in 1949 to the National Security Act created the post of chairman of the Joint Chiefs who was to pass on to the President and Secretary of Defense the advice of the Joint Chiefs. The Act had given the Secretary of Defense authority "to eliminate unnecessary duplication . . . in the fields of procurement, supply, transportation, storage, health, and research." Few secretaries, however, wished to rouse the passions which might result from such actions, and not until the administration of Secretary McNamara in the Kennedy administration was the authorization taken very seriously.[5]

Paradoxically, McNamara's effectiveness as Secretary of Defense—even though he was ostensibly, and undoubtedly sincerely, the champion of civilian as opposed to military domination of the Defense establishment—clearly pointed to the problem of the increasing impact of militarism on American society. Writers on military affairs periodically warned of the dangers of this development; C. Wright Mills in his best seller *The Power Elite* provided a sociological analysis of the phenomenon. President Eisenhower in his farewell address warned against "the acquisition of unwarranted influence by the military-industrial complex." Indeed McNamara, former president of the Ford Motor Company, himself symbolized the military-industrial complex, and by making the Department of Defense more monolithic and efficient, he was creating the same kind of power that

5. Congress in 1958 gave the Secretary of Defense further authority to eliminate duplicating of services in the Military Department.

the states'-righters feared in witnessing the growth of Federal power at the expense of the states [5].

More clearly evident, however, was the effect of the budget in promoting the military-industrial complex. It is true that in spite of the relative military security enjoyed by the United States prior to World War II and the antimilitaristic views of its citizens, more Federal monies had almost without exception been annually used to pay for past and future wars than for purely civil functions.[6] Only during the depression of the 1930s did civil expenditures significantly predominate. Prior to the depression of the 1930s, however, Federal peacetime activities were so comparatively slight—being almost entirely restricted to government housekeeping, foreign affairs, and maintaining a token defense establishment—that military expenditures, even though they comprised the largest items in the Federal budget, had little impact on American society. In the 1920s, for example, total annual Federal expenditures were usually around $3 billion, and rarely exceeded 4 percent of the Gross National Product.

Between 1945 and 1962, on the other hand, the importance of Federal activities had tremendously increased. Total Federal expenditures were usually greater than 15 percent of the Gross National Product, and it was obvious that the hundred-billion-dollar budget was not far in the future. Moreover, well over half of the total budget went for items related to the national defense. In 1948, for example—almost $20 billion of a total of $33 billion spent went for past, present, or future wars. In 1960, approximately $62 billion of $77 billion, and in 1961 more than $64 out of $82 billion went for such expenditures. In 1961, it was estimated that the Defense Department alone allocated approximately $21 billion for the purchase of goods; it employed 947,000 civilians with a payroll of about $11 billion. Some corporations were almost entirely dependent for their existence upon government purchases. Military officers made many contracts without competitive bidding. Civilian government officials who made decisions regarding weapons and contracts had made their reputations in the very corporations from which goods were purchased. Leaders in government returned to corporate positions, and retired military officers assumed positions in corporate

6. I am including interest on the national debt and expenditures for veterans in the category "past and future wars."

enterprises still doing business with governmental offices staffed by their former military associates. Congressmen became a part of this military-industrial complex because of their interest in obtaining government contracts for their constituents. Always in the background lurked the specter of a depression if defense spending should stop.

Actually there was little danger that defense spending would stop. Disarmament negotiations, although continual, brought frustratingly negative results. The Soviet Union's explosion of an atomic bomb in 1949 and success in launching "Sputnik" in 1957, together with continual friction throughout the world, were convincing evidence that the United States could not let its defenses down. Indeed even though "Cold War" came to be the term used to describe the period, the fine line between cold war and hot war was shown in the intervention in Korea in 1950, in Viet Nam in 1962, and the imposition of a "quarantine" on offensive arms shipments to Cuba in the same year. The Korean intervention was perhaps the single most important event in American foreign policy in the 1950s because it put so many aspects of that policy to the test. In the first place, President Truman in his decisive action in ordering American forces into battle proved that the United States would enforce its containment policy. Truman's reasoning was obviously that inaction in the face of aggression in Korea would encourage further aggression, as had the Munich capitulations of 1938. The President's decision was apparently encouraged by a paper of the National Security Council, which he had approved in April, about two months before fighting broke out in Korea. This paper, designed to provide a guide to American foreign policy, urged armed resistance to aggressive thrusts, which were expected to occur, but, at the same time, called for simultaneous efforts to prevent any conflict from becoming a global, all-out war. In the second place, the episode demonstrated both the problems and possibilities of carrying out a nation's foreign policy within the framework of the United Nations. In the last analysis, the Korean intervention was sponsored by the UN which instructed its members to support the Korean Republic, and a handful of the member states responded to this directive with at least token forces. In the third place, the Korean episode demonstrated the inadequacy of a strategic concept which relied almost entirely on the atomic bomb. Having put almost complete reliance on the bomb, conventional forces, particularly army units, were pared to the bone. The United States, perhaps prepared to fight an all-out war with nuclear weapons, was not prepared to counter a Soviet strategy which correctly assumed that the United States would not fight an all-out war for seemingly remote trouble spots throughout the world. Finally the Korean War gave the President an opportunity to prove that local military objectives must be subordinated to global political objectives. When General Douglas MacArthur, the UN Commander in Korea, insisted on publicizing his differences with the directive which limited his actions toward Red China, Truman promptly removed him from command in spite of the General's public popularity [6].

Although congressional leadership, both Democrats and Republicans, at first had supported Truman's decision to intervene, Republicans were becoming restive under the cloak of bipartisanship. The removal of MacArthur, the failure of American policy in the Far East symbolized by the triumph of the Chinese Communists in 1949, and the illness of Senator Vandenberg in 1950 followed by his death in 1951, saw the cooperation of the immediate postwar years come to an end. Perhaps, as John Spanier has suggested, American society is so committed to one set of values that it is much more sensitive to the possibilities of internal subversion than a society which takes as a matter of course the existence of diverse ideologies. In any case, the external threat led to a search for those responsible for failure. It was assumed that they were in league with Soviet Russia, and that at least some of them were employed in the State Department. Even the highly respected Robert A. Taft collaborated in attempting to drive Dean Acheson, who had succeeded Marshall as Secretary of State in January, 1949, from the State Department, at least partially on the grounds that he was "soft on Communism."

Unfortunately there were grounds for the fear of Soviet espionage. During the 1930s and the war period when Russia was an ally, Communists did enter government service, and some of these were spies. President Truman, alerted to the possibility that some might still be in sensitive positions, launched an investigation of Federal employees in 1947, and by 1950 it had been completed. As a result of this loyalty check, some 2,000 employees resigned, and 212 were dismissed because of "reasonable doubt" of their loyalty. By this time, however, one espionage ring had succeeded in passing information to the Soviet Union which appreciably speeded up that nation's solution of the problem of the atomic bomb. Actually Dr. Emil Julius Klaus Fuchs, a British atomic scientist born in Germany who had participated in the Los Alamos project, was a Soviet spy. The FBI unraveled Fuchs' activities in 1949, and the British arrested him. Others involved with Fuchs included Julius and Ethel Rosenberg, who were convicted for wartime espionage in 1951 and executed two years later. In short, there was little question that Russia had agents in this country trying to find out military secrets, just as the CIA had agents in Russia with similar aims. No one questioned the need to guard against espionage. The principal questions arose over the extent to which being a Communist or having been a Communist, or having been associated with Communists, or having been a member of an organization suspected of being sympathetic with Communists constituted grounds for judging a person disloyal and thus subject to social and economic ostracism, whether or not the person involved were in a sensitive position where espionage might aid the enemy.

Unfortunately these questions were frequently not answered rationally, and a "Red Scare" developed in the early 1950s which probably had more sinister effects than the one after World War I. Much of this hysteria resulted from the irresponsibility of Joseph R. McCarthy, U.S. Senator from Wisconsin, whose name was soon to connote the character assassination and guilt-by-associationism of the age. McCarthy had defeated young Bob La Follette in a senatorial primary in 1946. He made no headlines until February 1950, when he accused the Secretary of State of knowingly harboring numerous Communists in the State Department. For the next four years, in both the Truman and Eisenhower administrations, he seriously inconvenienced the State Department by forcing its officials to spend much of their time in proving that the Department was not riddled with Communists. Few in public positions were courageous enough to stand up against him, and an anti-Communist fervor infected much of the land as moving-picture studios, television stations, schools, and even universities cleansed themselves of those who might be suspect [7].

McCarthy's star fell in 1954 even faster than it had risen—as the Army and the Senate together finally rallied against him. From then until his death in 1957 he was a virtual nonenity. The aftereffects remained, however, in blasted reputations, suspicion, and a retarded foreign policy. Moreover, McCarthyism provided a rather unfortunate basis for the sometimes more respectable rightist movements of the late 1950s and 1960s. Intellectuals such as William Buckley and Russell Kirk and politicians such as Barry Goldwater beat the anti-Communist drums and preached conservative economics. Less rational, though in many cases eminently respectable, were the members of the John Birch Society, whose anti-Communism was in some instances not far removed from McCarthyism.

Permeating this rightist activity was a tendency to accept nineteenth-century classical economic theory as the only true doctrine and to associate anyone who departed significantly from such theory as subversive. An implication was sometimes drawn from the case of Alger Hiss, who to many typified the intellectual New Dealer, and whose conviction for perjury in 1950 was based on the premise that he had been a Communist spy in the 1930s. The doctrinaire anti-Communist, associating the economic theories of the New Dealers with sympathy to Communism became more embittered toward those theories as the Cold War emphasized over and over again that Communism was the external enemy.

The question is what was the internal enemy. To some it was centralized government; to some it was Keynesian economics; to some it was government spending and high taxes. Those who thought, however, that the New Deal-Fair Deal-New Frontier progression was in some way related to the Communist conspiracy simply did not understand the nature of the Democratic coalition that had developed in the 1920s, had elected Franklin D. Roosevelt four consecutive times, and had continued into the 1950s. Indeed perhaps the most important fact of American political life of the period from 1945 to 1962 was that there were more Democrats than there were Republicans. The Republicans had had to face that unpalatable fact since 1936. Roosevelt and his associates had succeeded in forming a formidable coalition consisting of the traditional bulwark of the Democratic party, the Solid South and the City Machines in the East and the Midwest,

together with organized labor, the Negroes, a substantial number of Midwestern farmers, old-line progressives, and intellectual
reformers.

The coalition was an uneasy one. No philosophical tie held it
together, and except for the intellectuals and old-line progressives, its elements were not particularly interested in idealistic
reform. Labor was interested in legislation that would improve
wages, hours, and working conditions. Farmers were interested
in legislation that would raise their prices, and the Negroes were
interested in action that would promote racial equality. Many
Southern Democrats were restive in this coalition, and it is quite
possible that had it not been for the outbreak of World War II
it would have fallen apart in the late 1930s. Eisenhower, perhaps
mainly because he was a highly respected war hero, was able
to break it in 1952 and 1956.

When Roosevelt died in 1945, the question had immediately
been raised as to whether Truman would continue in the New
Deal tradition. Actually there should have been little uncertainty
on this point. Truman, with one or two minor exceptions, had
given solid support to the legislation of the New Deal from the
time that he had entered the Senate in 1934. Moreover, he was a
professional politician who had made a practice of winning elections in Missouri. He fully understood that the Democratic
majorities would continue only by retaining the support of the
heavily populated urban states of the Northeast, Midwest, and
Far West, and by assuming that most of the Southern states
would refuse to go Republican. Both from an ideological and
from a practical point of view, then, he pitched his program to
the industrial urban and the city dweller.

Thus he announced the Fair Deal: expanded social security,
higher minimum wages, repeal of the Taft-Hartley Act and a
return to the collective bargaining principles of the Wagner Act,
high price supports and storage for farm commodities, extension
of the Trades Agreement Act, extension of the principles of TVA
to other river valleys, more low-cost housing, Federal aid to
education, civil rights for racial, religious, and national minorities, and from the point of view of the economy in general
perhaps the most important of all, the Employment Act of 1946.
This enactment reflected the contrast in attitudes toward the role

of government between the postwar periods of the 1920s and of the 1950s. Although it did not promise "full employment" as some of its advocates wished, it did state clearly that it was the function of the Federal government "to promote maximum employment, production, and purchasing power." Moreover, it set up a Council of Economic Advisors to advise the President on economic matters, and created legislative machinery to translate this advice into legislation [8].

The political appeal of this program is illustrated by Truman's unexpected victory over Governor Thomas E. Dewey in the presidential election of 1948. In Congress, however, it met with only mixed success. Effective social security, minimum wage, and housing acts were passed; the Trades Agreements Act, with some restrictions, was renewed; high price supports and storage were provided farmers, although the Truman-supported Brannan plan failed to gain support; extensive flood control and power projects were approved and the TVA continued, but its organization was not extended to other valleys; the collective-bargaining principles of the Wagner Act were sustained, but the Taft-Hartley Act was not repealed. Moreover, Federal aid to education, medical insurance, and civil-rights legislation were not passed. Indeed, it is clear that the measures which won legislative approval during the Truman administrations were little more than extensions of enactments of the New Deal. Those that failed had never received significant backing by the Roosevelt administrations [9].

The same pattern prevailed in the Eisenhower administrations. In spite of criticism of the Democrats for extravagance and considerable talk about a partnership between the states and the Federal government, Eisenhower supported further moderate extension of social security, the minimum wage, housing, and Trades Agreements Acts, and certainly had no intention of abandoning price supports for farm products or collective bargaining. In addition, he put considerable emphasis on road building, supported grants to states for medical care for the aged, and permitted a tremendous expansion in aid for scientific and medical research and, in the National Defense Education Act of 1958, for higher education in general. In spite of the attempt to identify the New Deal with socialism or communism, the Eisenhower Administration seemed to offer proof that the New

Deal's principal features were firmly incorporated in American society [10].

The domestic issue of perhaps the greatest importance so far as its implications for democracy at home and abroad were concerned, was over the place of the Negro in American society. Undoubtedly one of the most important developments on the international scene in the 1950s was the rebellion of the colonial peoples of Asia and Africa against Western rule. Whether this revolt of the black, brown, and yellow races had any effect on developments in the United States may be questionable. An important feature of the Cold War, however, was the competition between the United States and the Soviet Union to win friends among previously subject peoples; and there is no question that the discrimination which characterized much of American society proved a handicap in this competition. At the same time, the American Negro emerged from the war with greater self-consciousness and with a professional, educated class able to provide leadership. Moreover, Northern politicians were quite aware of the fact that Negro voters would play an increasingly important role in deciding elections. In the northeast and north central states, for example, white population increased about 30 percent between 1920 and 1950, while Negro population almost tripled [11].

In 1946 President Truman appointed a distinguished committee to investigate and make recommendations concerning the rights of minorities in the United States. A year later in its report, "To Secure These Rights," the Committee provided what was perhaps the first important codification of recommendations regarding the rights of such minorities as Mexicans, Jews, Japanese, Pacific Islanders, Roman Catholics, and Negroes. The recommendations concerned voting, residence, education, and legal rights, and provided the basis for proposals by the Truman, Eisenhower, and Kennedy Administrations.

By incorporating the recommendations of the Civil Rights Committee into his legislative program, President Truman was obviously taking the political chance that he would not lose enough support in the South to overbalance what he would gain in the North. His gamble paid off in 1948 in that only four states of the deep South bolted and supported a States' Rights candidate. However, the Southern Democrats firmly entrenched in strategic committee positions and strong in the Senate were able to keep Congress from passing any significant Civil Rights legislation until 1957. Indeed, more often than not, debates over Civil Rights degenerated into debates over the desirability of putting limitations upon the right to filibuster. In 1957, two brilliant Texas political strategists, Speaker of the House Sam Rayburn and Majority Leader Lyndon Johnson, worked out a compromise which sufficiently weakened the Southern bloc to permit the passage of the first significant Civil Rights Act since 1875, and which created machinery designed to protect minority voting rights.

In the meantime, the Federal courts, using the Fourteenth and Fifteenth Amendments as their weapon, were gradually battering down the walls of publicly authorized discrimination. Even before World War II, the process had begun. Led by the National Association for the Advancement of Colored People, the Supreme Court theoretically eliminated the white primary in the Southern states and stipulated that states must provide graduate and professional education for their citizens. Restrictive land covenants, however, still made possible segregated housing, the separate-but-equal principle governed in education and transportation, and there were still numerous ways by which the Negro could be prevented from casting his ballot.

Between 1944 and 1962, the Supreme Court, in several epochal decisions, lowered most of these discriminating barriers. In 1948, for example, Chief Justice Vinson, speaking for a unanimous Court, ruled that although property owners might make private restrictive land covenants, no Federal or state court could enforce them. In 1951, again ruling for a unanimous court, Vinson upheld a petition of a Negro for admission to the law school of the University of Texas. Vinson pointed out that the Negro law school available in Texas was by no objective measurement equal to that of the University of Texas, and furthermore, he argued that the University law school "possesses to a far greater degree those qualities which are incapable of objective measurement but which make for greatness in a law school." In this decision, the Court had not completely closed the "separate but equal" loophole. It was, however, at least theoretically closed when the Court turned to the public schools in 1953, and in one of the century's most important decisions, Earl Warren, now

Chief Justice and again speaking for a unanimous court, ruled that "separate educational facilities are inherently unequal," and that they thus deprive students of the "equal protection of the laws guaranteed by the Fourteenth Amendment." In a later ruling, the Court instructed states to desegregate their schools with "deliberate speed" [12].

These rulings marked the beginning of a long series of legal suits and demonstrations which were still continuing in 1964. The most dramatic episodes in this series were President Eisenhower's use of Federal troops to enforce integration in a high school at Little Rock, Arkansas in 1957, and President Kennedy's even more dramatic battle with the governor of Mississippi to enroll a Negro in the State University in 1962. Throughout the South, however, race relations were marked by picketing, "sit-in" demonstrations in and around theaters, restaurants, and churches, and occasionally by closed schools. In Northern cities, too, the school boards examined their constituencies as they discovered that segregation patterns were by no means sectional, and Negroes began actively to protest their ghettolike existence.

Although Congress approved a Civil Rights Act in 1957 and another in 1960, and executive agencies under Truman, Eisenhower, and Kennedy used their authority to eliminate discriminatory practices, the courts continued to be at the center of the Civil Rights war. Indeed, to those rightist elements who favored the preservation of the *status quo* at all costs, the Supreme Court with Warren at its head seemed almost a subversive institution. Not only did it protect the civil rights of Negroes, but beginning particularly in 1956 its majority began to speak out more strongly to protect the rights of Communists or those suspected of having been Communists.

In 1962, moreover, the Court further disturbed conservative elements in the United States. Historically, a fundamental bulwark for conservative government was the fact that rural constituents usually controlled state legislatures. In spite of provisions in state constitutions for reapportionment in accord with changing population, rural delegates in control of the legislatures have refused to give urban areas additional delegates to represent increased population. Fantastic inequities developed during the twentieth century, but as late as 1946 the Supreme Court refused to get involved in a reapportionment case that was referred to it. Thus it was assumed that such "political thickets," as Justice Frankfurter called them, were out of the Court's bounds. In 1962, however, in a case that involved Tennessee, Justice William Brennan, for a Court majority, cautiously ruled that "arbitrary and capricious" districting might violate the "equal protection of the law" clause of the Constitution, and therefore might be brought before Federal courts. This invitation, cautious though it was, brought immediate action, and before the end of the Court's term urban complainants had instituted suits in about half the states, and had won a good many of them.

The implications of increased representation for urban areas in party politics and governmental policy are considerable. One obvious fact, for example, is that in the period from 1933 to 1962 Democratic Presidents have had serious differences with their Congresses. Indeed, except in extraordinary circumstances these Presidents—Roosevelt, Truman, and Kennedy—were not able to put across their legislative programs. A possible explanation for these differences is that the Democratic Presidents and their programs have usually had far greater popular support from the urban areas of the nation. In the election of Senators and Representatives, however, the districting gave the rural areas a decided advantage, and many more congressmen were elected from predominantly rural constituencies where a great deal of suspicion existed about the New Deal, Fair Deal, and New Frontier.

Probably even more disturbing to those who wished to think that the Court was subversive, however, was another decision in 1962 concerning the separation between church and state. In 1962, the Supreme Court by an 8 to 1 vote ruled that a prayer required in the New York schools was "composed by governmental officials as a part of a governmental program to further religious belief," and thus was contrary to the First Amendment.

The fact that apparently rational people suspected the Supreme Court of subversive action is another indication of the way in which the polarization of the world related almost every function of society to the Cold War. Increasingly as the decade of the 1950s passed, thoughtful people were raising the question as to whether the United States was really winning the Cold War. By the end of the decade it was becoming apparent that in choosing sides, previously subject peoples for some reason were not turning to the United States, the country of the Declaration of Independence. No one could deny that Russian technicians had beaten the United States in putting an artificial satellite in the sky. Serious studies were suggesting that in the development of new weapons the lead which the United States had in airplanes might give way to a Soviet lead in rockets and missiles. Even more shattering to a nation which had grown accustomed to thinking of itself as economically out of reach of any other nation or combination of nations was the fact that in the 1950s the economic growth of many other nations was considerably greater than that of the United States [13].

The argument that developed about comparative rates of economic growth involved to some extent what the future of the United States was as a civilization as well as whether the United States could win out in a long extended battle for the world. The two questions were closely related, and became issues as the election of 1960 approached. President Eisenhower had consciously been cutting the percentage of the national income that was being spent by the government of the United States, and the people had thus been able to spend a greater share. In spite of a recession or two, the decade saw the triumph of consumer goods and services. As individual family incomes soared to unprecedented heights, automobiles, television sets, freezers, dishwashers, and other signs of conspicuous consumption became characteristic of American society. All this would have been an "unalloyed delight," as Walter Lippmann put it, were it not clear that highways, schools, hospitals, parks and playgrounds were inadequate, streams were polluted, cities were deteriorating and, in the face of a worldwide population explosion, water supplies and other natural resources were being exhausted. Indeed, there was a growing fear that the wholesale use of chemical insecticide to protect fruits, vegetables, and human beings against the attacks of insects was itself upsetting the balance of nature by destroying more than it protected and even threatening human well-being [14]. Increasingly questions were also being raised concerning the effectiveness of the educational system. Was there sufficient emphasis in the public schools on tough subject matter? Were the universities turning out a sufficient number of scientists and engineers to meet the challenge of the Soviet Union? On the other hand, was there a danger, under the pressure of the Cold War, of deemphasizing the social sciences and humanities to the extent of turning out illiterates in technical fields?

Despite conspicuous consumption and high income, two or three easily recognizable recessions occurred in the 1950s, and there were never fewer than 3-5 percent of the labor force unemployed between 1945 and 1962.

Certain problem areas were of particular importance. One of these was the South. This section had made tremendous progress after 1929. Individual personal income had almost tripled—a much greater increase than in other sections. Educational facilities had improved and illiteracy had decreased. Yet there was still more illiteracy than in any other section. The percentage rate of increase in personal income slowed down in the 1950s to about the national average, and in 1960 per capita individual incomes varied from 53 percent ($1,173.00) of the national average in Mississippi to 89 percent in Florida ($1,988.00).[7] The lot of migratory workers throughout the nation continued to be an unhappy one. Particular areas, such as the West Virginia coal mines, contained chronic unemployment; and some basic industries such as the railroads were finding it difficult to stay alive.

A key question in determining whether the United States would meet the challenge of the postwar world was whether the continuing problems of labor relations could be solved. Organized labor had emerged from the war stronger than ever, with almost 36 percent organized of the total nonagricultural labor force in contrast to 12 percent in 1930 and 27 percent in 1940. The battles between the AFL and CIO had at least superficially been resolved in 1955 by a merger, and after a period of substantial labor unrest from 1945 to 1952, the number of strikes together with the number of workers involved dropped off markedly, from 4,985 and 4,600,000 workers in 1946 to a low point of 3,333 strikes and 1,320,000 workers in 1960.[8] Even the Taft-Hartley Act of 1946 did not prove to be so much of a slave-labor act as William Green, at the time president of the AFL, had proph-

7. *Statistical Abstract of the United States (1958),* pp. 311 and 314; *Americana Annual,* 1962.

8. See *Historical Statistics,* p. 98; and *Statistical Abstract of the United States (1962),* p. 243. Actually the high point in number of strikes was in 1952 and 1953, but fewer workers were involved.

esied, and the principle of collective bargaining seemed generally acceptable. At the end of the decade, however, the labor picture was a mixed one. A campaign to organize the South had only limited success. Membership measured as a percentage of the total labor force had actually declined slightly since 1945. Congressional investigation of labor union practices had revealed several notorious instances of racketeering, and in at least one case—that of the powerful Teamsters Union—the membership seemed quite unable to clean house. Featherbedding practices continued on the railroads and elsewhere, and the power of certain unions, such as the Steelworkers, to upset the entire economy by a work stoppage raised the question as to whether the nation had yet found an answer to strikes that ran contrary to the general welfare.

One of the basic problems facing organized labor was also one of the basic problems facing agriculture—that American producers were able to produce far more than could be sold at a profit. Whenever the farm problem had really been serious in the United States, from 1870 to 1896, from 1921 to 1941, and in the 1950s, overproduction was at its root. Massive efforts to control production since the days of the first AAA in 1933, did not prevent surpluses from piling up, except during the war years. In spite of the continuing decline of rural population, it was becoming apparent that there were just too many farmers. This situation might not have posed such a serious dilemma were it not at least in the realm of possibility that automation was resulting in too many industrial laborers also. There was no question that workers were being displaced—or at least not being replaced after deaths or retirement—by labor-saving devices. The question was the extent to which new industries, new services, and national needs could create jobs to take up the slack. President Kennedy in a press conference in 1962 called automation one of the most serious economic problems facing the United States. Sensible labor leaders such as Walter Reuther and George Meany agreed with him, particularly when in 1958 unemployment reached 6.8 percent of the labor force, and when the stock market crash of 1962 indicated that something was still fundamentally wrong with the economy [15].

The thesis of the New Frontier, adopted as John F. Kennedy's campaign slogan in 1960, was that the American economy was strong enough to devote a large share of the Gross National Product to the public sector—to national defense, health and education, urban renewal, roads, and conservation. He took vigorous issue with what, according to Walter Lippmann, had been implicit in President Eisenhower's philosophy of the budget: "that, though we have the richest economy in all history, our liberal system is such that we cannot afford a sure defense and adequate provision for the civil needs of our people." Although Lippmann and others believed that a new sense of national purpose would support an increase in taxes if necessary to direct more of the national income to the public sector, Kennedy's attention was focused more upon increasing economic growth—the promotion of full production and full employment. His budget message of 1962 demonstrated pointedly that he was willing to make conscious use of the budget to control the economy. As he put it, "under present economic circumstances a moderate surplus is the best policy." For the first time in history, according to Walter Lippmann, a President made the balancing of the budget a matter of "deliberate decision," not a "question of right or wrong" [16].

At the same time, Kennedy took cognizance of the fact of overproduction. Here the solution, as he saw it, was to sell an increasing amount of American products abroad. Yet sensational developments in Europe, particularly the rise of the Common Market with economic potentialities as great as the United States, threatened an actual decline of markets for American exports. Thus an essential ingredient in President Kennedy's plans for economic growth was not merely tax and spending policies at home and abroad, but a bold plan to give him the power to negotiate tariff agreements which might permit higher imports while at the same time opening markets abroad for American products.

By 1962, seventeen years had passed since the end of World War II. Seventeen years after Armistice Day 1918, the United States, almost completely disarmed, was concentrating upon meeting the problems of depression and passing neutrality acts in an attempt to remain isolated from the powder-keg activities in East and West. In 1962 the emphasis was upon national security, but national security meant not only efficient weapons and strong armed forces. According to President Kennedy, it meant also a strong economy, good health for the nation, and the protection of civil rights; it meant strengthening the Atlantic community and hemispheric relations; it meant a "creative" policy in relation to new nations; and it meant sustaining the United Nations. Without too much stretching of the imagination, almost anything of significance that happened in the nation could be made a function of national security. James Reston made this point clearly when he suggested that no more important problem of foreign policy existed in 1962 than the misrepresentative and undemocratic makeup and the antiquated procedures of the House of Representatives and the state legislatures. "The President can talk till doomsday about the changing patterns of world trade, mobilizing the brain power of the nation, and improving the health, education and spirit of the American people," he wrote, "but they will not be done with the present House, and the present House will not be changed very much until the state legislatures are changed."

Indeed, during his first year in office President Kennedy found it even more difficult than had Truman to go much beyond New Deal reforms. His program for aid to education, medical care for the aged, and a special department for urban affairs failed. The Congress had not received "the word" so far as domestic policy was concerned. On questions of defense, however, and even on matters of foreign trade and foreign aid, Congress was more willing to cooperate. Few could miss the realities of the global competition with Soviet Russia. The most exciting new frontier was that of space. Lieutenant Colonel John H. Glenn and Major Leroy G. Cooper were the new American pioneers as they whirled around the earth at 17,500 miles an hour. In spite of Glenn's and Cooper's achievements, however, the two-day, million-mile jaunts of Nikolayev and Popovich suggested that the Soviets were still in the lead so far as space exploration was concerned. In August, 1962 a highly publicized question was who would first reach the moon [17]. Unfortunately the race for space represented only the peaceful side of "peaceful" coexistence. Beneath the surface the issue of the control of Berlin constantly threatened to create a real crisis. In fact, it was sufficiently beneath the surface to make it possible for some to forget that a principal factor in the preservation of world peace was the existence of a balance of terror. What brought the American people out of this false calm was the knowledge that the Soviet Union had surreptitiously begun to emplace medium and intermediate-range missiles on the island of Cuba. President Kennedy's prompt reaction to this intelligence, imposing a selective blockade on Cuba and demanding the withdrawal of offensive weapons, demonstrated forcibly his fear that to permit the development of these bases would dangerously upset the balance of power. Khrushchev's capitulation to these demands indicated that the balance was not yet upset, and even suggested —what Americans hoped—that the nuclear deterrent of the United States was now more fearsome than that of the Soviets [18].

To some, Khrushchev's capitulation signified that the crisis was over. To others, Cuba simply dramatized a plateau of danger that still existed and would continue to exist until pressing problems in Europe and Asia were resolved.

1

The Atomic Bomb and the End of the War

Official Government Reports on the Bombing of Hiroshima

The explosion of the first atomic bomb on July 16, 1945 in a remote air base in New Mexico cast its shadow over the entire period
covered by this book. The documents included here are the first official report of this event sent by Major General Leslie R. Groves, the
officer in charge of the Manhattan District Project, to Secretary of War
Stimson; the press release giving the official explanation for the mys-
terious explosion which had occurred; a series of once-top-secret communications involving the decision to drop the bomb on Japan; and
President Truman's public statement on the occasion of the bomb's
being dropped on Hiroshima. See also Robert C. Batchelder, *The Irre-
versible Decision, 1939-1950* (Boston, 1962); Herbert Feis, *Japan
Subdued: The Atomic Bomb and the End of the War in the Pacific*
(Princeton, 1961); and Thomas Murray, *Nuclear Policy for War and
Peace* (New York, 1960).

In reading these documents note (1) the effectiveness of the early
nuclear bombs, (2) the problems of security, and (3) the relationship between Great Britain and the United States at the time.

No. 1305]

Department of the Army Files

The Commanding General, Manhattan District *Project* (*Groves*)
to the Secretary of War (*Stimson*)[1]

*Foreign Relations of the United States, Conference of Berlin (Potsdam)
1945*, Vol. II, pp. 1361-1378. The footnotes are in the original document.

1. Stimson's diary entry for July 21 contains the following information
relating to this document:

". . . At eleven thirty-five General Groves' special report was received by
special courier. It was an immensely powerful document, clearly and well

TOP SECRET   Washington, 18 July 1945

MEMORANDUM FOR THE SECRETARY OF WAR

SUBJECT: THE TEST.

1. This is not a concise, formal military report but an attempt to recite what I would have told you if you had been here on my return from New Mexico.

2. At 0530,[2] 16 July 1945, in a remote section of the Alamogordo Air Base, New Mexico, the first full scale test was made of the implosion type atomic fission bomb. For the first time in history there was a nuclear explosion. And what an explosion! ... The bomb was not dropped from an airplane but was exploded on a platform on top of a 100-foot high steel tower.

3. The test was successful beyond the most optimistic expectations of anyone. Based on the data which it has been possible to

---

written and with supporting documents of the highest importance. It gave a pretty full and eloquent report of the tremendous success of the test and revealed far greater destructive power than we expected in S—1. . . .

"At three o'clock I found that Marshall had returned from the Joint Chiefs of Staff, and to save time I hurried to his house and had him read Groves' report and conferred with him about it.

"I then went to the 'Little White House' and saw President Truman. I asked him to call in Secretary Byrnes and then I read the report in its entirety and we then discussed it. They were immensely pleased. The President was tremendously pepped up by it and spoke to me of it again and again when I saw him. He said it gave him an entirely new feeling of confidence and he thanked me for having come to the Conference and being present to help him in this way."

Stimson showed Groves' report to Arnold on July 22 (see document No. 1310, footnote 3).

Concerning the discussion of the report with Churchill, see *ante*, pp. 203, 225 [in original].

Truman later stated that, following receipt of news that the Alamogordo test had been successful, he had called together Byrnes, Stimson, Leahy, Marshall, Arnold, Eisenhower, and King and had asked them for their opinions as to whether the bomb should be used, and the consensus had been that it should. See Hillman, *Mr. President*, p. 248. Truman apparently also received at this meeting an oral estimate of the casualties to be expected in the assault on Japan if the new weapon were not used. *See ibid.*, and Wesley Frank Craven and James Lea Cate, eds., *The Army Air Forces in World War II* (Chicago, 1948-1958), vol. v, facsimile following p. 712 of a letter from Truman to Cate dated January 12, 1953.

2. i.e., 5:30 a.m. All times in this memorandum are expressed in military style, i.e., from 0001 hours (12.01 a.m.) to 2400 hours (midnight).

work up to date, I estimate the energy generated to be in excess of the equivalent of 15,000 to 20,000 tons of TNT; and this is a conservative estimate. Data based on measurements which we have not yet been able to reconcile would make the energy release several times the conservative figure. There were tremendous blast effects. For a brief period there was a lighting effect within a radius of 20 miles equal to several suns in midday; a huge ball of fire was formed which lasted for several seconds. This ball mushroomed and rose to a height of over ten thousand feet before it dimmed. The light from the explosion was seen clearly at Albuquerque, Santa Fe, Silver City, El Paso and other points generally to about 180 miles away. The sound was heard to the same distance in a few instances but generally to about 100 miles. Only a few windows were broken although one was some 125 miles away. A massive cloud was formed which surged and billowed upward with tremendous power, reaching the substratosphere at an elevation of 41,000 feet, 36,000 feet above the ground, in about five minutes, breaking without interruption through a temperature inversion at 17,000 feet which most of the scientists thought would stop it. Two supplementary explosions occurred in the cloud shortly after the main explosion. The cloud contained several thousand tons of dust picked up from the ground and a considerable amount of iron in the gaseous form. Our present thought is that this iron ignited when it mixed with the oxygen in the air to cause these supplementary explosions. Huge concentrations of highly radioactive materials resulted from the fission and were contained in this cloud.

4. A crater from which all vegetation had vanished, with a diameter of 1200 feet and a slight slope toward the center, was formed. In the center was a shallow bowl 130 feet in diameter and 6 feet in depth. The material within the crater was deeply pulverized dirt. The material within the outer circle is greenish and can be distinctly seen from as much as 5 miles away. The steel from the tower was evaporated. 1500 feet away there was a four-inch iron pipe 16 feet high set in concrete and strongly guyed. It disappeared completely.

5. One-half mile from the explosion there was a massive steel test cylinder weighing 220 tons. The base of the cylinder was solidly encased in concrete. Surrounding the cylinder was a

strong steel tower 70 feet high, firmly anchored to concrete foundations. This tower is comparable to a steel building bay that would be found in typical 15 or 20 story skyscraper or in warehouse construction. Forty tons of steel were used to fabricate the tower which was 70 feet high, the height of a six story building. The cross bracing was much stronger than that normally used in ordinary steel construction. The absence of the solid walls of a building gave the blast a much less effective surface to push against. The blast tore the tower from its foundations, twisted it, ripped it apart and left it flat on the ground. The effects on the tower indicate that, at that distance, unshielded permanent steel and masonry buildings would have been destroyed. I no longer consider the Pentagon a safe shelter from such a bomb. Enclosed are a sketch showing the tower before the explosion and a telephotograph showing what it looked like afterwards.[3] None of us had expected it to be damaged.

6. The cloud traveled to a great height first in the form of a ball, then mushroomed, then changed into a long trailing chimney-shaped column and finally was sent in several directions by the variable winds at the different elevations. It deposited its dust and radioactive materials over a wide area. It was followed and monitored by medical doctors and scientists with instruments to check its radioactive effects. While here and there the activity on the ground was fairly high, at no place did it reach a concentration which required evacuation of the population. Radioactive material in small quantities was located as much as 120 miles away. The measurements are being continued in order to have adequate data with which to protect the Government's interests in case of future claims. For a few hours I was none too comfortable about the situation.

7. For distances as much as 200 miles away, observers were stationed to check on blast effects, property damage, radioactivity and reactions of the population. While complete reports have not yet been received, I now know that no persons were injured nor was there any real property damage outside our Government area. As soon as all the voluminous data can be checked and correlated, full technical studies will be possible.

3. Neither reproduced.

8. Our long range weather predictions had indicated that we could expect weather favorable for our tests beginning on the morning of the 17th and continuing for four days. This was almost a certainty if we were to believe our long range forecasters. The prediction for the morning of the 16th was not so certain but there was about an 80% chance of the conditions being suitable. During the night there were thunder storms with lightning flashes all over the area. The test had been originally set for 0400 hours and all the night through, because of the bad weather, there were urgings from many of the scientists to postpone the test. Such a delay might well have had crippling results due to mechanical difficulties in our complicated test set-up. Fortunately, we disregarded the urgings. We held firm and waited the night through hoping for suitable weather. We had to delay an hour and a half, to 0530, before we could fire. This was 30 minutes before sunrise.

9. Because of bad weather, our two B-29 observation airplanes were unable to take off as scheduled from Kirtland Field at Albuquerque and when they finally did get off, they found it impossible to get over the target because of the heavy clouds and the thunder storms. Certain desired observations could not be made and while the people in the airplanes saw the explosion from a distance, they were not as close as they will be in action. We still have no reason to anticipate the loss of our plane in an actual operation although we cannot guarantee safety.

10. Just before 1100 the news stories from all over the state started to flow into the Albuquerque Associated Press. I then directed the issuance by the Commanding Officer, Alamogordo Air Base of a news release as shown on the inclosure. With the assistance of the Office of Censorship we were able to limit the news stories to the approved release supplemented in the local papers by brief stories from the many eyewitnesses not connected with our project. One of these was a blind woman who saw the light.

11. Brigadier General Thomas F. Farrell was at the control shelter located 10,000 yards south of the point of explosion. His impressions are given below:

"The scene inside the shelter was dramatic beyond words. In and around the shelter were some twenty-odd people concerned with last minute arrangements prior to firing the shot. Included were: Dr. Oppenheimer, the Director who had borne the great scientific burden of developing the weapon from the raw materials made in Tennessee and Washington and a dozen of his key assistants—Dr. Kistiakowsky, who developed the highly special explosives; Dr. Bainbridge, who supervised all the detailed arrangements for the test; Dr. Hubbard, the weather expert, and several others. Besides these, there were a handful of soldiers, two or three Army officers and one Naval officer. The shelter was cluttered with a great variety of instruments and radios.

"For some hectic two hours preceding the blast, General Groves stayed with the Director, walking with him and steadying his tense excitement. Every time the Director would be about to explode because of some untoward happening, General Groves would take him off and walk with him in the rain, counselling with him and reassuring him that everything would be all right. At twenty minutes before zero hour, General Groves left for his station at the base camp, first because it provided a better observation point and second, because of our rule that he and I must not be together in situations where there is an element of danger, which existed at both points.

"Just after General Groves left, announcements began to be broadcast of the interval remaining before the blast. They were sent by radio to the other groups participating in and observing the test. As the time interval grew smaller and changed from minutes to seconds, the tension increased by leaps and bounds. Everyone in that room knew the awful potentialities of the thing that they thought was about to happen. The scientists felt that their figuring must be right and that the bomb had to go off but there was in everyone's mind a strong measure of doubt. The feeling of many could be expressed by 'Lord, I believe; help Thou mine unbelief.' We were reaching into the unknown and we did not know what might come of it. It can be safely said that most of those present—Christian, Jew and Atheist—were praying and praying harder than they had ever prayed before. If the shot were successful, it was a justification of the several years of intensive effort of tens of thousands of people—statesmen, scientists, engineers, manufacturers, soldiers, and many others in every walk of life.

"In that brief instant in the remote New Mexico desert the tremendous effort of the brains and brawn of all these people came suddenly and startlingly to the fullest fruition. Dr. Oppenheimer, on whom had rested a very heavy burden, grew tenser as the last seconds ticked off. He scarcely breathed. He held on to a post to steady himself. For the last few seconds, he stared directly ahead and then when the announcer shouted 'Now!' and there came this tremendous burst of light followed shortly thereafter by the deep growling roar of the explosion, his face relaxed into an expression of tremendous relief. Several of the observers standing back of the shelter to watch the lighting effects were knocked flat by the blast.

"The tension in the room let up and all started congratulating each other. Everyone sensed 'This is it!' No matter what might happen now all knew that the impossible scientific job had been done. Atomic fission would no longer be hidden in the cloisters of the theoretical physicists' dreams. It was almost full grown at birth. It was a great new force to be used for good or for evil. There was a feeling in that shelter that those concerned with its nativity should dedicate their lives to the mission that it would always be used for good and never for evil.

"Dr. Kistiakowsky, the impulsive Russian,[4] threw his arms around Dr. Oppenheimer and embraced him with shouts of glee. Others were equally enthusiastic. All the pent-up emotions were released in those few minutes and all seemed to sense immediately that the explosion had far exceeded the most optimistic expectations and wildest hopes of the scientists. All seemed to feel that they had been present at the birth of a new age—The Age of Atomic Energy—and felt their profound responsibility to help in guiding into right channels the tremendous forces which had been unlocked for the first time in history.

"As to the present war, there was a feeling that no matter what else might happen, we now had the means to insure its speedy conclusion and save thousands of American lives. As to the future, there had been brought into being something big and something new that would prove to be immeasurably more important than the discovery of electricity or any of the other great discoveries which have so affected our existence.

"The effects could well be called unprecedented, magnificent, beautiful, stupendous and terrifying. No man-made phenomenon of such tremendous power had ever occurred before. The lighting effects beggared description. The whole country was lighted by a searing light with the intensity many times that of the midday sun. It was golden, purple, violet, gray and blue. It lighted every peak, crevasse and ridge of the nearby mountain range with a clarity and beauty that cannot be described but must be seen to be imagined. It was that beauty the great poets dream about but describe most poorly and inadequately. Thirty seconds after the explosion came first, the air blast pressing hard against the people and things, to be followed almost immediately by the strong, sustained, awesome roar which warned of doomsday and made us feel that we puny things were blasphemous to dare tamper with the forces heretofore reserved to The Almighty. Words are inadequate tools for the job of acquainting those not present with the physical, mental and psychological effects. It had to be witnessed to be realized."

12. My impressions of the night's high point follow:
After about an hour's sleep I got up at 0100 and from that

4. At this point is the following manuscript interpolation by Groves: "an American and Harvard professor for many years".

time on until about five I was with Dr. Oppenheimer constantly. Naturally he was nervous, although his mind was working at its usual extraordinary efficiency. I devoted my entire attention to shielding him from the excited and generally faulty advice of his assistants who were more than disturbed by their excitement and the uncertain weather conditions. By 0330 we decided that we could probably fire at 0530. By 0400 the rain had stopped but the sky was heavily overcast. Our decision became firmer as time went on. During most of these hours the two of us journeyed from the control house out into the darkness to look at the stars and to assure each other that the one or two visible stars were becoming brighter. At 0510 I left Dr. Oppenheimer and returned to the main observation point which was 17,000 yards from the point of explosion. In accordance with our orders I found all personnel not otherwise occupied massed on a bit of high ground.

At about two minutes of the scheduled firing time all persons lay face down with their feet pointing towards the explosion. As the remaining time was called from the loud speaker from the 10,000 yard control station there was complete silence. Dr. Conant said he had never imagined seconds could be so long. Most of the individuals in accordance with orders shielded their eyes in one way or another. There was then this burst of light of a brilliance beyond any comparison. We all rolled over and looked through dark glasses at the ball of fire. About forty seconds later came the shock wave followed by the sound, neither of which seemed startling after our complete astonishment at the extraordinary lighting intensity. Dr. Conant reached over and we shook hands in mutual congratulations. Dr. Bush, who was on the other side of me, did likewise. The feeling of the entire assembly was similar to that described by General Farrell, with even the uninitiated feeling profound awe. Drs. Conant and Bush and myself were struck by an even stronger feeling that the faith of those who had been responsible for the initiation and the carrying on of this Herculean project had been justified. I personally thought of Blondin crossing Niagara Falls on his tight rope, only to me this tight rope had lasted for almost three years and of my repeated confident-appearing assurances that such a thing was possible and that we would do it.

13. A large group of observers were stationed at a point about 27 miles north of the point of explosion. Attached is a memorandum written shortly after the explosion by Dr. E. O. Lawrence which may be of interest. [This document is not included.]

14. While General Farrell was waiting about midnight for a commercial airplane to Washington at Albuquerque—120 miles away from the site—he overheard several airport employees discussing their reaction to the blast. One said that he was out on the parking apron; it was quite dark; then the whole southern sky was lighted as though by a bright sun; the light lasted several seconds. Another remarked that if a few exploding bombs could have such an effect, it must be terrible to have them drop on a city.

15. My liaison officer at the Alamogordo Air Base, 60 miles away, made the following report:

"There was a blinding flash of light that lighted the entire northwestern sky. In the center of the flash, there appeared to be a huge billow of smoke. The original flash lasted approximately 10 to 15 seconds. As the first flash died down, there arose in the approximate center of where the original flash had occurred an enormous ball of what appeared to be fire and closely resembled a rising sun that was three-fourths above a mountain. The ball of fire lasted approximately 15 seconds, then died down and the sky resumed an almost normal appearance.

"Almost immediately, a third, but much smaller, flash and a billow of smoke of a whitish-orange color appeared in the sky, again lighting the sky for approximately 4 seconds. At the time of the original flash, the field was lighted well enough so that a newspaper could easily have been read. The second and third flashes were of much lesser intensity.

"We were in a glass-enclosed control tower some 70 feet above the ground and felt no concussion or air compression. There was no noticeable earth tremor although reports overheard at the Field during the following 24 hours indicated that some believed that they had both heard the explosion and felt some earth tremor."

16. I have not written a separate report for General Marshall as I feel you will want to show this to him. I have informed the necessary people here of our results. Lord Halifax after discussion with Mr. Harrison and myself stated that he was not sending a full report to his government at this time. I informed

him that I was sending this to you and that you might wish to show it to the proper British representatives.

17. We are all fully conscious that our real goal is still before us. The battle test is what counts in the war with Japan.

18. May I express my deep personal appreciation for your congratulatory cable to us[5] and for the support and confidence which I have received from you ever since I had this work under my charge.

19. I know that Colonel Kyle will guard these papers with his customary extraordinary care.

L R GROVES

[Enclosure 3]

BULLETIN[6]

Alamogordo, N.M., July 16—William O. Eareckson, commanding officer of the Alamogordo Army Air Base, made the following statement today:

"Several inquiries have been received concerning a heavy explosion which occurred on the Alamogordo Air Base reservation this morning.

"A remotely located ammunition magazine containing a considerable amount of high explosive and pyrotechnics exploded.

"There was no loss of life or injury to anyone, and the property damage outside of the explosives magazine itself was negligible.

"Weather conditions affecting the content of gas shells exploded by the blast may make it desirable for the Army to evacuate temporarily a few civilians from their homes."

No. 1306]

S/AE Files

Prime Minister Churchill to the Secretary of War (Stimson)

TOP SECRET
AND PERSONAL

MR. SECRETARY STIMSON: I enclose a photostat record of the

5. Not printed.
6. Identified in the source copy as a clipping from *The Albuquerque Tribune* for July 16, 1945.

Hyde Park Agreement on T.A., for which you asked the Chancellor of the Exchequer.[1]

This photograph was taken by a special photographic section of the Air Ministry, and flown out here in the charge of a trusted officer.

W[INSTON] S C[HURCHILL]

BERLIN, 18.7.45.

Enclosure

TOP SECRET

TUBE ALLOYS[2]

AIDE-MEMOIRE OF CONVERSATION BETWEEN THE PRESIDENT AND THE PRIME MINISTER AT HYDE PARK, SEPTEMBER 18, 1944[3]

1. The suggestion that the world should be informed regarding TUBE ALLOYS, with a view to an international agreement regarding its control and use, is not accepted. The matter should continue to be regarded as of the utmost secrecy; but when a "bomb" is finally available, it might perhaps, after mature consideration, be used against the Japanese, who should be warned that this bombardment will be repeated until they surrender.

2. Full collaboration between the United States and the British Government in developing TUBE ALLOYS for military and commercial purposes should continue after the defeat of Japan unless and until terminated by joint agreement.

F[RANKLIN] D R[OOSEVELT]   W[INSTON] S C[HURCHILL]

1. Sir John Anderson. Following the death of President Roosevelt, an authenticated text of the enclosed *aide-mémoire* was not available to responsible American officials. Before the Berlin Conference, Stimson had asked the British Government to supply a photocopy of the *aide-mémoire*.

2. The following manuscript notation appears in the top margin: "A copy of this *aide-mémoire* was left with Pres. Roosevelt. Another copy was given to Adl. Leahy to hand to Lord Cherwell. J[ohn] M[iller] M[artin]." The copy of the *aide-mémoire* in the Roosevelt Papers deposited in the Franklin D. Roosevelt Library at Hyde Park does not, of course, bear this notation nor that quoted in footnote 3, *infra*, but it does have a handwritten date, "18. 9," i.e., September 18, under Churchill's initials.

3. At this point there is the following marginal manuscript notation: "actually 19th J[ohn] M[iller] M[artin]."

No. 1307]

Department of the Army Files: Telegram

The Acting Chairman of the Interim Committee (Harrison) to the Secretary of War (Stimson)

TOP SECRET   Washington, 21 July 1945
URGENT

WAR 35987. Secretary of War EYES ONLY TopSec from Harrison.

All your local military advisors engaged in preparation definitely favor your pet city[1] and would like to feel free to use it as first choice if those on the ride select it out of four possible spots in the light of local conditions at the time.

No. 1308]

Department of the Army Files: Telegram

The Secretary of War (Stimson) to the Acting Chairman of the Interim Committee (Harrison)

TOP SECRET   Babelsberg, 21 July, 1945
URGENT

VICTORY 189. Reference WAR 35987[2] from Stimson to Pasco for Harrison's EYES ONLY. Message begins: Aware of no factors to change my decision. On the contrary new factors here tend to confirm it. End.

No. 1309]

Department of the Army Files: Telegram

The Acting Chairman of the Interim Committee (Harrison) to the Secretary of War (Stimson)

TOP SECRET   Washington, 21 July 1945
URGENT

WAR 35988. Secretary of War EYES ONLY top secret from Harrison.

1. The reference is to the selection of Kyoto as a possible target for atomic attack. See Stimson and Bundy, *On Active Service in Peace and War*, p. 625.
2. Document No. 1307.

Patient progressing rapidly and will be ready for final operation first good break in August. Complicated preparations for
use are proceeding so fast we should know not later than July
25 if any change in plans.

No. 1310]

Department of the Army Files: Telegram

*The Secretary of War (Stimson) to the Acting Chairman of the
Interim Committee (Harrison)*

TOP SECRET   Babelsberg, 23 July 1945
URGENT

VICTORY 218. To AGWar from Stimson to Pasco for Harrison[']s EYES ONLY. Reference your number War 35988.[1] We are
greatly pleased with apparent improvement in timing of
patient[']s progress. We assume operation may be any time after
the first of August. Whenever it is possible to give us a more
definite date please immediately advise us here where information is greatly needed. Also give name of place or alternate places,
always excluding the particular place against which I have decided.[2] My decision has been confirmed by highest authority.[3]

1. Document No. 1309.
2. Kyoto. See Stimson and Bundy, *On Active Service in Peace and War*,
p. 625.
3. i.e., Truman. Stimson's diary contains the following entries on this
subject:

"[July 22:] Called on President Truman at nine-twenty. . . .

"I also discussed with him Harrison's two messages [presumably documents Nos. 1307 and 1309]. He was intensely pleased by the accelerated
timetable. As to the matter of the special target which I had refused to
permit, he strongly confirmed my view and said he felt the same way. . . .

"At twelve-fifteen I called General Arnold over, showed him Harrison's
two cables, showed him my answer to them and showed him Groves' report [document No. 1305], which he read in its entirety. He told me that
he agreed with me about the target which I had struck off the program. He
said that it would take considerable hard work to organize the operations
now that it was to move forward. . . . [For Arnold's account of his various
conversations on this subject with Stimson at Babelsberg, see H. H. Arnold,
Global Mission (New York, 1949), pp. 584-585, 588-591.]

"[July 24:] . . . We [Stimson and Truman] had a few words more about
the S-1 program, and I again gave him my reasons for eliminating one of

No. 1311]

Department of the Army Files: Telegram

The Acting Chairman of the Interim Committee (Harrison) to the Secretary of War (Stimson)

TOP SECRET   Washington, 23 July 1945
URGENT

WAR 36791. Top secret Secretary of War EYES ONLY from Harrison.

Reference my WAR 35987[1] and your VICTORY 218[2] Hiroshima, Kokura, Niigata in [*is?*] order of choice here.

No. 1312]

Department of the Army Files: Telegram

The Acting Chairman of the Interim Committee (Harrison) to the Secretary of War (Stimson)

TOP SECRET   Washington, 23 July 1945
OPERATIONAL PRIORITY

WAR 36792. Secretary of War EYES ONLY top secret from Harrison.

Operation may be possible any time from August 1 depending on state of preparation of patient and condition of atmosphere. From point of view of patient only, some chance August 1 to 3, good chance August 4 to 5 and barring unexpected relapse almost certain before August 10.

---

the proposed targets. He again reiterated with the utmost emphasis his own concurring belief on that subject, and he was particularly emphatic in agreeing with my suggestion that if elimination was not done, the bitterness which would be caused by such a wanton act might make it impossible during the long post-war period to reconcile the Japanese to us in that area rather than to the Russians. It might thus, I pointed out, be the means of preventing what our policy demanded, namely a sympathetic Japan to the United States in case there should be any aggression by Russia in Manchuria."

1. Document No. 1307.
2. Document No. 1310.

No. 1313]

Department of the Army Files: Telegram

The Secretary of War (Stimson) to the President

TOP SECRET   Washington, 30 July 1945[1]
URGENT

WAR 41011. To the President from the Secretary of War.

The time schedule on Groves' project is progressing so rapidly that it is now essential that statement for release by you be available not later than Wednesday, 1 August. I have revised draft of statement, which I previously presented to you,[2] in light of

(a) Your recent ultimatum,[3]

(b) Dramatic results of test and

(c) Certain minor suggestions made by British[4] of which Byrnes is aware.

While I am planning to start a copy by special courier tomorrow in the hope you can be reached, nevertheless in the event he does not reach you in time, I will appreciate having your authority to have White House release revised statement as soon as necessary.[5]

Sorry circumstances seem to require this emergency action.

No. 1314]

Truman Papers

Prime Minister Attlee to President Truman

Berlin, August 1, 1945

DEAR MR PRESIDENT[:] Thank you so much for your letter of

1. Stimson had left Babelsberg on July 25 and had returned to Washington.

2. The draft referred to has not been found.

3. Document No. 1382.

4. Not printed.

5. For the text of the statement as issued by the White House in Washington on August 6, see document No. 1315. Concerning the military orders issued from the Conference for the atomic attack on Japan, see Craven and Cate, eds., *The Army Air Forces in World War II*, vol. v, facsimile facing p. 697 and chapter 23.

to-day[1] about the new weapon to be used on Japan. If it is quite convenient to you, I will come to see you for a few minutes after the Plenary Session this afternoon.[2]

I am deeply touched by the very kind words you use about me and I, too, have been greatly encouraged by the unity which exists between our two countries on policies for world peace. I shall work with all my strength to maintain this unity unimpaired during the difficult years which lie before us.

May I also thank you warmly for the great personal consideration and kindness which you have shown to me and which has been such a help, especially during these last few days.

Your sincerely   C R ATTLEE

No. 1315]

White House Files

White House Press Release[3]

STATEMENT BY THE PRESIDENT OF THE UNITED STATES

Sixteen hours ago an American airplane dropped one bomb on Hiroshima, an important Japanese Army base. That bomb had more power than 20,000 tons of T. N. T. It had more than two thousand times the blast power of the British "Grand Slam" which is the largest bomb ever yet used in the history of warfare.

The Japanese began the war from the air at Pearl Harbor. They have been repaid many fold. And the end is not yet. With this bomb we have now added a new and revolutionary increase in

1. The index to the folder in which Attlee's letter was found contains the following entry: "6. *1 August 1945.* Letter from the President to Attlee regarding the Atomic Bomb. The President wrote in longhand and no copy is available." It appears that Attlee received his first news of the successful test of the atomic bomb from Truman during the Berlin Conference. See Lord Attlee, "The Hiroshima Choice," in *The Observer, September* 6, 1959, p. 16.

2. The Log records no private meeting between Truman and Attlee on August 1.

3. Released August 6, 1945. A draft of this statement had been discussed with the British (see document No. 1313) [in original source].

destruction to supplement the growing power of our armed forces. In their present form these bombs are now in production and even more powerful forms are in development.

It is an atomic bomb. It is a harnessing of the basic power of the universe. The force from which the sun draws its power has been loosed against those who brought war to the Far East.

Before 1939, it was the accepted belief of scientists that it was theoretically possible to release atomic energy. But no one knew any practical method of doing it. By 1942, however, we knew that the Germans were working feverishly to find a way to add atomic energy to the other engines of war with which they hoped to enslave the world. But they failed. We may be grateful to Providence that the Germans got the V-1's and the V-2's late and in limited quantities and even more grateful that they did not get the atomic bomb at all.

The battle of the laboratories held fateful risks for us as well as the battles of the air, land and sea, and we have now won the battle of the laboratories as we have won the other battles.

Beginning in 1940, before Pearl Harbor, scientific knowledge useful in war was pooled between the United States and Great Britain, and many priceless helps to our victories have come from that arangement. Under that general policy the research on the atomic bomb was begun. With American and British scientists working together we entered the race of discovery against the Germans.

The United States had available the large number of scientists of distinction in the many needed areas of knowledge. It had the tremendous industrial and financial resources necessary for the project and they could be devoted to it without undue impairment of other vital war work. In the United States the laboratory work and the production plants, on which a substantial start had already been made, would be out of reach of enemy bombing, while at that time Britain was exposed to constant air attack and was still threatened with the possibility of invasion. For these reasons Prime Minister Churchill and President Roosevelt agreed that it was wise to carry on the project here. We now have two great plants and many lesser works devoted to the production of atomic power. Employment during peak construction numbered 125,000 and over 65,000 individuals are even now engaged in operating the plants. Many have worked there for two and a half years. Few know what they have been producing. They see great quantities of material going in and they see nothing coming out of these plants, for the physical size of the explosive charge is exceedingly small. We have spent two billion dollars on the greatest scientific gamble in history—and won.

But the greatest marvel is not the size of the enterprise, its secrecy, nor its cost, but the achievement of scientific brains in putting together infinitely complex pieces of knowledge held by many men in different fields of science into a workable plan. And hardly less marvellous has been the capacity of industry to design, and of labor to operate, the machines and methods to do things never done before so that the brain child of many minds came forth in physical shape and performed as it was supposed to do. Both science and industry worked under the direction of the United States Army, which achieved a unique success in managing so diverse a problem in the advancement of knowledge in an amazingly short time. It is doubtful if such another combination could be got together in the world. What has been done is the greatest achievement of organized science in history. It was done under high pressure and without failure.

We are now prepared to obliterate more rapidly and completely every productive enterprise the Japanese have above ground in any city. We shall destroy their docks, their factories, and their communications. Let there be no mistake; we shall completely destroy Japan's power to make war.

It was to spare the Japanese people from utter destruction that the ultimatum of July 26[2] was issued at Potsdam. Their leaders promptly rejected that ultimatum.[3] If they do not now accept our terms they may expect a rain of ruin from the air, the like of which has never been seen on this earth. Behind this air attack will follow sea and land forces in such numbers and power as they have not yet seen and with the fighting skill of which they are already well aware.

The Secretary of War, who has kept in personal touch with

2. Document No. 1382.
3. See document No. 1258 [in original source].

all phases of the project, will immediately make public a statement giving further details.[4]

His statement will give facts concerning the sites at Oak Ridge near Knoxville, Tennessee, and at Richland near Pasco, Washington, and an installation near Santa Fe, New Mexico. Although the workers at the sites have been making materials to be used in producing the greatest destructive force in history they have not themselves been in danger beyond that of many other occupations, for the utmost care has been taken of their safety.

The fact that we can release atomic energy ushers in a new era in man's understanding of nature's forces. Atomic energy may in the future supplement the power that now comes from coal, oil, and falling water, but at present it cannot be produced on a basis to compete with them commercially. Before that comes there must be a long period of intensive research.

It has never been the habit of the scientists of this country or the policy of this Government to withhold from the world scientific knowledge. Normally, therefore, everything about the work with atomic energy would be made public.

But under present circumstances it is not intended to divulge the technical processes of production or all the military applications, pending further examination of possible methods of protecting us and the rest of the world from the danger of sudden destruction.

I shall recommend that the Congress of the United States consider promptly the establishment of an appropriate commission to control the production and use of atomic power within the United States. I shall give further consideration and make further recommendations to the Congress as to how atomic power can become a powerful and forceful influence towards the maintenance of world peace.

4. For the text of Stimson's statement of August 6, 1945, see Raymond Dennett and Robert K. Turner, eds., *Documents on American Foreign Relations, July 1, 1945-December 31, 1946* (Princeton, 1948), p. 413.

2

Philosophical Basis of the Policy of Containment

George F. Kennan's
"The Sources of Soviet Conduct"

George F. Kennan may correctly be called the scholar-diplomat.
Born in Milwaukee, Wisconsin in 1904, he attended Princeton University and graduated in 1925. He entered the newly formed Foreign
Service of the State Department immediately upon graduation and remained in it until 1953. As a diplomat he considered it his responsibility to steep himself in the culture of those countries in which he
might be stationed, and he became one of the leading authorities in
the United States on the Soviet Union. During the final year of World
War II he served under Ambassador Harriman in the Embassy at
Moscow. In 1946 he sent a long telegram to the State Department in
which he brilliantly analyzed Russo-American relations. Secretary of
State Marshall appointed him Director of the newly formed Policy
Planning Staff of the State Department in 1947, and in July of the
same year his article, signed by "Mr. X" and entitled "Sources of
Soviet Conduct," appeared in *Foreign Affairs*. This article, which
provided the philosophical basis for the policy of containment, was
reprinted in Kennan's *American Diplomacy, 1900-1950*. By 1958, however, Kennan had shifted his views, and first in a BBC address and
then in *Russia, the Atom and the West* (1958) he called for the withdrawal of both Russian and NATO forces from central Europe, the
neutralization of Germany, and its reunification. In 1959 he became
particularly critical of what he considered an undue reliance upon
nuclear weapons. He was ambassador to Russia in 1952, and in 1961
President Kennedy appointed him ambassador to Yugoslavia. He has
written a two-volume study of Russo-American relations during and
after World War I, the first of which, *Russia Leaves the War* (1956)
won several prizes, including the Pulitzer prize for history. Additional
useful reading can be found in John Lukacs, *A History of the Cold
War* (New York, 1961). In reading "Sources of Soviet Conduct," note

"The Sources of Soviet Conduct" first appeared in *Foreign Affairs*, XXV
(July 1947) pp. 566-582, and is reprinted here with the permission of
the editor. Copyrighted by the Council on Foreign Relations, Inc. Footnotes in the text are Mr. Kennan's.

(1) what reasons the Soviet leaders found for retaining absolute power; (2) what has been the significance of the idea of "the innate antagonism between capitalism and socialism" for Russia's foreign relations; (3) the effects Kennan sees of Soviet absolutism upon the Russian society and people; and (4) Kennan's conclusions respecting American policy toward the Soviet Union.

I]

THE POLITICAL PERSONALITY OF SOVIET POWER AS WE know it today is the product of ideology and circumstances: ideology inherited by the present Soviet leaders from the movement in which they had their political origin, and circumstances of the power which they now have exercised for nearly three decades in Russia. There can be few tasks of psychological analysis more difficult than to try to trace the interaction of these two forces and the relative role of each in the determination of official Soviet conduct. Yet the attempt must be understood and effectively countered.

It is difficult to summarize the set of ideological concepts with which the Soviet leaders came into power. Marxian ideology, in its Russian-Communist projection, has always been in process of subtle evolution. The materials on which it bases itself are extensive and complex. But the outstanding features of Communist thought as it existed in 1916 may perhaps be summarized as follows: (*a*) that the central factor in the life of man, the factor which determines the character of public life and the "physiognomy of society," is the system by which material goods are produced and exchanged; (*b*) that the capitalist system of production is a nefarious one which inevitably leads to the exploitation of the working class by the capital-owning class and is incapable of developing adequately the economic resources of society or of distributing fairly the material goods produced by human labor; (*c*) that capitalism contains the seeds of its own destruction and must, in view of the inability of the capital-owning class to adjust itself to economic change, result eventually and inescapably in a revolutionary transfer of power to the working class; and (*d*) that imperialism, the final phase of capitalism, leads directly to war and revolution.

The rest may be outlined in Lenin's own words: "Unevenness of economic and political development is the inflexible law of capitalism. It follows from this that the victory of Socialism may come originally in a few capitalist countries or even in a single capitalist country. The victorious proletariat of that country, having expropriated the capitalists and having organized Socialist production at home, would rise against the remaining capitalist world, drawing to itself in the process the oppressed classes of other countries."[1] It must be noted that there was no assumption that capitalism would perish without proletarian revolution. A final push was needed from a revolutionary proletariat movement in order to tip over the tottering structure. But it was regarded as inevitable that sooner or later that push be given.

For fifty years prior to the outbreak of the Revolution, this pattern of thought had exercised great fascination for the members of the Russian revolutionary movement. Frustrated, discontented, hopeless of finding self-expression—or too impatient to seek it—in the confining limits of the Tsarist political system, yet lacking wide popular support for their choice of bloody revolution as a means of social betterment, these revolutionists found in Marxist theory a highly convenient rationalization for their own instinctive desires. It afforded pseudo-scientific justification for their impatience, for their categoric denial of all value in the Tsarist system, for their yearning for power and revenge and for their inclination to cut corners in the pursuit of it. It is therefore no wonder that they had come to believe implicitly in the truth and soundness of the Marxian-Leninist teachings, so congenial to their own impulses and emotions. Their sincerity need not be impugned. This is a phenomenon as old as human nature itself. It has never been more aptly described than by Edward Gibbon, who wrote in *The Decline and Fall of the Roman Empire*: From enthusiasm to imposture the step is perilous and slippery; the demon of Socrates affords a memorable instance how a wise man may deceive himself; how a good man may deceive others, how the conscience may slumber in a mixed and middle state between self-illusion and voluntary fraud." And it was with this set of conceptions that the members of the Bolshevik Party entered into power.

1. *Concerning the Slogans of the United States of Europe, August 1915* (Official Soviet edition of Lenin's works).

Now it must be noted that through all the years of preparation for revolution, the attention of these men, as indeed of Marx himself, had been centered less on the future form which Socialism[2] would take than on the necessary overthrow of rival power which, in their view, had to precede the introduction of Socialism. Their views, therefore, on the positive program to be put into effect, once power was attained, were for the most part nebulous, visionary and impractical. Beyond the nationalization of industry and the expropriation of large private capital holdings, there was no agreed program. The treatment of the peasantry, which according to the Marxist formulation was not of the proletariat, had always been a vague spot in the pattern of Communist thought; and it remained an object of controversy and vacillation for the first ten years of Communist power.

The circumstances of the immediate post-Revolution period— the existence in Russia of civil war and foreign intervention, together with the obvious fact that the Communists represented only a tiny minority of the Russian people—made the establishment of dictatorial power a necessity. The experiment with "war Communism" and the abrupt attempt to eliminate private production and trade had unfortunate economic consequences and caused further bitterness against the new revolutionary regime. While the temporary relaxation of the effort to communize Russia, represented by the New Economic Policy, alleviated some of this economic distress and thereby served its purpose, it also made it evident that the "capitalistic sector of society" was still prepared to profit at once from any relaxation of governmental pressure, and would, if permitted to continue to exist, always constitute a powerful opposing element to the Soviet regime and a serious rival for influence in the country. Somewhat the same situation prevailed with respect to the individual peasant who, in his own small way, was also a private producer.

Lenin, had he lived, might have proved a great enough man to reconcile these conflicting forces to the ultimate benefit of Russian society, though this is questionable. But be that as it may, Stalin, and those whom he led in the struggle for succession to Lenin's position of leadership, were not the men to tolerate rival political forces in the sphere of power which they coveted. Their sense of

2. Here and elsewhere in this paper "Socialism" refers to Marxist or Leninist Communism, not to liberal Socialism of the Second International variety.

insecurity was too great. Their particular brand of fanaticism, unmodified by any of the Anglo-Saxon traditions of compromise, was too fierce and too jealous to envisage any permanent sharing of power. From the Russian-Asiatic world out of which they had emerged they carried with them a skepticism as to the possibilities of permanent and peaceful coexistence of rival forces. Easily persuaded of their own doctrinaire "rightness," they insisted on the submission or destruction of all competing power. Outside of the Communist Party, Russian society was to have no rigidity. There were to be no forms of collective human activity or association which would not be dominated by the Party. No other force in Russian society was to be permitted to achieve vitality or integrity. Only the Party was to have structure. All else was to be an amorphous mass.

And within the Party the same principle was to apply. The mass of Party members might go through the motions of election, deliberation, decision and action; but in these motions they were to be animated not by their own individual wills but by the awesome breath of the Party leadership and the overbrooding presence of "the word."

Let it be stressed again that subjectively these men probably did not seek absolutism for its own sake. They doubtless believed —and found it easy to believe—that they alone knew what was good for society and that they would accomplish that good once their power was secure and unchallengeable. But in seeking that security of their own rule they were prepared to recognize no restrictions, either of God or man, on the character of their methods. And until such time as that security might be achieved, they placed far down on their scale of operational priorities the comforts and happiness of the peoples entrusted to their care.

Now the outstanding circumstance concerning the Soviet regime is that down to the present day this process of political consolidation has never been completed and the men in the Kremlin have continued to be predominantly absorbed with the struggle to secure and make absolute the power which they seized in November 1917. They have endeavored to secure it primarily against forces at home, within Soviet society itself. But they have also endeavored to secure it against the outside world. For ideology, as we have seen, taught them that the outside world was hostile and that it was their duty eventually to overthrow the political forces beyond their borders. The powerful hands of Russian history and tradition reached up to sustain them in this feeling. Finally, their own aggressive intransigence with respect to the outside world began to find its own reaction; and they were soon forced, to use another Gibbonesque phrase, "to chastise the contumacy" which they themselves had provoked. It is an undeniable privilege of every man to prove himself right in the thesis that the world is his enemy; for if he reiterates it frequently enough and makes it the background of his conduct he is bound eventually to be right.

Now it lies in the nature of the mental world of the Soviet leaders, as well as in the character of their ideology, that no opposition to them can be officially recognized as having any merit or justification whatsoever. Such opposition can flow, in theory, only from the hostile and incorrigible forces of dying capitalism. As long as remnants of capitalism were officially recognized as existing in Russia, it was possible to place on them, as an internal element, part of the blame for the maintenance of a dictatorial form of society. But as these remnants were liquidated, little by little, this justification fell away; and when it was indicated officially that they had been finally destroyed, it disappeared altogether. And this fact created one of the most basic of the compulsions which came to act upon the Soviet regime; since capitalism no longer existed in Russia and since it could not be admitted that there could be serious or widespread opposition to the Kremlin springing spontaneously from the liberated masses under its authority, it became necessary to justify the retention of the dictatorship by stressing the menace of capitalism abroad.

This began at an early date. In 1924, Stalin specifically defended the retention of the "organs of suppression," meaning, among others, the army and the secret police, on the ground that "as long as there is a capitalist encirclement there will be danger of intervention with all the consequences that flow from that danger." In accordance with that theory, and from that time on, all internal opposition forces in Russia have consistently been portrayed as the agents of foreign forces of reaction antagonistic to Soviet power.

By the same token, tremendous emphasis has been placed on the original Communist thesis of a basic antagonism between the capitalist and Socialist worlds. It is clear, from many indications, that this emphasis is not founded in reality. The real facts concerning it have been confused by the existence abroad of genuine resentment provoked by Soviet philosophy and tactics and occasionally by the existence of great centers of military power, notably the Nazi regime in Germany and the Japanese Government of the late 1930's, which did indeed have aggressive designs against the Soviet Union. But there is ample evidence that the stress laid in Moscow on the menace confronting Soviet society from the world outside its borders is founded not in the realities of foreign antagonism but in the necessity of explaining away the maintenance of dictatorial authority at home.

Now the maintenance of this pattern of Soviet power, namely, the pursuit of unlimited authority domestically, accompanied by the cultivation of the semi-myth of implacable foreign hostility, has gone far to shape the actual machinery of Soviet power as we know it today. Internal organs of administration which did not serve this purpose withered on the vine. Organs which did serve this purpose became vastly swollen. The security of Soviet power came to rest on the iron discipline of the Party, on the severity and ubiquity of the secret police, and on the uncompromising economic monopolism of the state. The "organs of suppression," in which the Soviet leaders had sought security from rival forces, became in large measure the masters of those whom they were designed to serve. Today the major part of the structure of Soviet power is committed to the perfection of the dictatorship and to the maintenance of the concept of Russia as in a state of siege, with the enemy lowering beyond the walls. And the millions of human beings who form that part of the structure of power must defend at all costs this concept of Russia's position, for without it they are themselves superfluous.

As things stand today, the rulers can no longer dream of parting with these organs of suppression. The quest for absolute power, pursued now for nearly three decades with a ruthlessness unparalleled (in scope at least) in modern times, has again produced internally, as it did externally, its own reaction. The excesses of the police apparatus have fanned the potential opposition to the regime into something far greater and more dangerous than it could have been before those excesses began. But least of all can the rulers dispense with the fiction by which the maintenance of dictatorial power has been defended. For this fiction has been canonized in Soviet philosophy by the excesses already committed in its name; and it is now anchored in the Soviet structure of thought by bonds far greater than those of mere ideology.

II]

So much for the historical background. What does it spell in terms of the political personality of Soviet power as we know it today?

Of the original ideology, nothing has been officially junked. Belief is maintained in the basic badness of capitalism, in the inevitability of its destruction, in the obligation of the proletariat to assist in that destruction and to take power into its own hands. But stress has come to be laid primarily on those concepts which relate most specifically to the Soviet regime itself: to its position as the sole truly Socialist regime in a dark and misguided world, and to the relationship of power within it.

The first of these concepts is that of the innate antagonism between capitalism and Socialism. We have seen how deeply that concept has become imbedded in foundations of Soviet power. It has profound implications for Russia's conduct as a member of international society. It means that there can never be on Moscow's side any sincere assumption of a community of aims between the Soviet Union and powers which are regarded as capitalist. It must invariably be assumed in Moscow that the aims of the capitalist world are antagonistic to the Soviet regime and, therefore, to the interests of the peoples it controls. If the Soviet Government occasionally sets its signature to documents which would indicate the contrary, this is to be regarded as a tactical maneuver permissible in dealing with the enemy (who is without honor) and should be taken in the spirit of *caveat emptor*. Basically, the antagonism remains. It is postulated. And from it flow many of the phenomena which we find disturbing in the Kremlin's conduct of foreign policy: the secretiveness, the lack of frankness, the duplicity, the war suspiciousness, and the basic unfriendliness of purpose. These phenomena are there to stay, for the foreseeable future. There can be variations of degree and of emphasis. When there is something the Russians want

from us, one or the other of these features of their policy may be
thrust temporarily into the background; and when that happens
there will always be Americans who will leap forward with
gleeful announcements that "the Russians have changed," and
some who will even try to take credit for having brought about
such "changes." But we should not be misled by tactical maneuvers. These characteristics of Soviet policy, like the postulate
from which they flow, are basic to the internal nature of Soviet
power, and will be with us, whether in the foreground or the
background, until the internal nature of Soviet power is changed.

This means that we are going to continue for a long time to
find the Russians difficult to deal with. It does not mean that they
should be considered as embarked upon a do-or-die program to
overthrow our society by a given date. The theory of the inevitability of the eventual fall of capitalism has the fortunate
connotation that there is no hurry about it. The forces of progress
can take their time in preparing the final *coup de grâce*. Meanwhile, what is vital is that the "Socialist fatherland"—that oasis of
power which has been already won for Socialism in the person
of the Soviet Union—should be cherished and defended by all
good Communists at home and abroad, its fortunes promoted, its
enemies badgered and confounded. The promotion of premature,
"adventuristic" revolutionary projects abroad which might
embarrass Soviet power in any way would be an inexcusable,
even a counter-revolutionary act. The cause of Socialism is the
support and promotion of Soviet power, as defined in Moscow.

This brings us to the second of the concepts important to
contemporary Soviet outlook. That is the infallibility of the
Kremlin. The Soviet concept of power, which permits no focal
points of organization outside the Party itself, requires that the
Party leadership remain in theory the sole repository of truth. For
if truth were to be found elsewhere, there would be justification
for its expression in organized activity. But it is precisely that
which the Kremlin cannot and will not permit.

The leadership of the Communist Party is therefore always
right, and has been always right ever since in 1929 Stalin formal-
ized his personal power by announcing that decisions of the
Politburo were being taken unanimously.

On the principle of infallibility there rests the iron discipline
of the Communist Party. In fact, the two concepts are mutually

self-supporting. Perfect discipline requires recognition of infallibility. Infallibility requires the observance of discipline. And the two together go far to determine the behaviorism of the entire Soviet apparatus of power. But their effect cannot be understood unless a third factor be taken into account: namely, the fact that the leadership is at liberty to put forward for tactical purposes any particular thesis which it finds useful to the cause at any particular moment and to require the faithful and unquestioning acceptance of that thesis by the members of the movement as a whole. This means that truth is not a constant but is actually created, for all intents and purposes, by the Soviet leaders themselves. It may vary from week to week, from month to month. It is nothing absolute and immutable—nothing which flows from objective reality. It is only the most recent manifestation of the wisdom of those in whom the ultimate wisdom is supposed to reside, because they represent the logic of history. The accumulative effect of these factors is to give to the whole subordinate apparatus of Soviet power an unshakeable stubbornness and steadfastness in its orientation. This orientation can be changed at will by the Kremlin but by no other power. Once a given party line has been laid down on a given issue of current policy, the whole Soviet governmental machine, including the mechanism of diplomacy, moves inexorably along the prescribed path, like a persistent toy automobile wound up and headed in a given direction, stopping only when it meets with some unanswerable force. The individuals who are the components of this machine are unamenable to argument or reason which comes to them from outside sources. Their whole training has taught them to mistrust and discount the glib persuasiveness of the outside world. Like the white dog before the phonograph, they hear only the "master's voice." And if they are to be called off from the purposes last dictated to them, it is the master who must call them off. Thus the foreign representative cannot hope that his words will make any impression on them. The most that he can hope is that they will be transmitted to those at the top, who are capable of changing the party line. But even those are not likely to be swayed by any normal logic in the words of the bourgeois representative. Since there can be no appeal to common purposes, there can be no appeal to common mental approaches. For this reason, facts speak louder than words to the ears of the Kremlin;

and words carry the greatest weight when they have the ring of reflecting, or being backed up by, facts of unchallengeable validity.

But we have seen that the Kremlin is under no ideological compulsion to accomplish its purposes in a hurry. Like the Church, it is dealing in ideological concepts which are of long-term validity, and it can afford to be patient. It has no right to risk the existing achievements of the revolution for the sake of vain baubles of the future. The very teachings of Lenin himself require great caution and flexibility in the pursuit of Communist purposes. Again, these precepts are fortified by the lessons of Russian history: of centuries of obscure battles between nomadic forces over the stretches of a vast unfortified plain. Here caution, circumspection, flexibility and deception are the valuable qualities; and their value finds natural appreciation in the Russian or the oriental mind. Thus the Kremlin has no compunction about retreating in the face of superior force. And being under the compulsion of no timetable, it does not get panicky under the necessity for such retreat. Its political action is a fluid stream which moves constantly, wherever it is permitted to move, toward a given goal. Its main concern is to make sure that it has filled every nook and cranny available to it in the basin of world power. But if it finds unassailable barriers in its path, it accepts these philosophically and accommodates itself to them. The main thing is that there should always be pressure, unceasing constant pressure, toward the desired goal. There is no trace of any feeling in Soviet psychology that that goal must be reached at any given time.

These considerations make Soviet diplomacy at once easier and more difficult to deal with than the diplomacy of individual aggressive leaders like Napoleon and Hitler. On the one hand it is more sensitive to contrary force, more ready to yield on individual sectors of the diplomatic front when that force is felt to be too strong, and thus more rational in the logic and rhetoric of power. On the other hand it cannot be easily defeated or discouraged by a single victory on the part of its opponents. And the patient persistence by which it is animated means that it can be effectively countered not by sporadic acts which represent the momentary whims of democratic opinion but only by intelligent long-range policies on the part of Russia's adversaries—

policies no less steady in their purpose, and no less variegated and resourceful in their application, than those of the Soviet Union itself.

In these circumstances it is clear that the main element of any United States policy toward the Soviet Union must be that of a long-term, patient but firm and vigilant containment of Russian expansive tendencies. It is important to note, however, that such a policy has nothing to do with outward histrionics: with threats or blustering or superfluous gestures of outward "toughness." While the Kremlin is basically flexible in its reaction to political realities, it is by no means unamenable to considerations of prestige. Like almost any other government, it can be placed by tactless and threatening gestures in a position where it cannot afford to yield even though this might be dictated by its sense of realism. The Russian leaders are keen judges of human psychology, and as such they are highly conscious that loss of temper and self-control is never a source of strength in political affairs. They are quick to exploit such evidences of weakness. For these reasons, it is a *sine qua non* of successful dealing with Russia that the foreign government in question should remain at all times cool and collected and that its demands on Russian policy should be put forward in such a manner as to leave the way open for a compliance not too detrimental to Russian prestige.

III]

In the light of the above, it will be clearly seen that the Soviet pressure against the free institutions of the Western world is something that can be contained by the adroit and vigilant application of counter-force at a series of constantly shifting geographical and political points, corresponding to the shifts and maneuvers of Soviet policy, but which cannot be charmed or talked out of existence. The Russians look forward to a duel of infinite duration, and they see that already they have scored great successes. It must be borne in mind that there was a time when the Communist Party represented far more of a minority in the sphere of Russian national life than Soviet power today represents in the world community.

But if ideology convinces the rulers of Russia that truth is on their side and that they can therefore afford to wait, those of us on whom that ideology has no claim are free to examine objectively the validity of that premise. The Soviet thesis not only implies complete lack of control by the West over its own economic destiny, it likewise assumes Russian unity, discipline and patience over an infinite period. Let us bring this apocalyptic vision down to earth, and suppose that the Western world finds the strength and resourcefulness to contain Soviet power over a period of ten to fifteen years. What does that spell for Russia itself?

The Soviet leaders, taking advantage of the contributions of modern technique to the arts of despotism, have solved the question of obedience within the confines of their power. Few challenge their authority; and even those who do are unable to make that challenge valid as against the organs of suppression of the state.

The Kremlin has also proved able to accomplish its purpose of building up in Russia, regardless of the interests of the inhabitants, an industrial foundation of heavy metallurgy, which is, to be sure, not yet complete but which is nevertheless continuing to grow and is approaching those of the other major industrial countries. All of this, however, both the maintenance of internal political security and the building of heavy industry, has been carried out at a terrible cost in human life and in human hopes and energies. It has necessitated the use of forced labor on a scale unprecedented in modern times under conditions of peace. It has involved the neglect or abuse of other phases of Soviet economic life, particularly agriculture, consumers' goods production, housing and transportation.

To all that, the war has added its tremendous toll of destruction, death and human exhaustion. In consequence of this, we have in Russia today a population which is physically and spiritually tired. The mass of the people are disillusioned, skeptical and no longer as accessible as they once were to the magical attraction which Soviet power still radiates to its followers abroad. The avidity with which people seized upon the slightest respite accorded to the Church for tactical reasons during the war was eloquent testimony to the fact that their capacity for faith and devotion found little expression in the purposes of the regime.

In these circumstances, there are limits to the physical and nervous strength of people themselves. These limits are absolute ones, and are binding even for the cruelest dictatorship, because beyond them people cannot be driven. The forced labor camps and the other agencies of constraint provide temporary means of compelling people to work longer hours than their own volition or mere economic pressure would dictate; but if people survive them at all they become old before their time and must be considered as human casualties to the demands of dictatorship. In either case their best powers are no longer available to society and can no longer be enlisted in the service of the state.

Here only the younger generation can help. The younger generation, despite all vicissitudes and sufferings, is numerous and vigorous; and the Russians are a talented people. But it still remains to be seen what will be the effects on mature performance of the abnormal emotional strains of childhood which Soviet dictatorship created and which were enormously increased by the war. Such things as normal security and placidity of home environment have practically ceased to exist in the Soviet Union outside of the most remote farms and villages. And observers are not yet sure whether that is not going to leave its mark on the over-all capacity of the generation now coming into maturity.

In addition to this, we have the fact that Soviet economic development, while it can list certain formidable achievements, has been precariously spotty and uneven. Russian Communists who speak of the "uneven development of capitalism" should blush at the contemplation of their own national economy. Here certain branches of economic life, such as the metallurgical and machine industries, have been pushed out of all proportion to other sectors of economy. Here is a nation striving to become in a short period one of the great industrial nations of the world while it still has no highway network worthy of the name and only a relatively primitive network of railways. Much has been done to increase efficiency of labor and to teach primitive peasants something about the operation of machines. But maintenance is still a crying deficiency of all Soviet economy. Construction is hasty and poor in quality. Depreciation must be enormous. And in vast sectors of economic life it has not yet been possible to instill into labor anything like that general

culture of production and technical self-respect which character-
izes the skilled worker of the West.

It is difficult to see how these deficiencies can be corrected at
an early date by a tired and dispirited population working
largely under the shadow of fear and compulsion. And as long
as they are not overcome, Russia will remain economically a
vulnerable, and in a certain sense an impotent, nation, capable
of exporting its enthusiasms and of radiating the strange charm
of its primitive political vitality but unable to back up those
articles of export by the real evidences of material power and
prosperity.

Meanwhile, a great uncertainty hangs over the political life of
the Soviet Union. That is the uncertainty involved in the transfer
of power from one individual or group of individuals to others.

This is, of course, outstandingly the problem of the personal
position of Stalin. We must remember that his succession to
Lenin's pinnacle of preeminence in the Communist movement
was the only such transfer of individual authority which the
Soviet Union has experienced. That transfer took twelve years
to consolidate. It cost the lives of millions of people and shook
the state to its foundations. The attendant tremors were felt all
through the international revolutionary movement, to the dis-
advantage of the Kremlin itself.

It is always possible that another transfer of preeminent power
may take place quietly and inconspicuously, with no repercussions anywhere. But again, it is possible that the questions
involved may unleash, to use some of Lenin's words, one of
those "incredibly swift transitions" from "delicate deceit" to
"wild violence" which characterize Russian history, and may
shake Soviet power to its foundations.

But this is not only a question of Stalin himself. There has
been, since 1938, a dangerous congealment of political life in the
higher circles of Soviet power. The All-Union Party Congress,
in theory the supreme body of the Party, is supposed to meet
not less often than once in three years. It will soon be eight full
years since its last meeting. During this period membership in
the Party has numerically doubled. Party mortality during the
war was enormous, and today well over half of the Party members are persons who have entered since the last Party Congress
was held. Meanwhile, the same small group of men has carried

on at the top through an amazing series of national vicissitudes. Surely there is some reason why the experiences of the war brought basic political changes to every one of the great governments of the West. Surely the causes of that phenomenon are basic enough to be present somewhere in the obscurity of Soviet political life, as well. And yet no recognition has been given to these causes in Russia.

It must be surmised from this that even within so highly disciplined an organization as the Communist Party there must be a growing divergence in age, outlook and interest between the great mass of Party members, only so recently recruited into the movement, and the little self-perpetuating clique of men at the top, whom most of these Party members have never met, with whom they have never conversed, and with whom they can have no political intimacy.

Who can say whether, in these circumstances, the eventual rejuvenation of the higher spheres of authority (which can only be a matter of time) can take place smoothly and peacefully, or whether rivals in the quest for higher power will not eventually reach down into these politically immature and inexperienced masses in order to find support for their respective claims. If this were ever to happen, strange consequences could flow for the Communist Party: for the membership at large has been exercised only in the practices of iron discipline and obedience and not in the arts of compromise and accommodation. And if disunity were ever to seize and paralyze the Party, the chaos and weakness of Russian society would be revealed in forms beyond description. For we have seen that Soviet power is only a crust concealing an amorphous mass of human beings among whom no independent organizational structure is tolerated. In Russia there is not even such a thing as local government. The present generation of Russians have never known spontaneity of collective action. If, consequently, anything were ever to occur to disrupt the unity and efficacy of the Party as a political instrument, Soviet Russia might be changed overnight from one of the strongest to one of the weakest and most pitiable of national societies.

Thus the future of Soviet power may not be by any means as secure as Russian capacity for self-delusion would make it appear to the men in the Kremlin. That they can keep power themselves, they have demonstrated. That they can quietly and easily turn it over to others remains to be proved. Meanwhile, the hardships of their rule and the vicissitudes of international life have taken a heavy toll of the strength and hopes of the great people on whom their power rests. It is curious to note that the ideological power of Soviet authority is strongest today in areas beyond the frontiers of Russia, beyond the reach of its police power. This phenomenon brings to mind a comparison used by Thomas Mann in his great novel *Buddenbrooks*. Observing that human institutions often show the greatest outward brilliance at a moment when inner decay is in reality farthest advanced, he compared the Buddenbrook family in the days of its greatest glamour to one of those stars whose light shines most brightly on this world when in reality it has long since ceased to exist. And who can say with assurance that the strong light still cast by the Kremlin on the dissatisfied peoples of the Western world is not the powerful afterglow of a constellation which is in actuality on the wane? This cannot be proved. And it cannot be disproved. But the possibility remains (and in the opinion of this writer it is a strong one) that Soviet power, like the capitalist world of its conception, bears within it the seeds of its own decay, and that the sprouting of these seeds is well advanced.

IV]

It is clear that the United States cannot expect in the foreseeable future to enjoy political intimacy with the Soviet regime. It must continue to regard the Soviet Union as a rival, not a partner, in the political arena. It must continue to expect that Soviet policies will reflect no abstract love of peace and stability, no real faith in the possibility of a permanent happy coexistence of the Socialist and capitalist worlds, but rather a cautious, persistent pressure toward the disruption and weakening of all rival influence and rival power.

Balanced against this are the facts that Russia, as opposed to the Western world in general, is still by far the weaker party, that Soviet policy is highly flexible, and that Soviet society may well contain deficiencies which will eventually weaken its own total potential. This would of itself warrant the United States entering with reasonable confidence upon a policy of firm containment, designed to confront the Russians with unalterable counter-force at every point where they show signs of encroaching upon the interests of a peaceful and stable world.

But in actuality the possibilities for American policy are by no means limited to holding the line and hoping for the best. It is entirely possible for the United States to influence by its actions the internal developments, both within Russia and throughout the international Communist movement, by which Russian policy is largely determined. This is not only a question of the modest measure of informational activity which this government can conduct in the Soviet Union and elsewhere, although that, too, is important. It is rather a question of the degree to which the United States can create among the peoples of the world generally the impression of a country which knows what it wants, which is coping successfully with the problems of its internal life and with the responsibilities of a World Power, and which has a spiritual vitality capable of holding its own among the major ideological currents of the time. To the extent that such an impression can be created and maintained, the aims of Russian Communism must appear sterile and quixotic, the hopes and enthusiasm of Moscow's supporters must wane, and added strain must be imposed on the Kremlin's foreign policies. For the palsied decrepitude of the capitalist world is the key-stone of Communist philosophy. Even the failure of the United States to experience the early economic depression which the ravens of the Red Square have been predicting with such complacent confidence since hostilities ceased would have deep and important repercussions throughout the Communist world.

By the same token, exhibitions of indecision, disunity and internal disintegration within this country have an exhilarating effect on the whole Communist movement. At each evidence of these tendencies, a thrill of hope and excitement goes through the Communist world; a new jauntiness can be noted in the Moscow tread; new groups of foreign supporters climb on to what they can only view as the band wagon of international politics; and Russian pressure increases all along the line in international affairs.

It would be an exaggeration to say that American behavior unassisted and alone could exercise a power of life and death over the Communist movement and bring about the early fall of

THE UNITED STATES IN THE CONTEMPORARY WORLD

Soviet power in Russia. But the United States has it in its power to increase enormously the strains under which Soviet policy must operate, to force upon the Kremlin a far greater degree of moderation and circumspection than it has had to observe in recent years, and in this way to promote tendencies which must eventually find their outlet in either the break-up or the gradual mellowing of Soviet power. For no mystical, Messianic movement—and particularly not that of the Kremlin—can face frustration indefinitely without eventually adjusting itself in one way or another to the logic of that state of affairs.

Thus the decision will really fall in large measure in this country itself. The issue of Soviet-American relations is in essence a test of the over-all worth of the United States as a nation among nations. To avoid destruction the United States need only measure up to its own best traditions and prove itself worthy of preservation as a great nation.

Surely, there was never a fairer test of national quality than this. In the light of these circumstances, the thoughtful observer of Russian-American relations will find no cause for complaint in the Kremlin's challenge to American society. He will rather experience a certain gratitude to a Providence which, by providing the American people with this implacable challenge, has made their entire security as a nation dependent on their pulling themselves together and accepting the responsibilities of moral and political leadership that history plainly intended them to bear.

3

The Marshall Plan for European Recovery

Secretary Marshall's Report to the Senate Committee on Foreign Affairs

One of the principal devices used by the United States to aid the Allies in their war against the Axis Powers had been H.R. 1776, the famous Lend Lease Act, passed in 1941. Until June 30, 1947, Lend Lease continued to function and provided almost fifty-one billion dollars in war and postwar aid. Additional relief was provided through the agency of the United Nations Relief and Rehabilitation Administration (UNNRA) supported largely by the United States. UNNRA also ceased its activities in 1947, but the United States continued to provide relief funds to individual countries. The State Department's Policy Planning Staff, recognizing the essentially negative nature of the "relief" approach, developed a plan that would revive European economics and make them self-supporting. On May 8, 1947, Undersecretary of State Dean Acheson outlined the requirements for European Reconstruction in an address at Cleveland, Mississippi, and sought to emphasize the need for an American Foreign Aid Program. A month later Secretary of State George C. Marshall himself delivered the famous address at Harvard in which he called on those nations who were interested to work out a cooperative program for recovery and submit it to the United States.

The invitation brought a quick response. Indeed, it was thought that Russia might cooperate with other European countries in working out a proposal. It soon became apparent, however, that Russia was in no mood to cooperate herself or to permit cooperation on the part of any of her allies. On July 12 sixteen other European nations met at Paris; they were later joined by West Germany. On September 22 they presented a bulky report to Secretary Marshall which outlined an enormous reconstruction plan.

For the rest of the year, studies and debates in various U.S. circles attempted to decide whether this country would finance a relief or a recovery program for Europe. Before the end of the year, Congress

Hearings before the Committee on Foreign Relations, U.S. Senate, 80th Cong., 2d Sess., 1948, on United States Assistance to European Economic Recovery, part 1, pp. 1-10.

had approved an appropriation of $880,000,000 for interim relief, and by the first of the new year was ready to begin a consideration of the long-range European Recovery Program.

The document produced here is Secretary Marshall's testimony before the Senate Committee on Foreign Relations in favor of the program. The measure was approved by Congress and signed by President Truman on April 3, 1948. For additional information consult Joseph M. Jones, *The Fifteen Weeks* (New York, 1955) and Harry B. Price, *The Marshall Plan and Its Meaning* (Ithaca, 1955). In reading this document, note (1) the general purposes of the European Recovery Program; (2) the principal arguments advanced by Marshall in favor of the program; and (3) the questions raised by Marshall about the proposal, and how he answered each one.

European Recovery Program]
Thursday, January 8, 1948]

UNITED STATES SENATE,
COMMITTEE ON FOREIGN RELATIONS,
WASHINGTON, D.C.

THE COMMITTEE MET, PURSUANT TO CALL, AT 10 A.M., in room 318, Senate Office Building, Senator Arthur H. Vandenberg (chairman) presiding.

Present: Senators Vandenberg (chairman), Capper, Wiley, Smith, Hickenlooper, Lodge, Connally, George, Thomas of Utah, Barkley, and Hatch.

Also present: Senators Lucas, Millikin, and Baldwin; Hon. Lewis W. Douglas, Ambassador to Great Britain.

The CHAIRMAN. The committee will come to order.

The committee has before it the proposed legislation for European recovery. The first witness will be the Secretary of State, Mr. Marshall. Mr. Secretary, will you take the stand?

Mr. Secretary, we will be very glad to have you proceed in your own way to present this subject.

Statement of Hon. George C. Marshall, Secretary of State]

Secretary MARSHALL. On December 19 the President placed before you the recommendations of the executive branch of the Government for a program of United States assistance to European economic recovery.

This program will cost our country billions of dollars. It will impose a burden on the American taxpayer. It will require sacrifices today in order that we may enjoy security and peace tomorrow. Should the Congress approve the program for European recovery, as I urgently recommend, we Americans will have made a historic decision of our peacetime history.

A nation in which the voice of its people directs the conduct of its affairs cannot embark on an undertaking of such magnitude and significance for light or purely sentimental reasons. Decisions of this importance are dictated by the highest considerations of national interest. There are none higher, I am sure, than the establishment of enduring peace and the maintenance of true freedom for the individual. In the deliberations of the coming weeks I ask that the European recovery program be judged in these terms and on this basis.

As the Secretary of State and as the initial representative of the executive branch of the Government in the presentation of the program to your committee, I will first outline my convictions as to the extent and manner in which American interests are involved in European recovery.

Without the reestablishment of economic health and vigor in the free countries of Europe, without the restoration of their social and political strength necessarily associated with economic recuperation, the prospect for the American people, and for free people everywhere, to find peace with justice and well-being and security for themselves and their children will be gravely prejudiced.

So long as hunger, poverty, desperation, and resulting chaos threaten the great concentrations of people in western Europe—some 270,000,000—there will steadily develop social unease and political confusion on every side. Left to their own resources there will be, I believe, no escape from economic distress so intense, social discontents so violent, political confusion so widespread, and hopes of the future so shattered that the historic base of western civilization, of which we are by belief and inheritance an integral part, will take on a new form in the image of the tyranny that we fought to destroy in Germany. The vacuum which the war created in western Europe will be filled by the forces of which wars are made. Our national security will be seriously threatened. We shall in effect live in an armed camp, regulated and controlled. But if we furnish effective aid to support the now visible reviving hope of Europe, the prospect should speedily change. The foundation of political vitality is economic recovery. Durable peace requires the restoration of western European vitality.

We have engaged in a great war. We poured out our resources to win that war. We fought it to make real peace possible. Though the war has ended the peace has not commenced. We must not fail to complete that which we commenced.

The peoples of western Europe have demonstrated their will to achieve a genuine recovery by entering into a great cooperative effort. Within the limits of their resources they formally undertake to establish the basis for the peace which we all seek, but they cannot succeed without American assistance. Dollars will not save the world, but the world today cannot be saved without dollars.

The Paris Report of the Committee of European Economic Cooperation was a notable achievement. For the first time in modern history representatives of 16 nations collectively disclosed their internal economic conditions and frailties and undertook, subject to stated conditions, to do certain things for the mutual benefit of all. The commitments each made to the other, if faithfully observed, will produce in western Europe a far more integrated economic system than any in previous history.

The report revealed the measure of outside assistance which in their judgment would be necessary to effect a lasting recovery of the participating nations. The executive branch, with help and advice from a great many sources, has developed from this report a program of American aid to Europe which gives substantial promise of achieving the goal of genuine recovery. The program is not one of a series of piecemeal relief measures. I ask that you note this difference, and keep it in mind throughout our explanations. The difference is absolutely vital.

I believe that this measure has received as concentrated study as has ever gone into the preparation of any proposal made to the Congress. The best minds in numerous related fields have worked for months on this vast and complicated subject. In addition, the best economic and political brains of 16 European nations have given us in an amazingly short time their analyses and conclusions.

The problem we face is enormously complex. It affects not only our country and Europe, but almost every other part of the globe.

We wish to present to you in the simplest possible way a full explanation of the executive branch recommendations for aid to Europe. Our presentation will entail the appearance of high officials from the agencies of the Government intimately concerned. Others will give you more detailed information on the many factors to be considered.

I will confine my remarks to the three basic questions involved: First, "Why does Europe need help?" Second, "How much help is needed?" And third, "How should help be given?"

The "why": Europe is still emerging from the devastation and dislocation of the most destructive war in history. Within its own resources Europe cannot achieve within a reasonable time economic stability. The war more or less destroyed the mechanism whereby Europe supported itself in the past and the initial rebuilding of that mechanism requires outside assistance under existing circumstances.

The western European participating countries, with a present population almost twice our own, constitute an interdependent area containing some of the most highly industrialized nations of the world. As a group, they are one of the two major workshops of the world. Production has become more and more specialized, and depends in large part on the processing of raw materials, largely imported from abroad, into finished goods and the furnishing of services to other areas. These goods and services have been sold throughout the world and the proceeds therefrom paid for the necessary imports.

The war smashed the vast and delicate mechanism by which European countries made their living. It was the war which destroyed coal mines and deprived the workshop of sufficient mechanical energy. It was the war which destroyed steel mills and thus cut down the workshop's material for fabrication. It was the war which destroyed transportation lines and equipment and thus made the ability to move goods and people inadequate. It was the war which destroyed livestock herds, made fertilizers unobtainable and thus reduced soil fertility. It was the war which destroyed merchant fleets and thus cut off accustomed income from carrying the world's goods. It was the war which destroyed or caused the loss of so much of foreign investments and the income which it has produced. It was the war which bled inventories and working capital out of existence. It was the war which shattered business relationships and markets and the sources of raw materials. The war disrupted the flow of vital raw materials from southeast Asia, thereby breaking the pattern of multilateral trade which formerly provided, directly or indirectly, large dollar earnings for western Europe. In the postwar period artificial and forcible reorientation to the Soviet Union of eastern European trade had deprived western Europe of sources of food-stuff and raw material from that area. Here and there the present European situation has been aggravated by unsound or destructive policies pursued in one or another country, but the basic dislocations find their source directly in the war.

The inability of the European workshop to get food and raw materials required to produce the exports necessary to get the purchasing power for food and raw materials is the worst of the many vicious circles that beset the European peoples. Not withstanding the fact that industrial output, except in western Germany, has almost regained its prewar volume, under the changed conditions this is not nearly enough. The loss of European investments abroad, the destruction of merchant fleets, and the disappearance of other sources of income, together with increases in populations to be sustained, make necessary an increase in production far above prewar levels, even sufficient for a living standard considerably below prewar standards.

This is the essence of the economic problem of Europe. This problem would exist even though it were not complicated by the ideological struggles in Europe between those who want to live as freemen and those small groups who aspire to dominate by the method of police states. The solution would be much easier, of course, if all the nations of Europe were cooperating. But they are not. Far from cooperating, the Soviet Union and the Communist parties have proclaimed their determined opposition to a plan for European economic recovery. Economic distress is to be employed to further political ends.

There are many who accept the picture that I have just drawn but who raise a further question: "Why must the United States carry so great a load in helping Europe?" The answer is simple. The United States is the only country in the world today which has the economic power and productivity to furnish the needed assistance.

I wish now to turn to the other questions which we must answer. These are "how much" aid is required and "how" should that aid be given.

Three principles should determine the amount and timing of our aid. It must be adequate. It must be prompt, it must be effectively applied.

The objective of the European recovery program submitted for your consideration is to achieve lasting economic recovery for western Europe; recovery in the sense that after our aid has terminated, the European countries will be able to maintain themselves by their own efforts on a sound economic basis.

Our assistance, if we determine to embark on this program to aid western Europe, must be adequate to do the job. The initial increment of our aid should be fully sufficient to get the program under way on a broad, sound basis and not in a piecemeal manner. An inadequate program would involve a wastage of our resources with an ineffective result. Either undertake to meet the requirements of the problem or don't undertake it at all.

I think it must be plain to all that the circumstances which have given birth to this program call for promptness in decision and vigor in putting the project into operation. The sooner this program can get under way the greater its chancess of success. Careful consideration and early action are not incompatible.

The interim-aid law which the Congress enacted last December was designated as a stop-gap measure to cover the period until April first of this year. In the meantime it would be possible to consider the long-term recovery measure which we are now discussing. Unless the program can be placed in operation on or soon after April 1, there will undoubtedly be a serious deterioration in some of the basic conditions upon which the whole project is predicated.

It is proposed that the Congress now authorize the program for its full four and one-quarter year duration, although appropriations are being requested only for the first 15 months. Annual decisions on appropriations will afford full opportunity for review and control. But a general authorization now for the longer term will provide a necessary foundation for the continuing effort and cooperation of the European countries in a progressive program of recovery.

The amounts, form, and conditions of the recommended program of American aid to European recovery have been presented in President Truman's message to the Congress on December 9, 1947. They were further explained in the proposed draft legislation and background material furnished to this committee at that time by the Department of State. Taking as the basis genuine European cooperation—the maximum of self-help and mutual help on the part of the participating European countries—the program aims to provide these countries until the end of June, 1952, with those portions of their essential imports from the Western Hemisphere which they themselves cannot pay for. These essential imports include not only the food, fuel, and other supplies but also equipment and materials to enable them to increase their productive capacity. They must produce and export considerably more goods than they did in prewar times if they are to become self-supporting even at a lower standard of living.

During the first 15 months, exports from the European countries will provide current revenue sufficient to cover almost their entire import needs from sources outside the Western Hemisphere and also about one-third of their requirements from the Western Hemisphere.

It is not proposed that the United States provide aid to the full extent of western Europe's remaining trade deficit with the Western Hemisphere. Funds from sources other than the United States Treasury are expected to carry part of the load. These will be, principally, credits and other forms of assistance from other countries in our hemisphere, loans from the International Bank and private sources, and a further slight reduction in European reserves. It is the final deficit, after all those other means of financing essential imports have been utilized, that it is proposed be covered by American aid.

In each succeeding year of the program, increased production and increased trade from Europe is expected to reduce the amount of assistance needed, until after mid-1952, when it is calculated that the participating countries will have recovered ability to support themselves.

The recommended program of $6,800,000,000 for the first 15 months reflects a searching and comprehensive investigation by the executive branch of European needs and of availabilities in the United States and other supplying countries, taking full account of the findings of the Harriman, Krug, and Nourse committees.

The program of the $6,800,000,000 for the first 15 months has been computed with precision. I wish to emphasize that this amount does not represent a generous estimate of requirements. It is not an "asking figure" based on anticipated reduction prior to approval. It reflects a rigorous screening of the proposals developed by the CEEC and a realistic appraisal of availabilities. In our judgment, American assistance in this magnitude is required to initiate a program of genuine recovery and to take both Europe and this Nation out of the blind alley of mere continuing relief.

The total estimated cost of the program is now put at somewhere between 15.1 to 17.8 billions. But this will depend on developments each year, the progress made, and unforeseeable variations in the weather as it affects crops. The over-all cost is not capable of precise determination so far in advance.

In developing the program of American assistance, no question has been more closely examined than the ability of the United States to provide assistance in the magnitudes proposed. Both in terms of physical resources and in terms of financial capacity our ability to support such a program seems clear. Representatives of the executive branch more closely familiar than I with the domestic economy will provide further testimony on this issue. But I should like to remind you of the conclusions of the three special committees which explored this matter in detail during the summer and fall.

The proposed program does involve some sacrifice on the part of the American people, but it should be kept in mind that the burden of the program diminishes rapidly after the first 15 months. Considerations of the cost must be related to the momentous objective, on the one hand, and to the probable price of the alternatives. The $6,800,000,000 proposed for the first 15 months is less than a single month's charge of the war. A world of continuing uneasy half-peace will create demands for constantly mounting expenditures for defense. This program should be viewed as an investment in peace. In those terms, the cost is low.

The third main consideration which, I feel, should be borne in mind in connection with this measure is that relating to conditions or terms upon which American assistance will be extended. It is the obvious duty of this government to insure insofar as possible that the aid extended should be effectively used to promote recovery and not diverted to other purposes, whatever their nature. This aspect of the program is perhaps the most delicate and difficult and one which will require the exercise of a mature judgment and intelligent understanding of the nature of the problem faced by the European governments and of our particular position of leadership in this matter. We must always have in mind that we are dealing with democratic governments of sovereign nations.

We will be working with a group of nations each with a long and proud history. The peoples of these countries are highly skilled, able, and energetic and justly proud of their cultures. They have ancient traditions of self-reliance and are eager to take the lead in working out their own salvation.

We have stated in many ways that American aid will not be used to interfere with the sovereign rights of these nations and their own responsibility to work out their own salvation. I cannot emphasize too much my profound conviction that the aid we furnish must not be tied to conditions which would, in effect, destroy the whole moral justification for our cooperative assistance toward European partnership.

We are dealing with democratic governments. One of the major justifications of asking the American people to make the sacrifice necessary under this program is the vital stake that the United States has in helping to preserve democracy in Europe. As democratic governments they are responsive, like our own, to the peoples of their countries—and we would not have it otherwise. We cannot expect any democratic government to take upon itself obligations or accept conditions which run counter to the basic national sentiment of its people. This program calls for free cooperation among nations mutually respecting one another's sincerity of purpose in the common endeavor—a cooperation which we hope will long outlive the period of American assistance.

The initial suggestion of June 5 last, the concept of American assistance to Europe, has been based on the premise that European initiative and cooperation are prerequisite to European recovery. Only the Europeans themselves can finally solve their problem.

The participating nations have signified their intention to retain the initiative in promoting their own joint recovery. They have pledged themselves to take effective cooperative measures. They have established ambitious production targets for themselves. They have recognized the need for financial and monetary stability and have agreed to take necessary steps in this direction. They have agreed to establish a continuing organization to make most effective their cooperative work and the application of American assistance. When our program is initiated we may expect that the participating European countries will reaffirm as an organic part of that program their multilateral agreements.

The fulfillment of the mutual pledges of these nations would have profound effects in altering for the better the future economic condition of the European Continent. The Paris Conference itself was one major step, and the participating nations have not waited on American action before taking further steps, many of which required a high order of practical courage. They have moved forward toward a practical working arrangement for the multilateral clearing of trade. France and Italy, whose financial affairs suffered greatly by war and occupation, are taking energetic measures to establish monetary stability—an essential prerequisite to economic recovery. British coal production is being increased more quickly than even the more hopeful forecasts, and there is prospect of the early resumption of exports to the Continent. The customs union among Belgium, the Netherlands, and Luxemburg is now in operation. Negotiations for a Franco-Italian customs union are proceeding.

Our aid will not be given merely by turning money over to the European governments. The European countries will prepare periodic statements of their needs, taking into account the developing programs of mutual aid worked out through the CEEC continuing organization. After review by the specialist economic cooperation officers in each country and by the special United States Ambassador to the continuing CEEC organization, they will be transmitted to the Administrator of the American agency carrying out our program of assistance.

The Administrator, in collaboration with other appropriate agencies of the Government, will determine to what extent the European requirements are justified and to what extent they can safely be met. The Administrator will also decide which specific requirements from among the over-all requirements will be financed by the United States, taking into account the ability of the country concerned to pay for some portion or all of its total needs. For those needs which cannot be paid for in cash, the Administrator will further decide, in consultation with the National Advisory Council, whether aid will be provided in loans—where a sound capacity to repay in the future exists—or in outright grants. When the program has been determined in detail, the Administrator will either advance requisite funds to the participating country concerned to enable the purchase of the approved imports or, more generally, he will reimburse the countries when they have procured and received these import items.

A substantial amount of the essential needs of Europe must come from countries of the Western Hemisphere other than the United States. In some cases the quantities required will not exist in the United States, in others the impact on the American economy will be greatly relieved if commodities can be procured elsewhere. A sizable proportion of the funds appropriated for the European recovery program should therefore be available for the financing of purchases made outside the United States.

The application of American assistance will be in accord with the bilateral agreements to be negotiated with each of the participating countries. The terms of these proposed agreements are outlined fully in the documents submitted to your committee on December 19 last.

The administration of the program will demand the best talent and the greatest efficiency that our country can muster. The organization bearing the central responsibility must be small and select. It must hold the full and complete confidence of the American people and of the Europeans. It should combine efficient, businesslike administration and operation with the qualities of judgment and discrimination necessary to achieve quick and lasting recovery in Europe at the least long-term cost to the American people and with the least impact on our economy.

The organization must fit into the complex mechanics of our world export picture. American food, steel, and other products are being exported to many areas other than Europe. In many categories American output represents the major source of shortage goods in the world. There is at present workable machinery in the Government for determining total export availabilities in the light of domestic needs and for allocating these items among the many bidders. We propose that this machinery be continued.

The organization must be granted flexibility in its operations. In my judgment this is the most vital single factor in effective administration. Without flexibility the organization will be unable to take advantage of favorable developments, to meet adverse emergencies, or to cushion the impact of the program on the domestic economy.

It has been suggested in some quarters that the administering agency should be established in the form of a Government corporation. It is claimed that a corporation can be vested with broader powers and flexibility than an independent executive agency. I do not believe that this is necessarily so.

The legislation establishing an agency can clothe it with any or all of the beneficial attributes of a Government corporation. On the other hand an executive agency under the responsible direction of one man, and fitted into the existing machinery of Government, will be better able to meet the requirements of the situation than a corporation directed by a board. This task of administration clearly calls for administration by a single responsible individual.

Finally, the operation of the program must be related to the foreign policy of the Nation. The importance of the recovery program in our foreign affairs needs no argument. To carry out this relationship effectively will require cooperation and teamwork, but I know of no other way by which the complexities of modern world affairs can be met. It should, I think, be constantly kept in mind that this great project, which would be difficult enough in a normal international political climate, must be carried to success against the avowed determination of the Soviet Union and the Communist Party to oppose and sabotage it at every turn. There has been comment that the proposed organization, the Economic Cooperation Administration, would be completely under the thumb of the Department of State. This is not so, should not be so, and need not be so. I have personally interested myself to see that it will not be so. The activities of this Administration will touch on many aspects of our internal American affairs and on our economy. In the multitude of activities of this nature the Department of State should have no direction.

But the activities of the ECA will be directly related to the affairs of the European nations, political as well as economic, and will also affect the affairs of other nations throughout the world. In this field, the constitutional responsibility of the President is paramount. Whether or not he chooses to ignore or eliminate the Secretary of State in the conduct of foreign relations is a Presidential decision. I think that in our effort to restore the stability of the governments of western Europe it would be unfortunate to create an entirely new agency of foreign policy for this Government. There cannot be two Secretaries of State. I do not wish to interfere in the proper operations of the ECA. The organizational structure we have proposed provides a means for giving appropriate direction and control in matters of foreign policy to the Administrator of the ECA with least interference in the businesslike conduct of his task. In this connection he must coordinate his affairs with the legal responsibilities charged to the Secretaries of Commerce and Agriculture.

The man who accepts the challenge of the great task of administering the European recovery program must be a man of great breadth, ability, and stature. I have no qualms but that with such a man, and the able aides he will choose, I and my staff can form a smoothly working team for handling the complicated problems in foreign relationships which will arise in the course of the programs. In my judgment, the organizational proposals which have been put forward represent a sound and practical arrangement of functions and a framework for successful administration.

What are the prospects of success of such a program for the economic recovery of a continent? It would be absurd to deny the existence of obstacles and risks. Weather and the extent of world crops are unpredictable. The possible extent of political sabotage and the effectiveness with which its true intentions are unmasked and thus made susceptible to control cannot be fully foreseen. All we can say is this program does provide the means for success and if we maintain the will for success I believe that success will be achieved.

To be quite clear, this unprecedented endeavor of the New World to help the Old is neither sure nor easy. It is a calculated risk. But there can be no doubts as to the alternatives. The way of life that we have known is literally in balance.

Our country is now faced with a momentous decision. If we decide that the United States is unable or unwilling effectively to assist in the reconstruction of western Europe, we must accept the consequences of its collapse into the dictatorship of police states.

I said a moment ago that this program does provide the means for success, and if we maintain the will for success, I believe that success will be achieved.

I think it is of the greatest importance in considering this program that the people, as well as the Congress, thoroughly understand the critical situation. We have heard the comment several times that we won a victory, but we still have not won a peace. It goes much further than that. In some portions of the world there is more fighting now than there was during the war. You are aware of that. There is political instability. There are efforts to almost change the face of Europe, contrary to the interests of mankind in advancing civilization, certainly as we understand and desire it. The whole situation is critical in the extreme.

We happen to be, very fortunately for ourselves, the strongest nation in the world today, certainly economically, and I think in most other respects. There will be requirements in this program for certain sacrifices. But I feel that when you measure those sacrifices against what we are fighting for you will get a very much better idea of the necessities of the case.

I would like to close by saying that this is a complex program. It is a difficult program. And you know, far better than I do, the political difficulties involved in this program. But there is no doubt whatever in my mind that if we decide to do this thing we can do it successfully, and there is no doubt in my mind that the whole world hangs in the balance, as to what it is to be, in connection with what we are endeavoring to put forward here.

Thank you.

The CHAIRMAN. Thank you very much, Mr. Secretary.

4

The Principle of Collective Action

NATO as an Instrument of International Peace

The year 1948 is an important one in the history of American foreign and defense policy because in that year the United States clearly abandoned the traditional principle of independent action which historians have customarily traced to Washington's Farewell Address. Being a member of the United Nations already symbolized the abandonment of that principle. The Charter of the UN, moreover, includes two articles which permitted further specific action to provide for the common defense of its members. Article 51 states that "Nothing in the present Charter shall impair the inherent right of individual or collective self-defense if an armed attack occurs against a Member of the United Nations, until the Security Council has taken the measures necessary to maintain international peace and security." Article 52 adds that "Nothing . . . precludes the existence of regional arrangements or agencies for dealing with such matters relating to the maintenance of international peace and security as are appropriate for regional action . . . consistent with the Purposes and Principles of the United Nations."

The first important regional pact in which the United States became involved within the framework of Article 52 was the Inter-American Treaty of Reciprocal Assistance. This treaty was adopted in 1947 at Rio de Janeiro during the Inter-American Conference for the Maintenance of Continental Peace and Security, and went into effect during the following year. It provided for "collective action by the American republics in the event of an armed attack against a Western Hemisphere nation, whether from within or without the Americas."

In the meantime, the United Kingdom, Belgium, France, the

For a brief discussion of the developments leading to the North Atlantic Treaty and for the text of the Vandenberg Resolution, see "Collective Security in the North Atlantic Area," *Foreign Affairs Outlines*, No. 19 (Spring 1949) Prepared by the Department of State. For the text of the North Atlantic Treaty, see "Documents relating to the North Atlantic Treaty," *Senate Document* No. 48. 81st Cong., 1st Sess.

Netherlands, and Luxemburg had signed the Brussels Treaty on March 17, 1948. This treaty was much more comprehensive than the treaty of Rio, and in addition to providing collective action against armed attack contained arrangements for economic cooperation and cultural understanding. The signatories to this pact recognized, however, that they did not possess sufficient military power to protect themselves against a Soviet attack. From the beginning, they hoped that the United States would cooperate with them. On March 17, 1948, President Truman expressed to Congress his belief that the development represented by the Brussels Treaty deserved the full support of the United States. On June 11, 1948, the Senate adopted the Vandenberg Resolution which, for the first time in history, proposed that "the United States associate itself in peacetime with countries outside the Western Hemisphere in collective security arrangements. . . ." In July, the Brussels Pact Nations suggested that their representatives meet with those from the United States and Canada to discuss methods of increasing the security of the nations concerned in some sort of defense pact "within the framework of the United Nations Charter." The North Atlantic Treaty which finally resulted was signed on April 4, 1949. For additional reading from varied points of view see Richard Leopold, *The Growth of American Foreign Policy* (New York, 1962); John W. Spanier, *American Policy Since World War II* (New York, 1960); and Robert E. Osgood, *NATO: The Entangling Alliance* (Chicago, 1962). Note (1) the relationships between the North Atlantic Treaty and the United Nations; (2) the action which other parties to the Treaty should take when there is a threat or an armed attack against any party to the pact; (3) provisions made for change or denunciation of the Treaty.

A. The Vandenberg Resolution]
June 11, 1948]

Whereas PEACE WITH JUSTICE AND THE DEFENSE OF human rights and fundamental freedoms require international cooperation through more effective use of the United Nations: Therefore be it

Resolved, That the Senate reaffirm the policy of the United States to achieve international peace and security through the United Nations so that armed force shall not be used except in the common interest, and that the President be advised of the sense of the Senate that this Government, by constitutional process, should particularly pursue the following objectives within the United Nations Charter:

(1) Voluntary agreement to remove the veto from all questions involving pacific settlements of international disputes and situations, and from the admission of new members.

(2) Progressive development of regional and other collective arrangements for individual and collective self-defense in accordance with the purposes, principles, and provisions of the Charter.

(3) Association of the United States, by constitutional process, with such regional and other collective arrangements as are based on continuous and effective self-help and mutual aid, and as affect its national security.

(4) Contributing to the maintenance of peace by making clear its determination to exercise the right of individual or collective self-defense under article 51 should any armed attack occur affecting its national security.

(5) Maximum efforts to obtain agreements to provide the United Nations with armed forces as provided by the Charter, and to obtain agreement among member nations upon universal regulation and reduction of armaments under adequate and dependable guaranty against violation.

(6) If necessary, after adequate effort toward strengthening the United Nations, review of the Charter at an appropriate time by a General Conference called under article 109 or by the General Assembly.

B. From the Text of the North Atlantic Treaty]
April 4, 1949]
Preamble]

THE PARTIES TO THIS TREATY REAFFIRM THEIR FAITH in the purposes and principles of the Charter of the United Nations and their desire to live in peace with all peoples and all governments.

They are determined to safeguard the freedom, common heritage and civilization of their peoples, founded on the principles of democracy, individual liberty and the rule of law.

They seek to promote stability and well-being in the North Atlantic area.

They are resolved to unite their efforts for collective defense and for the preservation of peace and security.

They therefore agree to this North Atlantic Treaty:

Article 1]

The Parties undertake, as set forth in the Charter of the United Nations, to settle any international disputes in which they may be involved by peaceful means in such a manner that international peace and security, and justice, are not endangered, and to refrain in their international relations from the threat or use of force in any manner inconsistent with the purposes of the United Nations.

Article 2]

The Parties will contribute toward the further development of peaceful and friendly international relations by strengthening their free institutions, by bringing about a better understanding of the principles upon which these institutions are founded, and by promoting conditions of stability and well-being. They will seek to eliminate conflict in their international economic policies and will encourage economic collaboration between any or all of them.

Article 3]

In order more effectively to achieve the objectives of this Treaty, the Parties, separately and jointly, by means of continuous and effective self-help and mutual aid, will maintain and develop their individual and collective capacity to resist armed attack.

Article 4]

The Parties will consult together whenever, in the opinion of any of them, the territorial integrity, political independence or security of any of the Parties is threatened.

Article 5]

The Parties agree that an armed attack against one or more of them in Europe or North America shall be considered an attack against them all; and consequently they agree that, if such an armed attack occurs, each of them, in exercise of the right of individual or collective self-defense recognized by Article 51 of the Charter of the United Nations, will assist the Party or Parties so attacked by taking forthwith, individually and in concert with the other Parties, such action as it deems necessary, including the use of armed force, to restore and maintain the security of the North Atlantic area.

Any such armed attack and all measures taken as a result thereof shall immediately be reported to the Security Council. Such measures shall be terminated when the Security Council has taken the measures necessary to restore and maintain international peace and security.

Article 6]

For the purpose of Article 5 an armed attack on one or more of the Parties is deemed to include an armed attack on the territory of any of the Parties in Europe or North America, on the Algerian departments of France, on the occupation forces of any Party in Europe, on the islands under the jurisdiction of any Party in the North Atlantic area north of the Tropic of Cancer or on the vessels or aircraft in this area of any of the Parties.

Article 7]

This Treaty does not affect, and shall not be interpreted as affecting, in any way the rights and obligations under the Charter of the Parties which are members of the United Nations, or the primary responsibility of the Security Council for the maintenance of international peace and security.

Article 8]

Each Party declares that none of the international engagements now in force between it and any other of the Parties or any third state is in conflict with the provisions of this Treaty, and undertakes not to enter into any international engagement in conflict with this Treaty.

Article 9]

The Parties hereby establish a council, on which each of them shall be represented, to consider matters concerning the implementation of this Treaty. The council shall be so organized as to be able to meet promptly at any time. The council shall set up such subsidiary bodies as may be necessary; in particular it shall establish immediately a defense committee which shall recommend measures for the implementation of Articles 3 and 5.

Article 10]

The Parties may, by unanimous agreement, invite any other European state in a position to further the principles of this Treaty and to contribute to the security of the North Atlantic area to accede to this Treaty. Any state so invited may become a party to the Treaty by depositing its instrument of accession with the Government of the United States of America. The Government of the United States of America will inform each of the Parties of the deposit of each such instrument of accession.

Article 11]

This Treaty shall be ratified and its provisions carried out by the Parties in accordance with their respective constitutional processes. The instruments of ratification shall be deposited as soon as possible with the Government of the United States of America, which will notify all the other signatories of each deposit. The Treaty shall enter into force between the states which have ratified it as soon as the ratifications of the majority of the signatories, including the ratifications of the majority of the signatories, including the ratifications of Belgium, Canada, France, Luxembourg, the Netherlands, the United Kingdom and the United States, have been deposited and shall come into effect with respect to other states on the date of the deposit of their ratifications.

Article 12]

After the Treaty has been in force for ten years, or at any time thereafter, the Parties shall, if any of them so requests, consult together for the purpose of reviewing the Treaty, having regard for the factors then affecting peace and security in the North Atlantic area, including the development of universal as well as regional arrangements under the Charter of the United Nations for the maintenance of international peace and security.

Article 13]

After the Treaty has been in force for twenty years, any Party may cease to be a party one year after its notice of denunciation has been given to the Government of the United States of America, which will inform the Governments of the other Parties of the deposit of each notice of denunciation.

Article 14]

This Treaty, of which the English and French texts are equally authentic, shall be deposited in the archives of the Government of the United States of America. Duly certified copies thereof will be transmitted by that Government to the Governments of the other signatories.

In witness whereof, the undersigned plenipotentiaries have signed this Treaty.

Done at Washington, the 4th day of April, 1949.

5

Military Capitalism and Prestige Politics

C. Wright Mills's *The Power Elite*

C. Wright Mills (1916-1962) received his Ph.D. at the University of Wisconsin in 1941, and taught at the University of Maryland from 1941 to 1945, from whence he moved to Columbia University. The publication of his first book, *The New Man of Power: America's Labor Leaders* (1948), won him the reputation as a sociologist who had drawn thought-provoking conclusions from scientific research. His succeeding publications including *White Collar: the American Middle Classes* (1951), and *The Sociological Imagination* (1959) sustained this reputation. The selection from *The Power Elite* (1956) which follows in some ways provides a theme for the consideration of the entire period 1945-1962. In reading it, note (1) the principal constituent elements of the Power Elite and its distinctive "current shape"; (2) the social homogeneity of the Power Elite; (3) the significance of this homogeneity; and (4) the criticisms of the concept of the Power Elite. The student might also consult with profit Fred J. Cook, *The Warfare State* (New York, 1962).

2]

WE STUDY HISTORY, IT HAS BEEN SAID, TO RID OUR-
selves of it, and the history of the power elite is a clear case for which this maxim is correct. Like the tempo of American life in general, the long-term trends of the power structure have been greatly speeded up since World War II, and certain newer trends within and between the dominant institutions have also set the shape of the power elite. . . .

I. In so far as the structural clue to the power elite today lies in the political order, that clue is the decline of politics as genu-

C. Wright Mills, *The Power Elite* (Fair Lawn, N.J.: Oxford University Press, Inc., 1957) pp. 274-297. Reprinted with the kind permission of the Oxford University Press, Inc.

ine and public debate of alternative decisions—with nationally responsible and policy-coherent parties and with autonomous organizations connecting the lower and middle levels of power with the top levels of decision. America is now in considerable part more a formal political democracy than a democratic social structure, and even the formal political mechanics are weak.

The long-time tendency of business and government to become more intricately and deeply involved with each other has . . . reached a new point of explicitness. The two cannot now be seen clearly as two distinct worlds. It is in terms of the executive agencies of the state that the rapprochement has proceeded most decisively. The growth of the executive branch of the government, with its agencies that patrol the complex economy, does not mean merely the 'enlargement of government' as some sort of autonomous bureaucracy: it has meant the ascendancy of the corporation's man as a political eminence.

During the New Deal the corporate chieftains joined the political directorate; as of World War II they have come to dominate it. Long interlocked with government, now they have moved into quite full direction of the economy of the war effort and of the postwar era. This shift of the corporation executives into the political directorate has accelerated the long-term relegation of the professional politicians in the Congress to the middle levels of power.

II. In so far as the structural clue to the power elite today lies in the enlarged and military state, that clue becomes evident in the military ascendancy. The warlords have gained decisive political relevance, and the military structure of America is now in considerable part a political structure. The seemingly permanent military threat places a premium on the military and upon their control of men, materiel, money, and power; virtually all political and economic actions are now judged in terms of military definitions of reality: the higher warlords have ascended to a firm position within the power elite. . . .

In part at least this has resulted from one simple historical fact, pivotal for the years since 1939: the focus of elite attention has been shifted from domestic problems, centered in the 'thirties around slump, to international problems, centered in the 'forties and 'fifties around war. Since the governing apparatus of the

United States has by long historic usage been adapted to and shaped by domestic clash and balance, it has not, from any angle, had suitable agencies and traditions for the handling of international problems. Such formal democratic mechanics as had arisen in the century and a half of national development prior to 1941, had not been extended to the American handling of international affairs. It is, in considerable part, in this vacuum that the power elite has grown.

III. In so far as the structural clue to the power elite today lies in the economic order, the clue is the fact that the economy is at once a permanent-war economy and a private-corporation economy. American capitalism is now in considerable part a military capitalism, and the most important relation of the big corporation to the state rests on the coincidence of interests between military and corporate needs, as defined by warlords and corporate rich. Within the elite as a whole, this coincidence of interest between the high military and the corporate chieftains strengthens both of them and further subordinates the role of the merely political men. Not politicians, but corporate executives, sit with the military and plan the organization of war effort.

The shape and meaning of the power elite today can be understood only when these three sets of structural trends are seen at their point of coincidence: the military capitalism of private corporations exists in a weakened and formal democratic system containing a military order already quite political in outlook and demeanor. Accordingly, at the top of this structure, the power elite has been shaped by the coincidence of interests between those who control the major means of production and those who control the newly enlarged means of violence; from the decline of the professional politician and the rise to explicit political command of the corporate chieftains and the professional warlords; from the absence of any genuine civil service of skill and integrity, independent of vested interests.

The power elite is composed of political, economic, and military men, but this instituted elite is frequently in some tension: it comes together only on certain coinciding points and only on certain occasions of 'crisis.' In the long peace of the nineteenth century, the military were not in the high councils of state, not

of the political directorate, and neither were the economic men—
they made raids upon the state but they did not join its directorate. During the 'thirties, the political man was ascendant.
Now the military and the corporate men are in top positions.

Of the three types of circle that compose the power elite today, it is the military that has benefited the most in its enhanced
power, although the corporate circles have also become more
explicitly intrenched in the more public decision-making circles.
It is the professional politician that has lost the most, so much
that in examining the events and decisions, one is tempted to
speak of a political vacuum in which the corporate rich and the
high warlord, in their coinciding interests, rule.

It should not be said that the three 'take turns' in carrying the
initiative, for the mechanics of the power elite are not often as
deliberate as that would imply. At times, of course, it is—as
when political men, thinking they can borrow the prestige of
generals, find that they must pay for it, or, as when during big
slumps, economic men feel the need of a politician at once safe
and possessing vote appeal. Today all three are involved in
virtually all widely ramifying decisions. Which of the three types
seems to lead depends upon 'the task of the period' as they, the
elite, define them. Just now, these tasks center upon 'defense'
and international affairs. Accordingly, as we have seen, the
military are ascendant in two senses: as personnel and as justify-
ing ideology. That is why, just now, we can most easily specify
the unity and the shape of the power elite in terms of the military ascendancy.

But we must always be historically specific and open to complexities. The simple Marxian view makes the big economic man
the *real* holder of power; the simple liberal view makes the big
political man the chief of the power system; and there are some
who would view the warlords as virtual dictators. Each of these
is an oversimplified view. It is to avoid them that we use the
term 'power elite' rather than, for example, 'ruling class.'*

* 'Ruling class' is a badly loaded phrase. 'Class' is an economic term;
'rule' a political one. The phrase, 'ruling class,' thus contains the theory that
an economic class rules politically. That short-cut theory may or may not at
times be true, but we do not want to carry that one rather simple theory
about in the terms that we use to define our problems; we wish to state the
theories explicitly, using terms of more precise and unilateral meaning.

In so far as the power elite has come to wide public attention, it has done so in terms of the 'military clique.' The power elite does, in fact, take its current shape from the decisive entrance into it of the military. Their presence and their ideology are its major legitimations, whenever the power elite feels the need to provide any. But what is called the 'Washington military clique' is not composed merely of military men, and it does not prevail merely in Washington. Its members exist all over the country, and it is a coalition of generals in the roles of corporation executives, of politicians masquerading as admirals, of corporation executives acting like politicians, of civil servants who become majors, of vice-admirals who are also the assistants to a cabinet officer, who is himself, by the way, really a member of the managerial elite.

Neither the idea of a 'ruling class' nor of a simple monolithic rise of 'bureaucratic politicians' nor of a 'military clique' is adequate. The power elite today involves the often uneasy coincidence of economic, military, and political power.

3]

Even if our understanding were limited to these structural trends, we should have grounds for believing the power elite a useful, indeed indispensable, concept for the interpretation of what is going on at the topside of modern American society. But we are not, of course, so limited: our conception of the power elite does not need to rest only upon the correspondence of the institutional hierarchies involved, or upon the many points at which their shifting interests coincide. The power elite, as we conceive it, also rests upon the similarity of its personnel, and

---

Specifically, the phrase 'ruling class,' in its common political connotations, does not allow enough autonomy to the political order and its agents, and it says nothing about the military as such. It should be clear to the reader by now that we do not accept as adequate the simple view that high economic men unilaterally make all decisions of national consequence. We hold that such a simple view of 'economic determinism' must be elaborated by 'political determinism' and 'military determinism'; that the higher agents of each of these three domains now often have a noticeable degree of autonomy; and that only in the often intricate ways of coalition do they make up and carry through the most important decisions. Those are the major reasons we prefer 'power elite' to 'ruling class' as a characterizing phrase for the higher circles when we consider them in terms of power. [Footnote in original.]

their personal and official relations with one another, upon their social and psychological affinities. In order to grasp the personal and social basis of the power elite's unity, we have first to remind ourselves of the facts of origin, career, and style of life of each of the types of circle whose members compose the power elite.

The power elite is *not* an aristocracy, which is to say that it is not a political ruling group based upon a nobility of hereditary origin. It has no compact basis in a small circle of great families whose members can and do consistently occupy the top positions in the several higher circles which overlap as the power elite. But such nobility is only one possible basis of common origin. That it does not exist for the American elite does not mean that members of this elite derive socially from the full range of strata composing American society. They derive in substantial proportions from the upper classes, both new and old, of local society and the metropolitan 400. The bulk of the very rich, the corporate executives, the political outsiders, the high military, derive from, at most, the upper third of the income and occupational pyramids. Their fathers were at least of the professional and business strata, and very frequently higher than that. They are native-born Americans of native parents, primarily from urban areas, and, with the exceptions of the politicians among them, overwhelmingly from the East. They are mainly Protestants, especially Episcopalian or Presbyterian. In general, the higher the position, the greater the proportion of men within it who have derived from and who maintain connections with the upper classes. The generally similar origins of the members of the power elite are underlined and carried further by the fact of their increasingly common educational routine. Overwhelmingly college graduates, substantial proportions have attended Ivy League colleges, although the education of the higher military, of course, differs from that of other members of the power elite.

But what do these apparently simple facts about the social composition of the higher circles really mean? In particular, what do they mean for any attempt to understand the degree of unity, and the direction of policy and interest that may prevail among these several circles? Perhaps it is best to put this question in a deceptively simple way: in terms of origin and career, who or what do these men at the top represent?

Of course, if they are elected politicians, they are supposed to represent those who elected them; and, if they are appointed, they are supposed to represent, indirectly, those who elected their appointers. But this is recognized as something of an abstraction, as a rhetorical formula by which all men of power in almost all systems of government nowadays justify their power of decision. At times it may be true, both in the sense of their motives and in the sense of who benefits from their decisions. Yet it would not be wise in any power system merely to assume it.

The fact that members of the power elite come from near the top of the nation's class and status levels does not mean that they are necessarily 'representative' of the top levels only. And if they were, as social types, representative of a cross-section of the population, that would not mean that a balanced democracy of interest and power would automatically be the going political fact.

We cannot infer the direction of policy merely from the social origins and careers of the policy-makers. The social and economic backgrounds of the men of power do not tell us all that we need to know in order to understand the distribution of social power. For: (1) Men from high places may be ideological representatives of the poor and humble. (2) Men of humble origin, brightly self-made, may energetically serve the most vested and inherited interests. Moreover (3), not all men who effectively represent the interests of a stratum need in any way belong to it or personally benefit by policies that further its interests. Among the politicians, in short, there are sympathetic *agents* of given groups, conscious and unconscious, paid and unpaid. Finally (4), among the top decision-makers we find men who have been chosen for their positions because of their 'expert knowledge.' These are some of the obvious reasons why the social origins and careers of the power elite do not enable us to infer the class interests and policy directions of a modern system of power.

Do the high social origin and careers of the top men mean

nothing, then, about the distribution of power? By no means. They simply remind us that we must be careful of any simple and direct inference from origin and career to political character and policy, not that we must ignore them in our attempt at political understanding. They simply mean that we must analyze the political psychology and the actual decisions of the political directorate as well as its social composition. And they mean, above all, that we should control, as we have done here, any inference we make from the origin and careers of the political actors by close understanding of the institutional landscape in which they act out their drama. Otherwise we should be guilty of a rather simple-minded biographical theory of society and history.

Just as we cannot rest the notion of the power elite solely upon the institutional mechanics that lead to its formation, so we cannot rest the notion solely upon the facts of the origin and career of its personnel. We need both, and we have both—as well as other bases, among them that of the status intermingling.

But it is not only the similarities of social origin, religious affiliation, nativity, and education that are important to the psychological and social affinities of the members of the power elite. Even if their recruitment and formal training were more heterogeneous than they are, these men would still be of quite homogeneous social type. For the most important set of facts about a circle of men is the criteria of admission, of praise, of honor, of promotion that prevails among them; if these are similar within a circle, then they will tend as personalities to become similar. The circles that compose the power elite do tend to have such codes and criteria in common. The co-optation of the social types to which these common values lead is often more important than any statistics of common origin and career that we might have at hand.

There is a kind of reciprocal attraction among the fraternity of the successful—not between each and every member of the circles of the high and mighty, but between enough of them to insure a certain unity. On the slight side, it is a sort of tacit, mutual admiration; in the strongest tie-ins, it proceeds by intermarriage. And there are all grades and types of connection between these extremes. Some overlaps certainly occur by means of cliques and clubs, churches and schools.

If social origin and formal education in common tend to make the members of the power elite more readily understood and trusted by one another, their continued association further cements what they feel they have in common. Members of the several higher circles know one another as personal friends and even as neighbors; they mingle with one another on the golf course, in the gentleman's clubs, at resorts, on transcontinental airplanes, and on ocean liners. They meet at the estates of mutual friends, face each other in front of the TV camera, or serve on the same philanthropic committee; and many are sure to cross one another's path in the columns of newspapers, if not in the exact cafes from which many of these columns originate. As we have seen, of 'The New 400' of cafe society, one chronicler has named forty-one members of the very rich, ninety-three political leaders, and seventy-nine chief executives of corporations. . . .

The multiplicity of high-prestige organizations to which the elite usually belong is revealed by even casual examination of the obituaries of the big businessman, the high-prestige lawyer, the top general and admiral, the key senator: usually, high-prestige church, business associations, plus high-prestige clubs, and often plus military rank. In the course of their lifetimes, the university president, the New York Stock Exchange chairman, the head of the bank, the old West Pointer—mingle in the status sphere, within which they easily renew old friendships and draw upon them in an effort to understand through the experience of trusted others those contexts of power and decision in which they have not personally moved.

In these diverse contexts, prestige accumulates in each of the higher circles, and the members of each borrow status from one another. Their self-images are fed by these accumulations and these borrowings, and accordingly, however segmental a given man's role may seem, he comes to feel himself a 'diffuse' or 'generalized' man of the higher circles, a 'broad-gauge' man. Perhaps such inside experience is one feature of what is meant by 'judgment.'

The key organizations, perhaps, are the major corporations themselves, for on the boards of directors we find a heavy overlapping among the members of these several elites. On the lighter side, again in the summer and winter resorts, we find that, in an intricate series of overlapping circles; in the course of time, each meets each or knows somebody who knows somebody who knows that one.

The higher members of the military, economic, and political orders are able readily to take over one another's point of view, always in a sympathetic way, and often in a knowledgeable way as well. They define one another as among those who count, and who, accordingly, must be taken into account. Each of them as a member of the power elite comes to incorporate into his own integrity, his own honor, his own conscience, the viewpoint, the expectations, the values of the others. If there are no common ideals and standards among them that are based upon an explicitly aristocratic culture, that does not mean that they do not feel responsibility to one another.

All the structural coincidence of their interests as well as the intricate, psychological facts of their origins and their education, their careers and their associations make possible the psychological affinities that prevail among them, affinities that make it possible for them to say of one another: He is, of course, one of us. And all this points to the basic, psychological meaning of class consciousness. Nowhere in America is there as great a 'class consciousness' as among the elite; nowhere is it organized as effectively as among the power elite. For by class consciousness, as a psychological fact, one means that the individual member of a 'class' accepts only those accepted by his circle as among those who are significant to his own image of self.

Within the higher circles of the power elite, factions do exist; there are conflicts of policy; individual ambitions do clash. There are still enough divisions of importance within the Republican party, and even between Republicans and Democrats, to make for different methods of operation. But more powerful than these divisions are the internal discipline and the community of interests that bind the power elite together, even across the boundaries of nations at war.

4]

Yet we must give due weight to the other side of the case which may not question the facts but only our interpretation of them. There is a set of objections that will inevitably be made to our whole conception of the power elite, but which has essentially to do with only the psychology of its members. It might well be put by liberals or by conservatives in some such way as this:

'To talk of a power elite—isn't this to characterize men by their origins and associations? Isn't such characterization both unfair and untrue? Don't men modify themselves, especially Americans such as these, as they rise in stature to meet the demands of their jobs? Don't they arrive at a view and a line of policy that represents, so far as they in their human weaknesses can know, the interests of the nation as a whole? Aren't they merely honorable men who are doing their duty?'

What are we to reply to these objections?

I. We are sure that they are honorable men. But what is honor? Honor can only mean living up to a code that one believes to be honorable. There is no one code upon which we are all agreed. That is why, if we are civilized men, we do not kill off all of those with whom we disagree. The question is not: are these honorable men? The question is: what are their codes of honor? The answer to that question is that they are the codes of their circles, of those to whose opinions they defer. How could it be otherwise? That is one meaning of the important truism that all men are human and that all men are social creatures. As for sincerity, it can only be disproved, never proved.

II. To the question of their adaptability—which means their capacity to transcend the codes of conduct which, in their life's work and experience, they have acquired—we must answer: simply no, they cannot, at least not in the handful of years most of them have left. To expect that is to assume that they are indeed strange and expedient: such flexibility would in fact involve a violation of what we may rightly call their character and their integrity. By the way, may it not be precisely because of the lack of such character and integrity that earlier types of

American politicians have not represented as great a threat as do these men of character?

It would be an insult to the effective training of the military, and to their indoctrination as well, to suppose that military officials shed their military character and outlook upon changing from uniform to mufti. This background is more important perhaps in the military case than in that of the corporate executives, for the training of the career is deeper and more total. . . .

Would it not be ridiculous, for example, to believe seriously that, in psychological fact, Charles Erwin Wilson represented anyone or any interest other than those of the corporate world? This is not because he is dishonest; on the contrary, it is because he is probably a man of solid integrity—as sound as a dollar. He is what he is and he cannot very well be anything else. He is a member of the professional corporation elite, just as are his colleagues, in the government and out of it; he represents the wealth of the higher corporate world; he represents its power; and he believes sincerely in his oft-quoted remark that 'what is good for the United States is good for the General Motors Corporation and vice versa.'

The revealing point about the pitiful hearings on the confirmation of such men for political posts is not the cynicism toward the law and toward the lawmakers on the middle levels of power which they display, nor their reluctance to dispose of their personal stock. The interesting point is how impossible it is for such men to divest themselves of their engagement with the corporate world in general and with their own corporations in particular. Not only their money, but their friends, their interests, their training—their lives in short—are deeply involved in this world. The disposal of stock is, of course, merely a purifying ritual. The point is not so much financial or personal interests in a given corporation, but identification with the corporate world. To ask a man suddenly to divest himself of these interests and sensibilities is almost like asking a man to become a woman.

III. To the question of their patriotism, of their desire to serve the nation as a whole, we must answer first that, like codes of honor, feelings of patriotism and views of what is to the whole nation's good, are not ultimate facts but matters upon which there exists a great variety of opinion. Furthermore, patriotic opinions too are rooted in and are sustained by what a man has become by virtue of how and with whom he has lived. This is no simple mechanical determination of individual character by social conditions; it is an intricate process, well established in the major tradition of modern social study. One can only wonder why more social scientists do not use it systematically in speculating about politics.

iv. The elite cannot be truly thought of as men who are merely doing their duty. They are the ones who determine their duty, as well as the duties of those beneath them. They are not merely following orders: they give the orders. They are not merely 'bureaucrats': they command bureaucracies. They may try to disguise these facts from others and from themselves by appeals to traditions of which they imagine themselves the instruments, but there are many traditions, and they must choose which ones they will serve. They face decisions for which there simply are no traditions.

Now, to what do these several answers add up? To the fact that we cannot reason about public events and historical trends merely from knowledge about the motives and character of the men or the small groups who sit in the seats of the high and mighty. This fact, in turn, does not mean that we should be intimidated by accusations that in taking up our problem in the way we have, we are impugning the honor, the integrity, or the ability of those who are in high office. For it is not, in the first instance, a question of individual character; and if, in further instances, we find that it is, we should not hesitate to say so plainly. In the meantime, we must judge men of power by the standards of power, by what they do as decision-makers, and not by who they are or what they may do in private life. Our interest is not in that: we are interested in their policies and in the *consequences* of their conduct of office. We must remember that these men of the power elite now occupy the strategic places in the structure of American society; that they command the dominant institutions of a dominant nation; that, as a set of men, they are in a position to make decisions with terrible consequences for the underlying populations of the world.

5]

Despite their social similarity and psychological affinities, the members of the power elite do not constitute a club having a permanent membership with fixed and formal boundaries. It is of the nature of the power elite that within it there is a good deal of shifting about, and that it thus does not consist of one small set of the same men in the same positions in the same hierarchies. Because men know each other personally does not mean that among them there is a unity of policy; and because they do not know each other personally does not mean that among them there is a disunity. The conception of the power elite does not rest, as I have repeatedly said, primarily upon personal friendship.

As the requirements of the top places in each of the major hierarchies become similar, the types of men occupying these roles at the top—by selection and by training in the jobs—become similar. This is no mere deduction from structure to personnel. That it is a fact is revealed by the heavy traffic that has been going on between the three structures, often in very intricate patterns. The chief executives, the warlords, and selected politicians came into contact with one another in an intimate, working way during World War II; after that war ended, they continued their associations, out of common beliefs, social congeniality, and coinciding interests. Noticeable proportions of top men from the military, the economic, and the political worlds have during the last fifteen years occupied positions in one or both of the other worlds: between these higher circles there is an interchangeability of position, based formally upon the supposed transferability of 'executive ability,' based in substance upon the co-optation by cliques of insiders. As members of a power elite, many of those busy in this traffic have come to look upon 'the government' as an umbrella under whose authority they do their work.

As the business between the big three increases in volume and importance, so does the traffic in personnel. The very criteria for selecting men who will rise come to embody this fact. The corporate commissar, dealing with the state and its military, is wiser to choose a young man who has experienced the state and its military than one who has not. The political director, often dependent for his own political success upon corporate decisions and corporations, is also wiser to choose a man with corporate experience. Thus, by virtue of the very criterion of success, the interchange of personnel and the unity of the power elite is increased.

Given the formal similarity of the three hierarchies in which the several members of the elite spend their working lives, given the ramifications of the decisions made in each upon the others, given the coincidence of interest that prevails among them at many points, and given the administrative vacuum of the American civilian state along with its enlargement of tasks—given these trends of structure, and adding to them the psychological affinities we have noted—we should indeed be surprised were we to find that men said to be skilled in administrative contacts and full of organizing ability would fail to do more than get in touch with one another. They have, of course, done much more than that: increasingly, they assume positions in one another's domains.

The unity revealed by the interchangeability of top roles rests upon the parallel development of the top jobs in each of the big three domains. The interchange occurs most frequently at the points of their coinciding interest, as between regulatory agency and the regulated industry; contracting agency and contractor. And, as we shall see, it leads to co-ordinations that are more explicit, and even formal.

The inner core of the power elite consists, first, of those who interchange commanding roles at the top of one dominant institutional order with those in another: the admiral who is also a banker and a lawyer and who heads up an important federal commission; the corporation executive whose company was one of the two or three leading war materiel producers who is now the Secretary of Defense; the wartime general who dons civilian clothes to sit on the political directorate and then becomes a member of the board of directors of a leading economic corporation.

Although the executive who becomes a general, the general

who becomes a statesman, the statesman who becomes a banker, see much more than ordinary men in their ordinary environments, still the perspectives of even such men often remain tied to their dominant locales. In their very career, however, they interchange roles within the big three and thus readily transcend the particularity of interest in any one of these institutional milieux. By their very careers and activities, they lace the three types of milieux together. They are, accordingly, the core members of the power elite.

These men are not necessarily familiar with every major arena of power. We refer to one man who moves in and between perhaps two circles—say the industrial and the military—and to another man who moves in the military and the political, and to a third who moves in the political as well as among opinion-makers. These in-between types most closely display our image of the power elite's structure and operation, even of behind-the-scenes operations. To the extent that there is any 'invisible elite,' these advisory and liaison types are its core. Even if—as I believe to be very likely—many of them are, at least in the first part of their careers, 'agents' of the various elites rather than themselves elite, it is they who are most active in organizing the several top milieux into a structure of power and maintaining it.

The inner core of the power elite also includes men of the higher legal and financial type from the great law factories and investment firms, who are almost professional go-betweens of economic, political and military affairs, and who thus act to unify the power elite. The corporation lawyer and the investment banker perform the functions of the 'go-between' effectively and powerfully. By the nature of their work, they transcend the narrower milieu of any one industry, and accordingly are in a position to speak and act for the corporate world or at least sizable sectors of it. The corporation lawyer is a key link between the economic and military and political areas; the investment banker is a key organizer and unifier of the corporate world and a person well versed in spending the huge amounts of money the American military establishment now ponders. When you get a lawyer who handles the legal work of investment bankers you get a key member of the power elite.

During the Democratic era, one link between private corpo-

rate organizations and governmental institutions was the investment house of Dillon, Read. From it came such men as James
Forrestal and Charles F. Detmar, Jr.; Ferdinand Eberstadt had
once been a partner in it before he branched out into his own
investment house from which came other men to political and
military circles. Republican administrations seem to favor the
investment firm of Kuhn, Loeb and the advertising firm of Bat-
ten, Barton, Durstine and Osborn.

Regardless of administrations, there is always the law firm of
Sullivan and Cromwell. Mid-West investment banker Cyrus
Eaton has said that 'Arthur H. Dean, a senior partner of Sullivan
& Cromwell of No. 48 Wall Street, was one of those who assisted
in the drafting of the Securities Act of 1933, the first of the series
of bills passed to regulate the capital markets. He and his firm,
which is reputed to be the largest in the United States, have
maintained close relations with the SEC since its creation, and
theirs is the dominating influence on the Commission.'

There is also the third largest bank in the United States: the
Chase National Bank of New York (now Chase-Manhattan).
Regardless of political administration, executives of this bank
and those of the International Bank of Reconstruction and Development have changed positions: John J. McCloy, who became Chairman of the Chase National in 1953, is a former
president of the World Bank; and his successor to the presidency
of the World Bank was a former vice-president of the Chase
National Bank. And in 1953, the president of the Chase National
Bank, Winthrop W. Aldrich, had left to become Ambassador to
Great Britain. . . .

When the power elite find that in order to get things done
they must reach below their own realms—as is the case when it
is necessary to get bills passed through Congress—they themselves must exert some pressure. But among the power elite, the
name for such high-level lobbying is 'liaison work.' There are
'liaison' military men with Congress, with certain wayward sections of industry, with practically every important element not
directly concerned with the power elite. The two men on the
White House staff who are *named* 'liaison' men are both experienced in military matters; one of them is a former investment banker and lawyer as well as a general.

Not the trade associations but the higher cliques of lawyers and investment bankers are the active political heads of the corporate rich and the members of the power elite. 'While it is generally assumed that the national associations carry tremendous weight in formulating public opinion and directing the course of national policy, there is some evidence to indicate that inter-action between associations on a formal level is not a very tight-knit affair. The general tendency within associations seems to be to stimulate activities around the specific interests of the organization, and more effort is made to educate its members rather than to spend much time in trying to influence other associations on the issue at hand . . . As media for stating and re-stating the over-all value structure of the nation they (the trade associations) are important . . . But when issues are firmly drawn, individuals related to the larger corporate interests are called upon to exert pressure in the proper places at the strategic time. The national associations may act as media for co-ordinat-ing such pressures, but a great volume of intercommunication between members at the apex of power of the larger corporate interests seems to be the decisive factor in final policy determi-nation.

Conventional 'lobbying,' carried on by trade associations, still exists, although it usually concerns the middle levels of power— usually being targeted at Congress and, of course, its own rank and file members. The important function of the National As-sociation of Manufacturers, for example, is less directly to influ-ence policy than to reveal to small businessmen that their interests are the same as those of larger businesses. But there is also 'high-level lobbying.' All over the country the corporate leaders are drawn into the circle of the high military and politi-cal through personal friendship, trade and professional associa-tions and their various subcommittees, prestige clubs, open political affiliation, and customer relationships. 'There is . . . an awareness among these power leaders,' one first-hand investiga-tor of such executive cliques has asserted, 'of many of the current major policy issues before the nation such as keeping taxes down, turning all productive operations over to private enterprises, increasing foreign trade, keeping governmental welfare and other domestic activities to a minimum, and strengthening and maintaining the hold of the current party in power nationally.

There are, in fact, cliques of corporate executives who are more important as informal opinion leaders in the top echelons of corporate, military, and political power than as actual participants in military and political organizations. Inside military circles and inside political circles and 'on the sidelines' in the economic area, these circles and cliques of corporation executives are in on most all major decisions regardless of topic. And what is important about all this high-level lobbying is that it is done within the confines of that elite. . . . [Section 6 omitted.]

7]

The idea of the power elite rests upon and enables us to make sense of (1) the decisive institutional trends that characterize the structure of our epoch, in particular, the military ascendancy in a privately incorporated economy, and more broadly, the several coincidences of objective interests between economic, military, and political institutions; (2) the social similarities and the psychological affinities of the men who occupy the command posts of these structures, in particular the increased interchangeability of the top positions in each of them and the increased traffic between these orders in the careers of men of power; (3) the ramifications, to the point of virtual totality, of the kind of decisions that are made at the top, and the rise to power of a set of men who, by training and bent, are professional organizers of considerable force and who are unrestrained by democratic party training.

Negatively, the formation of the power elite rests upon (1) the relegation of the professional party politician to the middle levels of power, (2) the semi-organized stalemate of the interests of sovereign localities into which the legislative function has fallen, (3) the virtually complete absence of a civil service that constitutes a politically neutral, but politically relevant, depository of brainpower and executive skill, and (4) the increased official secrecy behind which great decisions are made without benefit of public or even Congressional debate.

As a result, the political directorate, the corporate rich, and the ascendant military have come together as the power elite, and the expanded and centralized hierarchies which they head have encroached upon the old balances and have now relegated them to the middle levels of power. Now the balancing society is a conception that pertains accurately to the middle levels, and on that level the balance has become more often an affair of intrenched provincial and nationally irresponsible forces and demands than a center of power and national decision.

But how about the bottom? As all these trends have become visible at the top and on the middle, what has been happening to the great American public? If the top is unprecedentedly powerful and increasingly unified and willful; if the middle zones are increasingly a semi-organized stalemate—in what shape is the bottom, in what condition is the public at large? The rise of the power elite, we shall now see, rests upon, and in some ways is part of, the transformation of the publics of America into a mass society.

6

Strategic Controversy over Korea

Douglas MacArthur (1880-1964), graduated from West Point in 1903; he served in France during World War I and as Chief of Staff of the Army from 1930 to 1935. He was military advisor to the Philippine Commonwealth from 1935 until his return to active duty shortly before Japan attacked the United States in 1941. During World War II, he commanded American and Allied forces in the Philippines, the Southwest Pacific, and the Far East. From the Japanese surrender in 1945 until his removal in 1951, he commanded the occupational forces in Japan. When the North Korean forces attacked South Korea in 1950, President Truman ordered him to lead American and later United Nations' forces in meeting this attack.

Omar N. Bradley (1893-   ) graduated from West Point in 1915. He was known as a scholar in the Army, having attended most of its schools and served as an instructor at South Dakota State College and at West Point on two different occasions. After a distinguished planning and combat career during World War II, he was appointed Chief of Staff of the Army in 1948 and Chairman of the Joint Chiefs of Staff from 1949 to 1953.

Inclusion of the two documents below is designed to give some idea of the problem of global strategy that existed at the time of the Korean War. A dispute over strategy arose between General MacArthur and the Administration, and the General refused to accept the position endorsed by his Commander in Chief. Thereupon, President Truman removed General MacArthur from his various positions as Commander of the American and United Nations forces in the Far East. This dismissal aroused widespread emotional disapproval within the United States and led to a comprehensive Congressional

Hearings Before the Committee on Armed Services and the Committee on Foreign Relations, U.S. Senate, 82nd Cong., 1st Sess., to Conduct an Inquiry into the Military Situation in the Far East and the Facts Surrounding the Relief of General MacArthur . . ., part 1, May 5, 1961, pp. 729-741. "Communism a Global Enemy," speech by Douglas MacArthur, delivered before a joint meeting of the United States Congress, April 19, 1951, Vital Speeches, XVII 1950/51, pp. 430-433.

investigation not only of the dismissal but of the strategic Far Eastern policy of the Administration.

The first document is the speech that General MacArthur delivered to both Houses of Congress upon his return to the United States after his removal. In this document MacArthur explained why and how he thought the scope of the war should be enlarged. After the General's death in 1964 a controversy developed as to whether he recommended the use of radioactive cobalt and atomic bombs against the Chinese. In reading this document note (1) MacArthur's comments upon the revolt of colonial peoples; (2) his conclusion as to the new role of Asia; and (3) the philosophical and strategic bases for his criticism of the concept of limited war.

The second document consists of General Bradley's statement in support of the position of the Truman Administration at an important hearing conducted by the Senate Committees on Armed Services and Foreign Relations. Bradley's statement is in accord with a significant statement of American policy approved two months before the Korean War began that called for resisting aggression by arms if necessary, but striving to avoid all-out war. Note (1) Bradley's defense of the concept of limited war; and (2) his explanation of the grounds for the removal of General MacArthur. John W. Spanier reviewed the entire controversy in *The Truman-MacArthur Controversy and the Korean War* (Cambridge, 1959).

A. Don't Scuttle the Pacific—Communism a Global Enemy]

By Douglas MacArthur, General of the Army]

Delivered before a joint meeting of the United States Congress,]
Washington, D. C., April 19, 1951]

Mr. PRESIDENT, MR. SPEAKER AND DISTINGUISHED members of the Congress: I stand on this rostrum with a sense of deep humility and great pride—humility in the wake of those great American architects of our history who have stood here before me, pride in the reflection that this home of legislative debate represents human liberty in the purest form yet devised.

Here are centered the hopes and aspirations and faith of the entire human race.

I do not stand here as advocate for any partisan cause, for the issues are fundamental and reach quite beyond the realm of partisan considerations. They must be resolved on the highest plane of national interest if our course is to prove sound and our future protected.

I trust, therefore, that you will do me the justice of receiving that which I have to say as solely expressing the considered viewpoint of a fellow American.

I address you with neither rancor nor bitterness in the fading twilight of life, with but one purpose in mind: To serve my country.

Issues Global]

The issues are global, and so interlocked that to consider the problems of one sector oblivious to those of another is to court disaster for the whole. While Asia is commonly referred to as the gateway to Europe, it is no less true that Europe is the gateway to Asia, and the broad influence of the one cannot fail to have its impact upon the other.

There are those who claim our strength is inadequate to protect on both fronts, that we cannot divide our effort. I can think of no greater expression of defeatism.

If a potential enemy can divide his strength on two fronts, it is for us to counter his efforts. The Communist threat is a global one. Its successful advance in one sector threatens the destruction of every other sector. You cannot appease or otherwise surrender to communism in Asia without simultaneously undermining our efforts to halt its advance in Europe.

Beyond pointing out these general truisms, I shall confine my discussion to the general areas of Asia. . . .

New Strategic Frontier]

Of . . . direct and immediate bearing upon our national security are the changes wrought in the strategic potential of the Pacific Ocean in the course of the past war.

Prior thereto, the western strategic frontier of the United States lay on the littoral line of the Americas, with an exposed island salient extending out through Hawaii, Midway and Guam to the Philippines. That salient proved not an outpost of strength but an avenue of weakness along which the enemy could, and did, attack. The Pacifiic was a potential area of advance for any predatory force intent upon striking at the bordering land areas.

All this was changed by our Pacific victory. Our strategic frontier then shifted to embrace the entire Pacific Ocean, which became a vast moat to protect us as long as we held it. Indeed, it acts as a protective shield for all of the Americas and all free lands of the Pacific Ocean area. We control it to the shores of Asia by a chain of islands extending in an arc from the Aleutians to the Marianas, held by us and our free Allies.

From this island chain we can dominate with sea and air power every Asiatic port from Vladivostok to Singapore—with sea and air power, every port, as I said, from Vladivostok to Singapore—and prevent any hostile movement into the Pacific.

Any predatory attack from Asia must be an amphibious effort. No amphibious force can be successful without control of the sea lanes and the air over those lanes in its avenue of advance. With naval and air supremacy and modest ground elements to defend bases, any major attack from continental Asia toward us or our friends in the Pacific would be doomed to failure.

Under such conditions, the Pacific no longer represents menacing avenues of approach for a prospective invader. It assumes, instead, the friendly aspect of a peaceful lake.

Our line of defense is a natural one and can be maintained with a minimum of military effort and expense. It envisions no attack against anyone, nor does it provide the bastion essential for offensive operations, but properly maintained, would be an invincible defense against aggression.

The holding of this littoral defense line in the western Pacific is entirely dependent upon holding all segments thereof, for any major breach of that line by an unfriendly power would render vulnerable to determined attack every other major segment. This is a military estimate as to which I have yet to find a military leader who will take exception.

For that reason, I have strongly recommended in the past, as a matter of military urgency, that under no circumstances must Formosa fall under Communist control. Such an eventuality would at once threaten the freedom of the Philippines and the loss of Japan and might well force our western frontier back to the coast of California, Oregon and Washington.

To understand the changes which now appear upon the Chinese mainland, one must understand the changes in Chinese character and culture over the past fifty years. China up to fifty years ago was completely nonhomogeneous, being compartmented into groups divided against each other. The war-making tendency was almost non-existent as they still followed the tenets of the Confucian ideal pacifist culture.

At the turn of the century under the regime of Chang Tso-Lin efforts toward greater homogeneity produced the spark of a nationalist urge. This was further and more successfully developed under the leadership of Chiang Kai-shek, but has been brought to its great fruition under the present regime to the point that it has now taken on the character of a united nationalism of increasingly dominant aggressive tendencies.

New Dominant Power in Asia]

Through these past fifty years the Chinese people have thus become militarized in their concepts and in their ideals. They now constitute excellent soldiers, with competent staffs and commanders. This has produced a new and dominant power in Asia, which, for its own purposes, is allied with Soviet Russia but which in its own concepts and methods has become aggressively imperialistic, with a lust for expansion and increased power normal to this type of imperialism.

There is little of the ideological concept either one way or another in the Chinese make-up. The standard of living is so low and the capital accumulation has been so thoroughly dissipated by war that the masses are desperate and eager to follow any leadership which seems to promise the alleviation of local stringencies.

I have from the beginning believed that the Chinese Communists' support of the North Koreans was the dominant one. Their interests are at present parallel with those of the Soviet, but I believe that the aggressiveness recently displayed not only in Korea but also in Indo-China and Tibet and pointing potentially toward the South reflects predominantly the same lust for the expansion of power which has animated every would-be conqueror since the beginning of time.

The Japanese people since the war have undergone the greatest reformation recorded in modern history. With a commendable will, eagerness to learn, and marked capacity to understand, they have from the ashes left in war's wake erected in Japan an edifice dedicated to the primacy of individual liberty and personal dignity, and in the ensuing process there has been created a truly representative government committed to the advance of political morality, freedom of economic enterprise and social justice.

Politically, economically, and socially, Japan is now abreast of many free nations of the earth and will not again fail the universal trust. That it may be counted upon to wield a profoundly beneficial influence over the course of events in Asia is attested by the magnificent manner in which the Japanese people have met the recent challenge of war, unrest and confusion surrounding them from the outside, and checked communism within their own frontiers without the slightest slackening in their forward progress.

I sent all four of our occupation divisions to the Korean battlefront without the slightest qualms as to the effect of the resulting power vacuum upon Japan. The results fully justified my faith.

I know of no nation more serene, orderly and industrious, nor in which higher hopes can be entertained for future constructive service in the advance of the human race. . . .

With this brief insight into the surrounding areas, I now turn to the Korean conflict.

While I was not consulted prior to the President's decision to intervene in support of the Republic of Korea, that decision, from a military standpoint, proved a sound one. As I say, it proved a sound one, as we hurled back the invader and decimated his forces. Our victory was complete, and our objectives within reach, when Red China intervened with numerically superior ground forces.

New Situation in Korea]

This created a new war and an entirely new situtation, a situation not contemplated when our forces were committed against the North Korean invaders; a situation which called for new decisions in the diplomatic sphere to permit the realistic adjustment of military strategy. Such decisions have not been forthcoming.

While no man in his right mind would advocate sending our ground forces into continental China, and such was never given a thought, the new situation did urgently demand a drastic revision of strategic planning if our political aim was to defeat this new enemy as we had defeated the old.

Apart from the military need, as I saw it, to neutralize the sanctuary protection given the enemy north of the Yalu, I felt that military necessity in the conduct of the war made necesary—

(1) The intensification of our economic blockade against China.

(2) The imposition of a naval blockade against the China coast.

(3) Removal of restrictions on air reconnaissance of China's coastal area and of Manchuria.

(4) Removal of restrictions on the forces of the Republic of China on Formosa, with logistical support to contribute to their effective operations against the Chinese mainland.

For entertaining these views, all professionally designed to support our forces committed to Korea and bring hostilities to an end with the least possible delay and at a saving of countless American and Allied lives, I have been severely criticized in lay circles, principally abroad, despite my understanding that from a military standpoint the above views have been fully shared in the past by practically every military leader concerned with the Korean campaign, including our own Joint Chiefs of Staff.

The Position 'Forbade Victory']

I called for reinforcements, but was informed that reinforcements were not available. I made clear that if not permitted to destroy the enemy built-up bases north of the Yalu, if not permitted to utilize the friendly Chinese force of some 600,000 men on Formosa, if not permitted to blockade the China coast to prevent the Chinese Reds from getting succor from without, and if there were to be no hope of major reinforcements, the position of the command from the military standpoint forbade victory.

We could hold in Korea by constant maneuver and at an approximate area where our supply line advantages were in balance with the supply line disadvantages of the enemy, but we could hope at best for only an indecisive campaign with its terrible and constant attrition upon our forces if the enemy utilized his full military potential.

I have constantly called for the new political decisions essential to a solution.

Efforts have been made to distort my position. It has been said in effect that I was a warmonger. Nothing could be further from the truth.

I know war as few other men now living know it, and nothing to me is more revolting. I have long advocated its complete abolition, as its very destructiveness on both friend and foe has rendered it useless as a means of settling international disputes.

Problem Is Theological]

Indeed, on the second day of September, 1945, just following the surrender of the Japanese nation on the battleship Missouri, I formally cautioned as follows:

"Men since the beginning of time have sought peace. Various methods through the ages have been attempted to devise an international process to prevent or settle disputes between nations. From the very start workable methods were found in so far as individual citizens were concerned, but the mechanics of an instrumentality of larger international scope have never been successful.

"Military alliances, balances of power, leagues of nations, all in turn failed, leaving the only path to be by way of the crucible of war. The utter destructiveness of war now blocks out this alternative. We have had our last chance. If we will not devise some greater and more equitable system, our Armageddon will be at our door. The problem basically is theological and involves a spiritual recrudescence, an improvement of human character that will synchronize with our almost matchless advances in science, art, literature and all material and cultural developments of the past 2,000 years. It must be of the spirit if we are to save the flesh."

But once war is forced upon us, there is no other alternative than to apply every available means to bring it to a swift end. War's very object is victory not prolonged indecision.

In war there is no substitute for victory.

'I Could Not Answer']

There are some who for varying reasons would appease Red China. They are blind to history's clear lesson, for history teaches with unmistakable emphasis that appeasement but begets new and bloodier war. It points to no single instance where this end has justified that means, where appeasement has led to more than a sham peace.

Like blackmail, it lays the basis for new and successively greater demands until, as in blackmail, violence becomes the only other alternative. Why, my soldiers asked of me, surrender military advantages to an enemy in the field? I could not answer.

Some may say to avoid spread of the conflict into an all-out war with China. Others, to avoid Soviet intervention. Neither explanation seems valid, for China is already engaging with the maximum power it can commit, and the Soviet will not necessarily mesh its actions with our moves. Like a cobra, any new enemy will more likely strike whenever it feels that the relativity in military or other potential is in its favor on a world-wide basis.

The tragedy of Korea is further heightened by the fact that its military action is confined to its territorial limits. It condemns that nation, which it is our purpose to save, to suffer the devastating impact of full naval and air bombardment while the enemy's sanctuaries are fully protected from such attack and devastation.

Of the nations of the world, Korea alone, up to now, is the sole one which has risked its all against communism. The magnificence of the courage and fortitude of the Korean people defies description. They have chosen to risk death rather than slavery. Their last words to me were: "Don't scuttle the Pacific."

Old Soldiers 'Just Fade Away']

I have just left your fighting sons in Korea. They have met all tests there, and I can report to you without reservation that they are splendid in every way.

It was my constant effort to preserve them and end this savage conflict honorably and with the least loss of time and a minimum sacrifice of life. Its growing bloodshed has caused me the deepest anguish and anxiety. Those gallant men will remain often in my thoughts and in my prayers always.

I am closing my fifty-two years of military service. When I joined the Army, even before the turn of the century, it was the fulfillment of all my boyish hopes and dreams.

The world has turned over many times since I took the oath on the plain at West Point, and the hopes and dreams have long since vanished, but I still remember the refrain of one of the most popular barrack ballads of that day which proclaimed most proudly that old soldiers never die; they just fade away.

And like the old soldier of that ballad, I now close my military career and just fade away, an old soldier who tried to do his duty as God gave him the light to see that duty. Good bye.

B. Testimony of General of the Army Omar N. Bradley,]
Chairman of the Joint Chiefs of Staff]
May 15, 1951]

GENERAL BRADLEY. MR. CHAIRMAN AND MEMBERS of the committees, at the very outset, I want to make it clear that I would not say anything to discredit the long and illustrious career of Gen. Douglas MacArthur. We may have different views on certain aspects of our Government's military policy, but that is not unusual.

Certainly there have been no personal considerations in our differences of opinion. In matters of such great scope and of such importance many people have different ideas and might consequently recommend different courses of action.

As Chairman of the Joint Chiefs of Staff, I am one of the military advisers to the President, the Secretary of Defense, and the National Security Council, I pass on to them the collective advice and recommendations of the Joint Chiefs. When the Joint Chiefs of Staff express their opinion on a subject, it is from the military point of view, and is given with a full realization that considerations other than military may be overriding in making the final decision. The relative importance of the military aspect varies. In some cases it is greatly overshadowed by other considerations. In other cases, the military aspects may be the decisive ones.

When all of these aspects are considered the Government's policy is determined. As military men we then abide by the decision.

Before your interrogation on the details of our Government's policies in Korea and the Far East, I would like to ask myself this question: What is the great issue at stake in this hearing?

Principally I would say that you are trying to determine the course we should follow as the best road to peace. There are military factors which must be evaluated before a sound decision can be made. At present the issue is obscured in the public mind by many details which do not relate to the task of keeping the peace and making America secure.

Risk of Global War]

The fundamental military issue that has arisen is whether to increase the risk of a global war by taking additional measures that are open to the United States and its allies. We now have a localized conflict in Korea. Some of the military measures under discussion might well place the United States in the position of responsibility for broadening the war and at the same time losing most if not all of our allies.

General MacArthur has stated that there are certain additional measures which can and should be taken, and that by so doing no unacceptable increased risk of global war will result.

The Joint Chiefs of Staff believe that these same measures do increase the risk of global war and that such a risk should not be taken unnecessarily. At the same time we recognize the military advantages that might accrue to the United Nations' position in Korea and to the United States position in the Far East by these measures. While a field commander very properly estimates his needs from the viewpoint of operations in his own theater or sphere of action, those responsible for higher direction must necessarily base their actions on broader aspects, and on the needs, actual or prospective, of several theaters. The Joint Chiefs of Staff, in view of their global responsibilities and their perspective with respect to the world-wide strategic situation, are in a better position than is any single theater commander to assess the risk of general war. Moreover, the Joint Chiefs of Staff are best able to judge our own military resources with which to meet that risk.

Global Strategy Considered]

In order that all may understand the strategy which the Joint Chiefs of Staff believe the United States must pursue, I would like to discuss in broad terms this perspective in which we view our security problems.

As a background to our consideration of global strategy, we must realize that human beings have invented a great variety of techniques designed to influence other nations. Right now, nations are being subjected to persuasion by propaganda and coercion by force of arms. It is my conviction that broad and comprehensive knowledge of the strength, aims, and the policies of nations is basic to understanding the problem of security in a world of tension.

We must understand—as we conduct our foreign affairs and our military affairs—that while power and nationalism prevail, it is up to us to gain strength through cooperative efforts with other nations which have common ideals and objectives with our own. At the same time, we must create and maintain the power essential to persuasion, and to our own security in such a world. We must understand the role and nature, including the limitations, of this power if we are to exercise it wisely.

One of the great power potentials of this world is the United States of America and her allies. The other great power in this world is Soviet Russia and her satellites. As much as we desire peace, we must realize that we have two centers of power supporting opposing ideologies.

From a global viewpoint—and with the security of our Nation of prime importance—our military mission is to support a policy of preventing communism from gaining the manpower, the resources, the raw materials, and the industrial capacity essential to world domination. If Soviet Russia ever controls the entire

Eurasian land mass, then the Soviet-satellite imperialism may have the broad base upon which to build the military power to rule the world.

Plan of Korea, Berlin, Greece, and Turkey in Global Concept]

Three times in the past 5 years the Kremlin-inspired imperialism has been thwarted by direct action.

In Berlin, Greece, and Korea, the free nations have opposed Communist aggression with a different type of action. But each time the power of the United States has been called upon and we have become involved. Each incident has cost us money, resources, and some lives.

But in each instance we have prevented the domination of one more area, and the absorption of another source of manpower, raw materials, and resources.

Korea, in spite of the importance of the engagement, must be looked upon with proper perspective. It is just one engagement, just one phase of this battle that we are having with the other power center in the world which opposes us and all we stand for. For 5 years this "guerrilla diplomacy" has been going on. In each of the actions in which we have participated to oppose this gangster conduct, we have risked world war III. But each time we have used methods short of total war. As costly as Berlin and Greece and Korea may be, they are less expensive than the vast destruction would be inflicted upon all sides if a total war were to be precipitated.

Concept of Limited War in Korea]

I am under no illusion that our present strategy of using means short of total war to achieve our ends and oppose communism is a guarantee that a world war will not be thrust upon us. But a policy of patience and determination without provoking a world war, while we improve our military power, is one which we believe we must continue to follow.

As long as we keep the conflict within its present scope, we are holding to a minimum the forces we must commit and tie down.

The strategic alternative, enlargement of the war in Korea to include Red China, would probably delight the Kremlin more than anything else we could do. It would necessarily tie down additional forces, especially our sea power and our air power, while the Soviet Union would not be obliged to put a single man into the conflict.

Under present circumstances, we have recommended against enlarging the war. The course of action often described as a "limited war" with Red China would increase the risk we are taking by engaging too much of our power in an area that is not the critical strategic prize.

Red China is not the powerful nation seeking to dominate the world. Frankly, in the opinion of the Joint Chiefs of Staff, this strategy would involve us in the wrong war, at the wrong place, at the wrong time, and with the wrong enemy.

Role of JCS in Planning Policy]

There are some other considerations which have tended to obscure this main issue. Some critics have not hesitated to state that the policy our Government is following, and its included strategy, is not that which has been recommended by the Joint Chiefs of Staff.

Statements have been made that the President, as Commander in Chief, and the Secretary of State and the Secretary of Defense, have a policy all their own, and that the Joint Chiefs of Staff have been overridden.

This is just not so. The Joint Chiefs of Staff have continually given their considered opinion—always from a military viewpoint—concerning our global capabilities and responsibilities and have recommended our present strategy in and for Korea. This has been the course of action which the Secretary of Defense and the Commander in Chief have adopted as far as practicable.

I pointed out earlier that many times the international policy considerations, including the views of our allies, are also considered and in some instances modify the course of action.

In other instances, even after the international considerations and the views of our allies have been considered, the proposed military strategy has not been altered.

Our over-all policy has been one of steadfast patience and determination in opposing Communist aggression without provoking unnecessarily a total war.

Advisability of a "Show-down" Now]

There are many critics who have become impatient with this strategy and who would like to call for a show-down. From a purely military viewpoint, this is not desirable. We are not in the best military position to seek a show-down, even if it were the Nation's desire to forfeit the chances for peace by precipitating a total war.

Undoubtedly, this statement will be misconstrued by some critics who will say, "Why are the Joint Chiefs of Staff advertising the fact that we are not militarily in a position to have a show-down?"

I can assure those critics that with the methods we must pursue in a democracy in order to support a military establishment —including this present investigation of our strategy in the Far East—our capabilities are not unknown to the Communists.

They are apt students of military power, and fully realize that although we are not prepared to deliver any ultimatum, we could hurt them badly if they attacked us or our friends.

They also know that with our potential, and the strength of our allies, in the long run they could not win a war with a United States that is alert, and continuously prepared.

I would not be a proponent of any policy which would ignore the military facts and rush us headlong into a show-down before we are ready. It is true that this policy of armed resistance to aggression, which we pursue while we are getting stronger, often risks a world war. But so far we have taken these risks without disastrous results.

I think our global strategy is paying off and I see no reason to let impatience alter it in the Far East. Certainly the course of action we are pursuing has avoided a total war which could only bring death and destruction to millions of Americans, both in the United States and on the battlefield. Our present course of action has at the same time won us respect and admiration everywhere in the world, both inside and outside the iron curtain.

Possible Results from Enlarging War to China]

There are also those who deplore the present military situation in Korea and urge us to engage Red China in a larger war to solve this problem. Taking on Red China is not a decisive move, does not guarantee the end of the war in Korea, and may not bring China to her knees. We have only to look back to the five long years when the Japanese, one of the greatest military powers of that time, moved into China and had almost full control of a large part of China, and yet were never able to conclude that war successfully. I would say that from past history one would only jump from a smaller conflict to a larger deadlock at greater expense. My own feeling is to avoid such an engagement if possible because victory in Korea would not be assured and victory over Red China would be many years away. We believe that every effort should be made to settle the present conflict without extending it outside Korea. If this proves to be impossible, then other measures may have to be taken.

In my consideration of this viewpoint, I am going back to the basic objective of the American people—as much peace as we can gain without appeasement.

Nature of Appeasement from Military Viewpoint]

Some critics of our strategy say if we do not immediately bomb troop concentration points and airfields in Manchuria, it is "appeasement." If we do not immediately set up a blockade of Chinese ports—which to be successful would have to include British and Russian ports in Asia—it is "appeasement." These same critics would say that if we do not provide the logistical support and air and naval assistance to launch Chinese Nationalist troops into China it is "appeasement."

These critics ignore the vital questions:

Will these actions, if taken, actually assure victory in Korea?

Do these actions mean prolongation of the war by bringing Russia into the fight?

Will these actions strip us of our allies in Korea and in other parts of the world?

From a military viewpoint, appeasment occurs when you give up something, which is rightfully free, to an aggressor without putting up a struggle, or making him pay a price. Forsaking Korea—withdrawing from the fight unless we are forced out— would be an appeasement to aggression. Refusing to enlarge the quarrel to the point where our global capabilities diminished, is certainly not appeasement but is a militarily sound course of action under the present circumstances.

It is my sincere hope that these hearings will encourage us as a Nation to follow a steadfast and determined course of action in this world, which would deny any free nation to Soviet imperialism, and at the same time preserve the peace for which so many men died in World War I, World War II, and in Greece, Indochina, Malaya, and Korea. . . .

Directive of January 12, Study of January 12,
and President's Letter of January 13, 1951]

Chairman RUSSELL. The memorandum of January 12 has played quite a large part in these hearings, General Bradley.

I wish you would outline for the committee your understanding of the four items in the January 12 memorandum to which General MacArthur referred, with special reference to whether that was a directive or whether there were any contingencies involved in the four items to which he referred.

General BRADLEY. Mr. Chairman, if I might, I would like to go back a little on that, because I think there has been some confusion on this memorandum, because there are really three things that took place about that time.

There was a directive, dated January 12. There was a study which you speak of, dated January 12, and there was a letter from the President to General MacArthur, dated January 13. In other words, there are three things in this period. I will confine my remarks now to the study which you speak about. . . .

In late November, in fact November 28, when things were looking pretty bad in Korea, the Joint Chiefs of Staff directed one of their Joint Staff committees to make a study of possible lines of action which might be taken if the war in Korea developed into an all-out war against China, either declared or undeclared.

Now that was a directive which finally ended up with the January 12 study. They came up first with a study which was not agreed upon. There were split views in it between the services.

Then they reworked that paper and came up with another one, another version of it, dated January 3, which was also not acceptable, and that one was reworked and we finally got down to a paper on which the Chiefs agreed, dated January 12.

Now, when we consider one of these studies which are primarily for our own use, we consider a whole series, so to us we were thinking of this in terms of the conditions under which we started the study.

However, as we went forward in writing these different studies, the preamble or the reason for the study dropped out of it, so when we got up to the January 12 study, taken by itself it does not have the conditions under which we started the study, and at that time it was boiled down to merely the statement that it is tentatively agreed, was the term used, on the following objectives and possible lines of action.

I want to emphasize again that it was not a directive. It was a study, and I would like to explain right there that when we send a directive to the Commander in Chief, Far East, we draw up a draft of the study, a draft of the directive, take it to the Secretary of Defense, who approves or disapproves it, and if he approves it, if it has political implications we then discuss it with the Secretary of State or Department of State and then it is taken to the President who O.K.'s it or passes judgment on it.

It is then sent out as a directive. This particular study never went through that routine. In other words, it was never intended as a prospective directive to be handled in that way. It was a study for consideration along with other things that were going on at that time in trying to determine the policy, future policy toward Korea, and it was used for that purpose.

Chairman RUSSELL. Well, what was the directive now as contrasted with this study or memorandum?

Genesis of January 12 Directive]

General BRADLEY. On January the 10th General MacArthur came in with a message pointing out that under the present conditions he thought we were going to have difficulty in staying in Korea. He pointed out that the morale of the troops was not too good after a long fight and some of the remarks that had been made about them at various places in the world, and it was rather a gloomy message.

The Chiefs proposed an answer to that, and it was discussed

with the Department of State and they wanted to put certain political reasons also in this directive. The Joint Chiefs of Staff objected to that. It ended up in a discussion at the White House with the President, and the decision was made that the military part of this discussion would be pulled out and sent as a directive to General MacArthur, and then the State Department would prepare with the President a letter on political policy which he would send separately. So, the military part of that was pulled out and sent in the directive of January the 12th.

The political part of it was pulled out and fixed up with the President, and he sent it under his signature on the 13th.

Chairman RUSSELL. Now the January 12th directive was then in response to this communication from General MacArthur?

General BRADLEY. It was in response to his communication 2 days before; yes.

Chairman RUSSELL. Will you give us the broad outlines of that directive?

General BRADLEY. Yes, sir. It directed him to defend in successive positions if necessary, and always with the understanding that the security of his troops was paramount.

That is in brief form what it was. It told him, as I say, to defend in successive positions; in other words, to stay in Korea. In addition to that, we were so concerned with the situation as painted in General MacArthur's wire of January 10 that two of the Chiefs, General Collins and General Vandenberg, left on the evening of the 12th right after we had cleared the directive and went to Japan and on into Korea to see for themselves just what the situation was. Fortunately, about that time the situation began to improve, and from then on the position was stabilized and we even started to come back.

Chairman RUSSELL. The January 12th directive then was to the effect that he should stay in Korea if that could be done without endangering the security of his forces?

General BRADLEY. I can give you a paraphrase of that message if you desire, Mr. Chairman.

Chairman RUSSELL. Well, that will be all right, give a paraphrase. I have been somewhat uncertain as to the sequence, the reason for these three papers since these hearings opened, and I want them clarified.

General BRADLEY. Yes, sir. I would like to emphasize again that the one that was started back in November ended up as a study. This one was a directive which took—the formulation of it took—place over 2 days, and the political one really over 3 days.

Senator MORSE. Do you have the page from which the general is reading, Mr. Chairman?

General BRADLEY. No, sir; I have a paraphrase of a message I will give you, sir, if I may.

Senator MORSE. I thought you were reading from an exhibit.

Paraphrase of January 12 Directive]

General BRADLEY. I am reading from a note I have in my book, sir.

We are forced to the conclusion, based upon all the factors known to us, including particularly those presented in your recent message, that it is infeasible under existing conditions, including sustained major effort by Communist China, to hold the position in Korea for a protracted period.

It would be to our national interests, however, and also to the interests of the UN, before you issue firm instructions for initiation of evacuation of troops from Korea to gain some further time for essential military and diplomatic consultations with UN countries participating in Korean effort.

It is important also to the future of UN and NATO organizations, to the United States prestige world-wide, and to efforts to organize anti-Communist resistance in Asia, that maximum practical punishment be inflicted on Communist aggressors and that Korea not be evacuated unless actually forced by military considerations. In Washington it is not possible to evaluate present state of morale and combat efficiency of UN forces.

[Deleted.]

In your messages of 30 December 1950 and 4 January 1951, you had indicated it would not be necessary to make an anticipatory decision to evacuate until our forces had arrived at the old Pusan beachhead.

Including consideration of the factors outlined above, your estimate is desired as to timing and conditions under which you will have to issue instructions to evacuate Korea.

Directive contained in paragraph (c) of our message of 9 January meanwhile remains in effect.

That was, as I said, to fight in successive positions.

Nature of January 12, 1951, Study by JCS]

Chairman RUSSELL. Now, did you construe the four paragraphs which were outlined by General MacArthur in his address, I believe, the bombing of the bases, or air reconnaissance, and the use of Chinese troops, blockade of the coast of China—I believe that is the gist of it—did you construe that as having been contained in any order that was issued to General Mac-Arthur or any instructions of approval of any policy he had promulgated, or was it perfectly clear that that was a matter that was still under study, in your opinion?

General BRADLEY. Well, Mr. Chairman, to us it was clear that it was a study. Maybe it wasn't, and apparently it was not, to General MacArthur; but to us it was perfectly apparent that it was a study and was never handled as a proposed directive. It was a study which we used in the National Security Council in considering future actions if this thing developed into war against China.

Chairman RUSSELL. How was that forwarded to General Mac-Arthur?

General BRADLEY. It was forwarded in two ways. General Collins carried it to him, and discussed it with him when he arrived there on January 14. It was also sent to him later by the Army for information several days later; in fact, in a rather short form by message, by radio. So, it was actually sent to him in two ways, sir.

Chairman RUSSELL. Of course, General Collins would be the proper person to inquire of as to the nature of the conversations he had with General MacArthur?

General BRADLEY. Yes, sir. I do not know the nature, the full nature, of those discussions.

Reasons for January 13 Letter from President]

Chairman RUSSELL. Did I understand you to say now that the Joint Chiefs objected at a conference that was held at the White House to include the political considerations in the directive of January 12?

General BRADLEY. Yes, sir. We thought that the military part and the political part should be sent separately.

Chairman RUSSELL. And that accounts for the fact that the President's letter, I believe you said, followed this directive, and these instructions, this study?

General BRADLEY. Yes, sir; and the one that was sent on the 12th was a military directive. The one that was sent on the 13th, outlining certain political reasons, specifically said: "This is not a directive."

Bradley's First Awareness of Move to Relieve MacArthur]

Chairman RUSSELL. When did you first learn or when were you first consulted with respect to the advisability of relieving General MacArthur of his several commands? When did you first learn that that was under discussion? When was your opinion first asked?

General BRADLEY. If you don't mind, I will refer to notes, because when you start referring to back dates, unless you refer to notes, you are apt to get confused.

Chairman RUSSELL. All right, sir.

General BRADLEY. My first information that there was some concern being shown by the President over this was late the afternoon of Thursday, the 5th of April. When I received the information—I don't remember where from, but I think I received it from a telephone from someone—I called the Joint Chiefs of Staff together for about 30 minutes, from 5 to 5:30 in the afternoon, and told them that the President was concerned about some statements that had been made by General Mac-Arthur, and that they should begin studying the military aspects of it. There was nothing more than that said about it.

Chairman RUSSELL. When were you next approached with respect to this?

General BRADLEY. On Friday, the 6th of April, there was a meeting in the President's office, right after a Cabinet meeting, at which they asked me to join certain others, including Secretary Acheson, General Marshall, Mr. Harriman; and we were with the President, I would say, from around 11:30 to 12:30, and that is the first time I had heard first-hand the concern of the President in the matter.

Discussions of JCS on MacArthur Removal]

Chairman RUSSELL. Did you subsequently call another conference of the Joint Chiefs?

General BRADLEY. Yes, sir. There were subsequent meetings with the same four people—I believe General Marshall has explained that to you—and then on Saturday we were told that the President would like to have the views of the Joint Chiefs of Staff.

Chairman RUSSELL. What day of the month would that be?

General BRADLEY. That was Saturday, April 7. We were told they would like to have the views of the Joint Chiefs of Staff, and we should give them to General Marshall at 4 o'clock Sunday afternoon. That would have been Sunday, the 8th of April.

So, I called the Chiefs together at 2 p.m. Sunday, the 8th of April, in my office, at which time I presented to them the concern of the President and what he had in mind, and two or three other subjects were discussed between the time we met at 2 o'clock and 4 o'clock, when we went up to join General Marshall, and at 4 o'clock we went up to join him in a further conference, which lasted for about an hour, I guess.

Chairman RUSSELL. Were all of the Joint Chiefs present?

General BRADLEY. All the Chiefs were present.

Chairman RUSSELL. Were their opinions asked individually as to the wisdom of the course that was under consideration?

General BRADLEY. Yes, sir. After we discussed it and went up to General Marshall's office, he asked each of the three Chiefs their individual views, and there was some discussion in which they were all in agreement on the reasons that they advanced why they thought, from a military point of view, alone, he should be relieved.

Chairman RUSSELL. Were the Joint Chiefs unanimous in their opinion that, from the military standpoint, General MacArthur should be relieved?

General BRADLEY. Yes, sir.

Chairman RUSSELL. Were you present when the final decision was taken to relieve General MacArthur?

General BRADLEY. Yes. The final decision was made on Monday, the 9th of April, at the White House; and I was present when that decision was made.

Chairman RUSSELL. Did the recommendations of the Joint Chiefs—did they approve of the immediate relief of General MacArthur? Was there any discussion as to delay in time, or did any of them express any objection to the immediate relief of General MacArthur?

General BRADLEY. I don't remember that the exact time of the relief was discussed. Maybe some of the Chiefs will remember. I didn't include it in my notes I made immediately afterward, as to the timing of it.

The question of whether or not he could be left in part of his position and relieved of the command in Korea was discussed and from a military point of view, the Chiefs thought that was not feasible.

Chairman RUSSELL. They were unanimous in that opinion?

General BRADLEY. Yes. . . .

Danger of Russian Intervention if War Extended]

Chairman RUSSELL. Now, in your opening statement, General, you referred to the fact that the Chiefs were in agreement as to the danger of Russian intervention if the war in Asia were extended as recommended by General MacArthur.

Was that finding as to the danger of Russian intervention a unanimous decision on the part of the Joint Chiefs?

General BRADLEY. Yes, sir; they all feel that way.

Senator SALTONSTALL. Will you repeat that question, please, Mr. Chairman.

Chairman RUSSELL. I asked him if the decision of the Joint Chiefs as to the danger of Russian intervention in the event of the adoption of the MacArthur program was unanimous.

Is that danger regarded as being remote or very real by the Joint Chiefs?

General BRADLEY. Well, we think there is a real danger. Now the degree of that is anybody's opinion, Mr. Chairman. In our case we believe it is a risk which we should not take at this time.

Chairman RUSSELL. What do you base your opinion on?

General BRADLEY. Well, the strength that they have in the Far East—I mean that the Russians have in the Far East; the fact that they have been supporting China in its operation; they were supporting North Korea previously; the question of whether or not they can afford to lose in Korea; and the fact that they have an arrangement with China whereby if China is attacked under certain conditions Russia will come to her assistance.

7

Communists in the Army: "No Sense of Decency"

Excerpt from the Army-McCarthy Hearing

April 22, 1954

Probably the most important factor in the decline in influence of Senator Joseph R. McCarthy was the hearing in March and April, 1954, conducted by a special subcommittee of the Government Operations Committee of the Senate on charges made by McCarthy and others against the Army and especially Secretary of the Army, Robert Stevens. In the portion of the hearing here reproduced, three of the most significant participants are represented:

Joseph Nye Welch (1890-1960) son of an Iowa farmer, a graduate of the Harvard Law School, and a senior partner in the distinguished Boston law firm of Hale and Dorr, had been a skillful trial lawyer for many years when he was appointed the Army's counsel for the hearing. So little known that he did not appear in the 1950-51 edition of *Who's Who in America,* after the hearing he won a television contract for *Omnibus* and a role in the motion picture *Anatomy of a Murder* on the basis of his devastating yet witty interrogation of those called to testify at the hearing.

Roy M. Cohn (1927-   ), a graduate of Columbia Law School in 1947, served in the United States District Attorney's office from then until 1952 and became chief counsel of the U.S. senate permanent investigations subcommittee in 1953 and 1954. In 1953 he and another subcommittee consultant, G. David Schine, made a highly publicized eighteen-day trip to American bases in Europe which resulted in accusations of serious Communist infiltration of these bases. After the hearing Cohn went on to material success as a lawyer, teacher of law at New York University, and controversial businessman.

Joseph R. McCarthy (1909-1957), after practicing law, sitting as a

Government Operations Committee, Senate, Special Senate Investigation on Charges and Countercharges involving Secretary of the Army, Robert T. Stevens. Hearings before Special Subcommittee on Investigations, 83d Congress, 2d Session, pursuant to S. Res. 189, March 16-April 26, 1954, 2424-2430.

circuit judge in Wisconsin, and serving with the Marines from 1942 to 1945, defeated young Robert La Follette in the race for U.S. Senate from Wisconsin in 1946. He made no headlines until February 1950, when in Wheeling, West Virginia, he accused the State Department of being "thoroughly infested with Communists." He continued an anti-Communist campaign and was aided by the Republican victory in 1952 which resulted in his becoming chairman of the Senate Committee on Government Operations.

In the document below, Mr. Welch seeks to show that Cohn was perhaps more concerned with publicity than in rooting Communists out of the Army; McCarthy uses a technique which had already led to the coining of the term "McCarthyism"; and Welch gave McCarthy his come-uppance in one of the most dramatic moments of the hearing. Later in the year the Senate officially approved a resolution of censure against its junior member from Wisconsin. For further reading, see Richard H. Rovere, *Senator Joe McCarthy* (New York, 1959); William F. Buckley, Jr. and L. Brent Bozell, *McCarthy and His Enemies* (Chicago, 1954); Michael Straight, *Trial by Television* (Boston, 1954).

In reading this document note (1) the principal point that Welch is trying to make in his questioning of Roy Cohn; (2) the basis for Welch's irritation at Senator McCarthy; and (3) the reason that Welch did not permit Fred Fisher to participate as an assistant in the congressional investigation.

Aʟʟ ʀɪɢʜᴛ, ᴍʀ. ᴡᴇʟᴄʜ, ʏᴏᴜ ʜᴀᴠᴇ ᴀɴᴏᴛʜᴇʀ 10 minutes.

Mr. WELCH. I want to come back, Mr. Cohn, to the item that we were talking about this morning. I gathered, to sum it up a little, that as early as the spring, which must mean March or April, you knew about this situation of possible subversives and security risks, and even spies at Fort Mommouth, is that right?

Mr. COHN. Yes, sir.

Mr. WELCH. And I think you have used the word "disturbing," that you found it a disturbing situation?

Mr. COHN. Yes, sir.

Mr. WELCH. And you had, so to speak, only a sort of glimpse in it, you couldn't tell how big it was or how little it was, could you?

Mr. COHN. Not at the beginning, sir.

Mr. WELCH. And you probably knew enough about Fort Monmouth or found out quickly enough about Fort Monmouth, to know it was a sensitive place, didn't you?

Mr. COHN. Yes, sir.

Mr. WELCH. And I am sure the knowledge that you had was a source, Mr. Cohn, to one in your position, of some anxiety for the Nation's safety, wasn't it?

Mr. COHN. It was one situation among a number of serious situations; yes, sir.

Mr. WELCH. Well, I don't know how many worries you have, but I am sure that was, to you, a disturbing and alarming situation.

Mr. COHN. Well, sir, it was certainly serious enough for me to want to check into it and see how many facts we could check out and—

Mr. WELCH. And stop it as soon as possible?

Mr. COHN. Well, it was a question of developing the—

Mr. WELCH. But the thing that we have to do is stop it, isn't it?

Mr. COHN. Stop what, sir?

Mr. WELCH. Stop the risk.

Mr. COHN. Stop the risk, sir?

Mr. WELCH. Yes.

Mr. COHN. Yes, what we had to do was stop the risk and——

Mr. WELCH. That is right, get the people suspended or get them on trial or fire them or do something, that is right, isn't it?

Mr. COHN. Partly, sir.

Mr. WELCH. Sir?

Mr. COHN. Partly, sir.

Mr. WELCH. But it is primarily the thing, isn't it?

Mr. COHN. Well, the thing came up—

Mr. WELCH. Mr. Cohn, if I told you now that we had a bad situation at Monmouth, you would want to cure it by sundown, if you could, wouldn't you?

Mr. COHN. I am sure I couldn't, sir.

Mr. WELCH. But you would like to, if you could?

Mr. COHN. Sir—

Mr. WELCH. Isn't that right?

Mr. COHN. No, what I want—

Mr. WELCH. Answer me. That must be right. It has to be right.

Mr. COHN. What I would like to do and what can be done are two different things.

Mr. WELCH. Well, if you could be God and do anything you wished, you would cure it by sundown, wouldn't you?

Mr. COHN. Yes, sir.

Mr. WELCH. And you were that alarmed about Monmouth?

Mr. COHN. It doesn't go that way.

Mr. WELCH. I am just asking how it does go. When you find there are Communists and possible spies in a place like Monmouth, you must be alarmed, aren't you?

Mr. COHN. Now you have asked me how it goes, and I am going to tell you.

Mr. WELCH. No; I didn't ask you how it goes. I said aren't you alarmed when you find it is there?

Mr. COHN. Whenever I hear that people have been failing to act on FBI information about Communists, I do think it is alarming, I would like the Communists out, and I would like to be able to advise this committee of why people who have the responsibility for getting them out haven't carried out their responsibility.

Mr. WELCH. Yes, but what you want first of all, Mr. Cohn, and let's be fair with each other, what you want first of all, if it is within your power, is to get them out, isn't it?

Mr. COHN. I don't know if I draw a distinction as to what ought to come first, Mr. Welch.

M. WELCH. It certainly ranks terrifically high, doesn't it?

Mr. COHN. It was a situation that I thought should be developed, and we did develop it.

Mr. WELCH. When did you first meet Secretary Stevens?

Mr. COHN. I first met Secretary Stevens September 7 I believe it was.

Mr. WELCH. September 7? Where were you, sir?

Mr. COHN. Washington.

Mr. WELCH. Where in Washington?

Mr. COHN. I don't remember where I was when I met him. It was in this building, either at lunch or in a hearing room, something like that.

Mr. WELCH. And you knew that he was the new Secretary of the Army?

Mr. COHN. Yes; I did know he was the Secretary of the Army.

Mr. WELCH. And you must have had high hopes about him, didn't you?

Mr. COHN. I don't think I gave it too much thought, sir.

Mr. WELCH. Anybody wants the Secretary of the Army to do well, no matter what party he is from, do we not?

Mr. COHN. Surely, sir.

Mr. WELCH. And on September 7, when you met him, you had in your bosom this alarming situation about Monmouth, is that right?

Mr. COHN. Yes; I knew about Monmouth, then. Yes, sir.

Mr. WELCH. And you didn't tug at his lapel and say, "Mr. Secretary, I know something about Monmouth that won't let me sleep nights"? You didn't do it, did you?

Mr. COHN. I don't—as I testified, Mr. Welch, I don't know whether I talked to Mr. Stevens about it then or not. I know that on the 16th I did. Whether I talked to him on the 7th or not, is something I don't know.

Mr. WELCH. Don't you know that if you had really told him your fears were, and substantiated them to any extent, he could have jumped in the next day with suspensions?

Mr. COHN. No, sir.

Mr. WELCH. Did you then have any reason to doubt his fidelity?

Mr. COHN. No, sir.

Mr. WELCH. Or his honor?

Mr. COHN. No.

Mr. WELCH. Or his patriotism?

Mr. COHN. No.

Mr. WELCH. And yet, Mr. Cohn, you didn't tell him what you knew?

Mr. COHN. I don't know whether I did or not. I told him some of the things I knew, sir. I don't think I told him everything I knew on the first occasion. After the first 2 or 3 occasions, I think he had a pretty good idea of what we were working on.

Mr. WELCH. Mr. Cohn, tell me once more: Every time you

learn of a Communist or a spy anywhere, is it your policy to get them out as fast as possible?

Mr. COHN. Surely, we want them out as fast as possible, sir.

Mr. WELCH. And whenever you learn of one from now on, Mr. Cohn, I beg of you, will you tell somebody about them quick?

Mr. COHN. Mr. Welch, with great respect, I work for the committee here. They know how we go about handling situations of Communist infiltration and failure to act on FBI information about Communist infiltration. If they are displeased with the speed with which I and the group of men who work with me proceed, if they are displeased with the order in which we move, I am sure they will give me appropriate instructions along those lines, and I will follow any which they give me.

Mr. WELCH. May I add my small voice, sir, and say whenever you know about a subversive or a Communist or a spy, please hurry. Will you remember those words?

Senator McCARTHY. Mr. Chairman.

Mr. COHN. Mr. Welch, I can assure you, sir, as far as I am concerned, and certainly as far as the chairman of this committee and the members, and the members of the staff, are concerned, we are a small group, but we proceed as expeditiously as is humanly possible to get out Communists and traitors and to bring to light the mechanism by which they have been permitted to remain where they were for so long a period of time.

Senator McCARTHY. Mr. Chairman, in view of that question—

Senator MUNDT. Have you a point of order?

Senator McCARTHY. Not exactly, Mr. Chairman, but in view of Mr. Welch's request that the information be given once we know of anyone who might be performing any work for the Communist Party, I think we should tell him that he has in his law firm a young man named Fisher whom he recommended, incidentally, to do work on this committee, who has been for a number of years a member of an organization which was named, oh, years and years ago, as the legal bulwark of the Communist Party, an organization which always swings to the defense of anyone who dares to expose Communists. I certainly assume that Mr. Welch did not know of this young man at the time he recommended him as the assistant counsel for this committee, but he has such terror and such a great desire to know where anyone is located who may be serving the Communist cause, Mr. Welch, that I thought we should just call to your attention the fact that your Mr. Fisher, who is still in your law firm today, whom you asked to have down here looking over the secret and classified material, is a member of an organization, not named by me but named by various committees, named by the Attorney General, as I recall, and I think I quote this verbatim, as "the legal bulwark of the Communist Party." He belonged to that for a sizable number of years, according to his own admission, and he belonged to it long after it had been exposed as the legal arm of the Communist Party.

Knowing that, Mr. Welch, I just felt that I had a duty to respond to your urgent request that before sundown, when we know of anyone serving the Communist cause, we let the agency know. We are now letting you know that your man did belong to this organization for either 3 or 4 years, belonged to it long after he was out of law school.

I don't think you can find anyplace, anywhere, an organization which has done more to defend Communists—I am again quoting the report—to defend Communists, to defend espionage agents, and to aid the Communist cause, than the man whom you originally wanted down here at your right hand instead of Mr. St. Clair.

I have hesitated bringing that up, but I have been rather bored with your phony requests to Mr. Cohn here that he personally get every Communist out of government before sundown. Therefore, we will give you information about the young man in your own organization.

I am not asking you at this time to explain why you tried to foist him on this committee. Whether you knew he was a member of that Communist organization or not, I don't know. I assume you did not, Mr. Welch, because I get the impression that, while you are quite an actor, you play for a laugh, I don't think you have any conception of the danger of the Communist Party. I don't think you yourself would ever knowingly aid the Communist cause. I think you are unknowingly aiding it when you try to burlesque this hearing in which we are attempting to bring out the facts, however.

Mr. WELCH. Mr. Chairman.

Senator MUNDT. Mr. Welch, the Chair should say he has no recognition or no memory of Mr. Welch's recommending either Mr. Fisher or anybody else as counsel for this committee.

I will recognize Mr. Welch.

Senator McCARTHY. Mr. Chairman, I will give you the news story on that.

Mr. WELCH. Mr. Chairman, under these circumstances I must have something approaching a personal privilege.

Senator MUNDT. You may have it, sir. It will not be taken out of your time.

Mr. WELCH. Senator McCarthy, I did not know—Senator, sometimes you say "May I have your attention?"

Senator McCARTHY. I am listening to you. I can listen with one ear.

Mr. WELCH. This time I want you to listen with both.

Senator McCARTHY. Yes.

Mr. WELCH. Senator McCarthy, I think until this moment—

Senator McCARTHY. Jim, will you get the news story to the effect that this man belonged to this Communist-front organization? Will you get the citations showing that this was the legal arm of the Communist Party, and the length of time that he belonged, and the fact that he was recommended by Mr. Welch? I think that should be in the record.

Mr. WELCH. You won't need anything in the record when I have finished telling you this.

Until this moment, Senator, I think I never really gaged your cruelty or your recklessness. Fred Fisher is a young man who went to the Harvard Law School and came into my firm and is starting what looks to be a brilliant career with us.

When I decided to work for this committee I asked Jim St. Clair, who sits on my right, to be my first assistant. I said to Jim, "Pick somebody in the firm who works under you that you would like." He chose Fred Fisher and they came down on an afternoon plane. That night, when he had taken a little stab at trying to see what the case was about, Fred Fisher and Jim St. Clair and I went to dinner together. I then said to these two young men, "Boys, I don't know anything about you except I have always liked you, but if there is anything funny in the life of either one of you that would hurt anybody in this case you speak up quick."

Fred Fisher said, "Mr. Welch, when I was in law school and for a period of months after, I belonged to the Lawyers Guild," as you have suggested, Senator. He went on to say, "I am secretary of the Young Republicans League in Newton with the son of Massachusetts' Governor, and I have the respect and admiration of my community and I am sure I have the respect and admiration of the 25 lawyers or so in Hale & Dorr."

I said, "Fred, I just don't think I am going to ask you to work on the case. If I do, one of these days that will come out and go over national television and it will just hurt like the dickens."

So, Senator, I asked him to go back to Boston.

Little did I dream you could be so reckless and so cruel as to do injury to that lad. It is true he is still with Hale & Dorr. It is true that he will continue to be with Hale & Dorr. It is, I regret to say, equally true that I fear he shall always bear a scar needlessly inflicted by you. If it were in my power to forgive you for your reckless cruelty, I will do so. I like to think I am a gentleman, but your forgiveness will have to come from someone other than me.

Senator McCARTHY. Mr. Chairman.

Senator MUNDT. Senator McCarthy?

Senator McCARTHY. May I say that Mr. Welch talks about this being cruel and reckless. He was just baiting; he has been baiting Mr. Cohn here for hours, requesting that Mr. Cohn, before sundown, get out of any department of Government anyone who is serving the Communist cause.

I just give this man's record, and I want to say, Mr. Welch, that it has been labeled long before he became a member, as early as 1944—

Mr. WELCH. Senator, may we not drop this? We know he belonged to the Lawers Guild, and Mr. Cohn nods his head at me. I did you, I think, no personal injury, Mr. Cohn.

Mr. COHN. No, sir.

Mr. WELCH. I meant to do you no personal injury, and if I did, I beg your pardon.

Let us not assassinate this lad further, Senator. You have done enough. Have you no sense of decency, sir, at long last? Have you left no sense of decency?

Senator McCARTHY. I know this hurts you, Mr. Welch. But I may say, Mr. Chairman, on a point of personal privilege, and I would like to finish it—

Mr. WELCH. Senator, I think it hurts you, too, sir.

Senator McCARTHY. I would like to finish this.

Mr. Welch has been filibustering this hearing, he has been talking day after day about how he wants to get anyone tainted with communism out before sundown. I know Mr. Cohn would rather not have me go into this. I intend to, however, Mr. Welch talks about any sense of decency. If I say anything which is not the truth, then I would like to know about it.

The foremost legal bulwark of the Communist Party, its front organizations, and controlled unions, and which, since its inception, has never failed to rally to the legal defense of the Communist Party, and individual members thereof, including known espionage agents.

Now, that is not the language of Senator McCarthy. That is the language of the Un-American Activities Committee. And I can go on with many more citations. It seems that Mr. Welch is pained so deeply he thinks it is improper for me to give the record, the Communist-front record, of the man whom he wanted to foist upon this committee. But it doesn't pain him at all—there is no pain in his chest about the unfounded charges against Mr. Frank Carr; there is no pain there about the attempt to destroy the reputation and take the jobs away from the young men who were working in my committee.

And, Mr. Welch, if I have said anything here which is untrue, then tell me. I have heard you and every one else talk so much about laying the truth upon the table that when I hear—and it is completely phony, Mr. Welch, I have listened to you for a long time—when you say "Now, before sundown, you must get these people out of Government," I want to have it very clear, very clear that you were not so serious about that when you tried to recommend this man for this committee.

And may I say, Mr. Welch, in fairness to you, I have reason to believe that you did not know about his Communist-front record at the time you recommended him. I don't think you would have recommended him to the committee if you knew that.

I think it is entirely possible you learned that after you recommended him.

Senator MUNDT. The Chair would like to say again that he does not believe that Mr. Welch recommended Mr. Fisher as counsel for this committee, because he has through his office all the recommendations that were made. He does not recall any that came from Mr. Welch, and that would include Mr. Fisher.

Senator McCARTHY. Let me ask Mr. Welch. You brought him down, did you not, to act as your assistant?

Mr. WELCH. Mr. McCarthy, I will not discuss this with you further. You have sat within 6 feet of me, and could have asked me about Fred Fisher. You have brought it out. If there is a God in heaven, it will do neither you nor your cause any good. I will not discuss it further. I will not ask Mr. Cohn any more questions. You, Mr. Chairman, may, if you will, call the next witness.

8

The Fair Deal at Home and Abroad
Harry S. Truman's State of the Union Message, 1948

Harry S. Truman, (1884-   ), farmer and professional politician
from the state of Missouri, was elected to the U.S. Senate in 1934 and
reelected in 1940. In 1941, he was appointed chairman of a special
senatorial committee to investigate war production. So vigorously and
effectively did he carry out this investigation that by 1944 he probably knew as much about the war effort as anybody in the United
States. This fact, together with political considerations which made
others "unavailable," led Franklin D. Roosevelt to approve him as
his running mate in 1944. The Democratic Convention nominated him,
and the Roosevelt-Truman ticket triumphed. President Roosevelt died
on April 12, 1945, just three months after the beginning of his fourth
term. Truman succeeded to the Presidency with the sympathy and
pledges of support seemingly from all. By January 1948, however,
the scene had fundamentally changed. Rebellion within the Democratic Party was threatening from Southern elements on the one side
and from the followers of Henry Wallace on the other. Even middle-
of-the-road New Dealers were looking for another candidate who
might be more likely than Truman to win in the November presidential election. In his State of the Union Message, Truman formulated
his personal platform. In reading this document, note (1) the philosophical basis for Truman's domestic and foreign policy; (2) his
specific goals in domestic policy (the Fair Deal); (3) his specific goals
in foreign and defense policy; and (4) the means by which the
realization of these goals were to be financed. Useful additional reading may be found in *Memoirs by Harry S. Truman* Volume I, *Year of
Decisions* (New York, 1955), and Volume II, *Years of Trial and Hope*
(New York, 1956); and Jonathan Daniels, *The Man from Independence* (Philadelphia, 1950).

I SINCERELY HOPE THAT ALL OF YOU HAD A PLEASANT holiday season and that you won't have too much hard work in the coming year.

Mr. President, Mr. Speaker and members of the Eightieth Congress:

We are here today to consider the state of the Union.

On this occasion, above all others, the Congress and the President should concentrate their attention, not upon party, but upon the country; not upon the things which divide us but upon those which bind us together—the enduring principles of our American system, and our common aspirations for the future welfare and security of the United States.

The United States has become great because we, as a people, have been able to work together for great objectives even while differing about details.

The elements of our strength are many. They include our democratic government, our economic system, our great natural resources. But these are only partial explanations.

The basic source of our strength is spiritual. For we are a people with a faith. We believe in the dignity of man. We believe that he was created in the image of the Father of us all.

We do not believe that men exist merely to strengthen the state or to be cogs in an economic machine. We do believe that governments are created to serve the people and that economic systems exist to minister to their wants. We have a profound devotion to the welfare and rights of the individual as a human being.

The faith of our people has particular meaning at this time in history because of the unsettled and changing state of the world.

The victims of war in many lands are striving to rebuild their lives, and are seeking assurance that the tragedy of war will not occur again. Throughout the world new ideas are challenging the old. Men of all nations are re-examining the beliefs by which they live. Great scientific and industrial changes have released new forces which will affect the future course of civilization.

The state of our Union reflects the changing nature of the

modern world. On all sides there is heartening evidence of great energy—of capacity for economic development—and even more important, capacity for spiritual growth. But accompanying this great activity there are equally great questions—great anxieties and great aspirations. They represent the concern of an enlightened people that conditions should be so arranged as to make life more worthwhile.

Dictators and Destruction]

We must devote ourselves to finding answers to these anxieties and aspirations. We seek answers which will embody the moral and spiritual elements of tolerance, unselfishness and brotherhood upon which true freedom and opportunity must rest.

As we examine the state of our Union today, we can benefit from viewing it on a basis of the accomplishments of the last decade and of our goals for the next. How far have we come during the last ten years and how far can we go in the next ten?

It was ten years ago that the determination of dictators to wage war upon mankind became apparent. The years that followed brought untold death and destruction.

We shared in the human suffering of the war, but we were fortunate enough to escape most of war's destruction. We were able through these ten years to expand the productive strength of our farms and factories.

More important, however, is the fact that these years brought us new courage and new confidence in the ideals of our free democracy. Our deep belief in freedom and justice was reinforced in the crucible of war.

On the foundations of our greatly strengthened economy and our renewed confidence in democratic values, we can continue to move forward.

There are some who look with fear and distrust upon planning for the future. Yet our great national achievements have been attained by those with vision. Our Union was formed, our frontiers were pushed back and our great industries were built by men who looked ahead.

I propose that we look ahead today toward those goals for the future which have the greatest bearing upon the foundation of our democracy and the happiness of our people.

I do so, confident in the thought that with clear objectives and with firm determination, we can, in the next ten years, build upon the accomplishments of the past decade to achieve a glorious future. Year by year, beginning now, we must make a substantial part of this progress.

Our First Goal Defined]

Our first goal is to secure fully the essential human rights of our citizens.

The United States has always had a deep concern for human rights. Religious freedom, free speech and freedom of thought are cherished realities in our land. Any denial of human rights is a denial of the basic beliefs of democracy and of our regard for the worth of each individual.

Today, however, some of our citizens are still denied equal opportunity for education, for jobs and economic advancement, and for the expression of their views at the polls. Most serious of all, some are denied equal protection under the laws. Whether discrimination is based on race, or creed, or color, or land or origin, it is utterly contrary to American ideals of democracy.

The recent report of the President's Committee on Civil Rights points the way to corrective action by the Federal Government and by state and local governments. Because of the need for effective Federal action, I shall send a special message to the Congress on this important subject.

We should also consider our obligations to assure the fullest possible measure of civil rights to the people of our territories and possessions. I believe that the time has come for Alaska and Hawaii to be admitted to the Union as states.

Our second goal is to protect and develop our human resources.

The safeguarding of the rights of our citizens must be accompanied by an equal regard for their opportunities for development and their protection from economic insecurity. In this nation the ideals of freedom and equality can be given specific meaning in terms of health, education, social security and housing.

Over the past twelve years we have erected a sound framework of social security legislation. Many millions of our citizens are now protected against the loss of income which can come with unemployment, old-age, or the death of wage-earners. Yet our system has gaps and inconsistencies; it is only half-finished.

We should now extend unemployment compensation, old-age benefits and survivors' benefits to millions who are not now protected. We should also raise the level of benefits.

The greatest gap in our Social Security structure is the lack of adequate provision for the nation's health. We are rightly proud of the high standards of medical care we know how to provide in the United States. The fact is, however, that most of our people cannot afford to pay for the care they need.

I have often and strongly urged that this condition demands a national health program. The heart of the program must be a national system of payment for medical care based on well-tried insurance principles. This great nation cannot afford to allow its citizens to suffer needlessly from the lack of proper medical care.

Our ultimate aim must be a comprehensive insurance system to protect all our people equally against insecurity and ill-health.

Another fundamental aim of our democracy is to provide an adequate education for every person.

Our educational systems face a financial crisis. It is deplorable that in a nation as rich as ours there are millions of children who do not have adequate schoolhouses or enough teachers for a good elementary or secondary education. If there are educational inadequacies in any state the whole nation suffers. The Federal Government has a responsibility for providing financial aid to meet this crisis.

Requirements of Democracy]

In addition, we must make possible greater equality of opportunity to all our citizens for an education. Only by so doing can we insure that our citizens will be capable of understanding and sharing the responsibilities of democracy.

The Government's program for health, education and security are of such great importance to our democracy that we should now establish an executive department for their administration.

Health and education have their beginning in the home. No matter what our hospitals or schools are like, the youth of our nation are handicapped when millions of them live in city slums and country shacks. Within the next decade we must see that every American family has a decent home.

As an immediate step we need the long-range housing program which I have recommended on many occasions to this Congress. This should include financial aids designed to yield more housing at lower prices. It should provide public housing for low-income families, and vigorous development of new techniques to lower the cost of building.

Until we can overcome the present drastic housing shortage we must extend and strengthen rent control.

We have had, and shall continue to have, a special interest in the welfare of our veterans. Over 14 million men and women who served in the armed forces in World War II have now returned to civilian life. Over two million veterans are being helped through school. Millions have been aided while finding jobs, and have been helped in buying homes, in obtaining medical care, and in adjusting themselves to physical handicaps.

All but a very few veterans have successfully made the transition from military life to their home communities. The success of our veterans' program is proved by this fact. This nation is proud of the eagerness shown by our veterans to become self-reliant and self-supporting citizens.

Our third goal is to conserve and use our natural resources so that they can contribute most effectively to the welfare of the people.

The resources given by nature to this country are rich and extensive. The material foundations of our growth and economic development are the bounty of our fields, the wealth of our mines and forests, and the energy of our waters. As a nation we are coming to appreciate more each day the close relationship between the conservation of these resources and the preservation of our national strength.

We are doing far less than we know how to do to make use of our resources without destroying them. Both the public and private use of these resources must have the primary objective of maintaining and increasing these basic supports for an expanding future.

We must continue to take specific steps toward this goal. We must vigorously defend our natural wealth against those who would misuse it for selfish gain.

We need accurate and comprehensive knowledge of our mineral resources and must intensify our efforts to develop new supplies and to acquire stockpiles of scarce materials.

We need to protect and restore our land—public and private—through combating erosion and rebuilding the fertility of the soil.

We must expand our reclamation program to bring millions of acres of arid land into production, and to improve water supplies for additional millions of acres. This will provide new opportunities for veterans and others, particularly in the West, and aid in providing a rising living standard for a growing population.

We must protect and restore our forests by sustained-yield forestry and by planting new trees in areas now slashed and barren.

For Power Development]

We must continue to erect multiple-purpose dams on our great rivers—not only to reclaim land, but also to prevent floods, to extend our inland waterways and to provide hydroelectric power. This public power must not be monopolized for private gain. Only through well-established policies of transmitting power directly to its market and thus encouraging wide-spread use at low rates can the Federal Government assure the people of their full share of its benefits. Additional power—public and private—is needed to raise the ceilings now imposed by power shortages on industrial and agricultural development.

We should achieve the wise use of resources through the integrated development of our great river basins. We can learn much from our Tennessee Valley experience. We should no longer delay in applying the lessons of that vast undertaking to our other great river basins.

Our fourth goal is to lift the standard of living for all our people by strengthening our economic system and sharing more broadly among our people the goods we produce.

The amazing economic progress of the past ten years points the way for the next ten.

Today fourteen more million people have jobs than in 1938.

Our yearly output of goods and services has increased by two-thirds.

The average income of our people, measured in dollars of equal purchasing power, has increased—after taxes—by more than 50 per cent.

In no other ten years have farmers, business men and wage-earners made such great gains.

We may not be able to expand as rapidly in the next decade as in the last, because we are now starting from full employment and very high production. But we can increase our annual output by at least one-third above the present level. We can lift our standard of living to nearly double what it was ten years ago.

If we distribute these gains properly we can go far toward stamping out poverty in our generation.

To do this agriculture, business and labor must move forward together.

Permanent farm prosperity and agricultural abundance will be achieved only as our whole economy grows and prospers. The farmer can sell more food at good prices when the incomes of wage-earners are high and when there is full employment. Adequate diet for every American family, and the needs of our industries at full production, will absorb a farm output well above our present levels.

Although the average farmer is now better off than ever before, farm families as a whole have only begun to catch up with the standards of living enjoyed in the cities. In 1946 the average income of farm people was $779, contrasted with an average income of $1,288 for nonfarm people. Within the next decade we should eliminate elements of inequality in these living standards.

To this end our farm program should enable the farmer to market his varied crops at fair price levels and to improve his standard of living.

We need to continue price supports for major farm commodities on a basis which will afford reasonable protection against fluctuations in the levels of production and demand. The present price support program must be re-examined and modernized.

Crop insurance should be strengthened and its benefits extended in order to protect the farmer against the special hazards to which he is subject.

We also need to improve the means for getting farm products

into the markets and into the hands of consumers. Cooperatives which directly or indirectly serve this purpose must be encouraged—not discouraged. The school lunch program should be continued and adequately financed.

We need to go forward with the rural electrification program to bring the benefits of electricity to all our farm population.

We can, and must, aid and encourage farmers to conserve their soil resources and restore the fertility of land that has suffered from neglect or unwise use.

All of these are practical measures upon which we should act immediately to enable agriculture to make its full contribution to our prosperity.

Industrial Expansion Urged]

We must also strengthen our economic system within the next decade by enlarging our industrial capacity within the framework of our free enterprise system.

We are today far short of the industrial capacity we need for a growing future. At least $50 billions should be invested by industry to improve and expand our productive facilities over the next few years. But this is only the beginning. The industrial application of atomic energy and other scientific advances will constantly open up further opportunities for expansion. Farm prosperity and high employment will call for an immensely increased output of goods and services.

Growth and vitality in our economy depend on vigorous private enterprise. Free competition is the key to industrial development, full production and employment, fair prices and an ever-improving standard of living. Competition is seriously limited today in many industries by the concentration of economic power and other elements of monopoly. The appropriation of sufficient funds to permit proper enforcement of the present antitrust laws is essential. Beyond that we should go on to strengthen our legislation to protect competition.

Another basic element of a strong economic system is the well-being of the wage-earner.

We have learned that the well-being of workers depends on high production and consequent high employment. We have learned equally well that the welfare of industry and agriculture depends on high incomes for our workers.

The Government has wisely chosen to set a floor under wages. But our 40-cent minimum wage is inadequate and obsolete. I recommend the lifting of the minimum wage to 75 cents an hour.

In general, however, we must continue to rely on our sound system of collective bargaining to set wage scales. Workers' incomes should increase at a rate consistent with the maintenance of sound price, profit and wage relationships with increased productivity.

The Government's part in labor-management relations is now largely controlled by the terms of the Labor-Management Relations Act of 1947. I made my attitude clear on this act in my veto message to the Congress last June. Nothing has occurred since to change my opinion of this law. As long as it remains the law of the land, however, I shall carry out my constitutional duty and administer it.

As we look ahead we can understand the crucial importance of restraint and wisdom in arriving at new labor-management contracts. Work stoppages would result in a loss of production— a loss which could bring higher prices for our citizens and could also deny the necessities of life to the hard-pressed peoples of other lands. It is my sincere hope that the representatives of labor and of industry will bear in mind that the nation as a whole has a vital stake in the success of their bargaining efforts.

If we surmount our current economic difficulties, we can move ahead to a great increase in our national income which will enable all our people to enjoy richer and fuller lives.

All of us must advance together. One-fifth of our families now have average annual incomes of less than $850. We must see that our gains in national income are made more largely available to those with low incomes, whose need is greatest. This will benefit us all through providing a stable foundation of buying power to maintain prosperity.

Business, labor, agriculture and government, working together, must develop the policies which will make possible the realization of the full benefits of our economic system.

Our fifth goal is to achieve world peace based on principles of freedom and justice and the equality of all nations.

Twice within our generation world wars have taught us that we cannot isolate ourselves from the rest of the world.

We have learned that the loss of freedom in any area of the world means a loss of freedom to ourselves—that the loss of independence by any nation adds directly to the insecurity of the United States and all free nations.

We have learned that a healthy world economy is essential to world peace—that economic distress is a disease whose evil effects spread far beyond the boundaries of the afflicted nation.

Our Policies for Peace]

For these reasons the United States is vigorously following policies designed to achieve a peaceful and prosperous world.

We are giving, and will continue to give, our full support to the United Nations. While that organization has encountered unforeseen and unwelcome difficulties, I am confident of its ultimate success. We are also devoting our efforts toward world economic recovery and the revival of world trade. These actions are closely related and mutually supporting.

We believe that the United States can be an effective force for world peace only if it is strong. We look forward to the day when nations will decrease their armaments. Yet so long as there remains serious opposition to the ideals of a peaceful world, we must maintain strong armed forces.

The passage of the National Security Act by the Congress at its last session was a notable step in providing for the security of this country. A further step which I consider of even greater importance is the early provision for universal training. There are many elements in a balanced national security program, all interrelated and necessary, but universal training should be the foundation for them all. A favorable decision by the Congress at an early date is of world importance. I am convinced that such action is vital to the security of this nation and to the maintenance of its leadership.

The United States is engaged today in many international activities directed toward the creation of lasting peaceful relationships among nations.

We have been giving substantial aid to Greece and Turkey to assist these nations in preserving their integrity against foreign pressures. Had it not been for our aid, their situation today might well be radically different. The continued integrity of those countries will have a powerful effect upon other nations in the Middle East and in Europe struggling to maintain their independence while they repair the damages of war.

The United States has special responsibilities with respect to the countries in which we have occupation forces: Germany, Austria, Japan and Korea. Our efforts to reach agreements on peace settlements for these countries have so far been blocked. But we shall continue to exert our utmost efforts to obtain satisfactory settlements for each of these nations.

Many thousands of displaced persons, still living in camps overseas, should be allowed entry into the United States. I again urge the Congress to pass suitable legislation at once so that this nation may do its share in caring for the homeless and suffering refugees of all faiths. I believe that the admission of these persons will add to the strength and energy of this nation.

We are moving toward our goal of world peace in many ways. But the most important effort which we are now making are those which support world economic reconstruction. We are seeking to restore the world trading system which was shattered by the war and to remedy the economic paralysis which grips many countries.

To restore world trade we have recently taken the lead in bringing about the greatest reduction of world tariffs that the world has ever seen. The extension of the provisions of the Reciprocal Trade Agreements Act, which made this achievement possible, is of extreme importance. We must also go on to support the International Trade Organization, through which we hope to obtain world-wide agreement on a code of fair conduct in international trade.

Our present major effort toward economic reconstruction is to support the program for recovery developed by the countries of Europe. In my recent message to the Congress I outlined the reasons why it is wise and necessary for the United States to extend this support.

I want to reaffirm my belief in the soundness and promise of this proposal. When the European economy is strengthened, the product of its industry will be of benefit to many other areas of economic distress. The ability of free men to overcome hunger and despair will be a moral stimulus to the entire world.

Special Aid to China Planned]

We intend to work also with other nations in achieving world economic recovery. We shall continue our cooperation with the nations of the Western Hemisphere. A special program of assistance to China, to provide urgent relief needs and to speed reconstruction, will be submitted to the Congress.

Unfortunately, not all Governments share the hope of the people of the United States that economic reconstruction in many areas of the world can be achieved through cooperative effort among nations. In spite of these differences we will go forward with our efforts to overcome economic paralysis.

No nation by itself can carry these programs to success; they depend upon the cooperative and honest efforts of all participating countries. Yet the leadership is inevitably ours.

I consider it of the highest importance that the Congress should authorize support for the European Recovery Program for the period from April 1, 1948, to June 30, 1952, with an initial amount for the first fifteen months of $6,800,000,000, I urge the Congress to act promptly on this vital measure of our foreign policy—on this decisive contribution to world peace.

We are following a sound, constructive and practical course in carrying out our determination to achieve peace.

We are fighting poverty, hunger and suffering.

This leads to peace—not war.

We are building toward a world where all nations, large and small alike, may live free from the fear of aggression.

This leads to peace—not war.

Above all else, we are striving to achieve a concord among the peoples of the world based upon the dignity of the individual and the brotherhood of man.

This leads to peace—not war.

We can go forward with confidence that we are following sound policies, both at home and with other nations, which will lead us toward our great goals for economic, social and moral achievement.

As we enter the new year, we must surmount one major problem which affects all our goals. That is the problem of inflation.

Already inflation in this country is undermining the living

standards of millions of families. Food costs too much. Housing has reached fantastic price levels. Schools and hospitals are in financial distress. Inflation threatens to bring on disagreement and strife between labor and management.

Worst of all, inflation holds the threat of another depression, just as we had a depression after the unstable boom following the first World War.

When I announced last October that the Congress was being called into session, I described the price increases which had taken place since June, 1946. Wholesale prices had increased 40 per cent and retail prices had increased 23 per cent.

Since October prices have continued to rise. Wholesale prices have gone up at an annual rate of 18 per cent. Retail prices have gone up at an annual rate of 10 per cent.

The events which have occurred since I presented my ten-point anti-inflation program to the Congress in November have made it even clearer that all ten points are essential.

High prices must not be our means of rationing.

We must deal effectively and at once with the high cost of living. We must stop the spiral of inflation.

I trust that within the shortest possible time the Congress will make available to the Government the weapons that are so desperately needed in the fight against inflation.

One of the most powerful anti-inflationary factors in our economy today is the excess of Government revenues over expenditures.

Government expenditures have been and must continue to be held at the lowest safe levels. Since V-J Day Federal expenditures have been sharply reduced. They have been cut from more than $63 billion in the fiscal year 1946 to less than $38 billion in the present fiscal year. The number of civilian employes has been cut nearly in half—from 3¾ million down to 2 million.

Opposes Cut in Revenues]

On the other hand, Government revenues must not be reduced. Until inflation has been stopped there should be no cut in taxes that is not offset by additions at another point in our tax structure.

Certain adjustments should be made within our existing tax structure that will not affect total receipts, yet will adjust the tax burden so that thost least able to pay will have their burden lessened by the transfer of a portion of it to those best able to pay.

Many of our families today are suffering hardship because of the high cost of living. At the same time profits of corporations have reached an all-time record in 1947. Corporate profits totaled $17,000,000,000 after taxes. This compared with $12,500,-000,000 in 1946, the previous high year.

Because of this extraordinarily high level of profit corporations can well afford to carry a larger share of the tax load at this time.

During this period in which the high cost of living is bearing down on so many of our families tax adjustments should be made to ease their burden. The low-income group particularly is being pressed very hard. To this group a tax adjustment would result in a saving that could be used to buy the necessities of life.

I recommend, therefore, that, effective January 1, 1948, a cost of living tax credit be extended to our people consisting of a credit of $40 to each individual taxpayer and an additional credit of $40 for each dependent. Thus the income tax of a man with a wife and two children would be reduced $160. The credit would be extended to all taxpayers, but it would be particularly helpful to those in the low-income group.

It is estimated that such a tax credit would reduce the Federal revenue by $3,200,000,000. This reduction should be made up by increasing the tax on corporate profits in an amount that will produce this sum—with appropriate adjustments for small corporations.

This is the proper method of tax relief at this time. It gives relief to those who need it most without cutting the total tax revenue of the Government.

When the present danger of inflation has passed we should consider tax reduction based upon a revision of our entire tax structure.

When we have conquered inflation we shall be in a position to move forward toward our chosen goals.

As we do so let us keep ever before us our high purposes.

We are determined that every citizen of this nation shall have an equal right and an equal opportunity to grow in wisdom and in stature and to take his place in the control of his nation's destiny.

We are determined that the productive resources of this nation shall be used wisely and fully for the benefit of all.

We are determined that the democratic faith of our people and the strength of our resources shall contribute their full share to the attainment of an enduring peace in the world.

It is our faith in human dignity that underlies these purposes. It is this faith that keeps us a strong and vital people.

This is a time to remind ourselves of these fundamentals. For today the whole world looks to us for leadership.

This is the hour to rededicate ourselves to the faith in mankind that makes us strong.

This is the time to rededicate ourselves to the faith in God that gives us confidence as we face the challenge of the years ahead.

9

Opposition from a Conservative Republican

Robert A. Taft's Reply to Truman, January 8, 1948

Robert A. Taft (1889-1953), a son of President and Chief Justice William Howard Taft, graduated from Yale and received his LL.B. from Harvard. After practicing law in Ohio, he entered local politics, and in 1939 was elected U.S. Senator. He soon established his leadership among Republican Senators and skillfully developed a powerful coalition between his own party and certain Southern Democrats. When the Republicans won both houses of Congress in 1946, Taft was chosen chairman of the powerful Senate Republican Policy Committee. He could not be considered a rigid isolationist, but he was suspicious of long-term foreign aid, and had opposed Lend Lease in 1941. He stood for economy, labor controls, and economic "liberty," and yet at the same time he saw the need for Federal support for housing construction and for Federal grants to states for education and medical aid. For additional reading, see William S. White, *The Taft Story* (New York, 1954). When President Truman outlined his personal program for domestic and foreign policy in January 1948, Taft was the logical Republican to reply. In reading this document, note (1) the similarities and differences between the philosophies of government of Truman and Taft; (2) the ways in which Taft explains that freedom would be lost through the Truman program; and (3) the positive program that Taft would support.

I LISTENED YESTERDAY WITH GREAT INTEREST TO the President of the United States on the state of the Union. The message states in general terms the ideals and principles and program of the present Administration. The de-

New York Times, January 9, 1948, copyright by The New York Times. Reprinted by permission. A transcript of the radio speech made on Thursday, January 8, 1948.

tailed specifications for some actions have been already filled in by measures proposed, or presumably will be filled in by later messages.

No one can fail to agree with most of the ideals expressed by the President. No one can fail to agree with his general desire to bring about improved conditions in this country and throughout the world. No one can fail to agree with the five goals which he seeks. We all join with him in wishing the country a happy new year and a happy new ten years, happier than the fifteen years of New Deal Administration.

But when the President comes to fill out the methods by which he hopes to accomplish this happiness and these great purposes, while he still speaks in general terms, we can see that under the guise of American ideals the old New Deal has been revived in a more global form than ever before. In this picture, the Federal Government comes forward again as Santa Claus himself, with a rich present for every special group in the United States, and for everyone else who may not be included in any special group.

Linked to Wallace's Ideas]

If anyone has expressed a desire in a letter to Santa Claus, that desire is to be promptly fulfilled.

One cannot but feel that the recent announcement of Mr. Henry Wallace has had a substantial effect on the state of the Union. Henry himself will have a hard time to find anything to promise the people of this country which is not promised in this message.

The President is apparently determined that the Left Wing of the American Labor party and its labor-union friends throughout the country shall be bound to him and shall have no excuse to stray into the Wallace camp. He has raised all the ghosts of the old New Deal with new trappings that [Rexford G.] Tugwell* and Harry Hopkins never thought of.

The first point that occurs to me is that the New Deal administration has been in control of this Government for fifteen years.

---

*Rexford G. Tugwell was one of Franklin D. Roosevelt's original "Brains Trust." In addition to his other government positions, he was the first Resettlement Administrator and symbolized "radical" New Dealism to the New Deal's opponents. [Ed.]

If the country is crying for all these improvements in social welfare and every other field, what has the New Deal administration been doing for fifteen years?

They demanded and obtained from Congress infinite power so great that President Roosevelt said it would only be safe in his hands and not in those of the Republicans. They demanded and received huge sums of money. Plenty of that money was spent, but apparently little was accomplished. The President admits it. He says our social security system has gaps and inconsistencies, and is only half finished.

As a matter of fact, the old-age insurance system is utterly and completely inadequate. Today, many who have contributed to that system all their lives receive less in their old age than many receive from old-age assistance who have contributed nothing.

The President says there is still "lack of provision for the nation's health," and "that most of our people cannot afford to pay for the care they need." This is a gross exaggeration, but what has the New Deal been doing with all our money?

He says that millions of children do not have adequate *school houses* or enough teachers, and that millions of our youth live in city slums and country shacks. Surely, this is a more severe indictment of the Roosevelt Administration than any Republican has made, for that Administration had more power and more money to accomplish its purposes, widely advertised for political effect, than any administration in the history of the United States.

Wise "Leadership" Lacking]

Of course, the problem is not so simple as that. An improvement in social and economic welfare depends on intelligent planning, wise leadership, sound principles, and sound constructive work. Those we have not had.

Both parties—and Henry Wallace—wish to improve the condition of the people in the United States. That can be the only aim of anyone truly interested in government.

The Republican party is just as much concerned as Mr. Truman with speeding up and stabilizing the great economic machine which creates prosperity for this country. It wishes to adopt those measures which will bring the greatest good to the greatest number of people, and then alleviate the condition of the few who, through misfortune, may not benefit from that prosperity.

There are few indeed in public life who have the slightest interest in whether a few rich men prosper or do not prosper, whether corporations make profits, or don't make profits, except as their status may affect the people of the country and the welfare of their employes. There are few indeed who don't equal the New Dealers in their sincere and earnest desire for uplift and progress in America. But we do question the effect of New Deal measures and philosophy.

Most of their plans are more likely to interfere with prosperity than they are to bring it about, first, because they ignore the fundamental economic principles necessary for prosperity; second, because they promise something for nothing, and, third, because they ignore the vital necessity of maintaining the principles of freedom and justice to which they give a general lip service.

Measures which destroy the freedom of the individual, freedom of states and local communities, freedom of the farmers to run his own farm and the workman to do his own job, in the end do more harm than good, even to those supposed to be benefited. Measures which reduce the field in which the free competition of private enterprise can operate, reduce both freedom and production. Measures which ignore justice for social ends destroy the fundamental purpose of the American government.

The first principle of the New Deal was the spending of money. This message, in tax recommendations, admits that taxation is already too heavy on millions of people. Yet strangely enough the message proposes additional expenditures, far beyond the 40 billion dollars which is said to be included in the budget still to come. Nothing is said of additional taxation to take care of all the hand-outs that are proposed. The people are to get something for nothing from dear old Santa Claus.

Proposals Assailed as Vague]

What are these proposals likely to cost? They are so vague it is impossible to do more than make an intelligent guess. The level of benefits is to be raised for all unemployment compensation, old-age benefits, and survivors' benefits. In years to come this would amount to billions of dollars, mostly to be collected from employers, employes, and general taxation.

The national health-insurance system, which is not insurance at all, but the providing of free medical care to all the people of the United States, would require taxes, probably payroll taxes, in the neighborhood of four or five billion dollars a year.

The President says: "Our ultimate aim must be a comprehensive insurance system to protect all our people equally against insecurity and ill health." This seems to be a kind of catch-all . . . plan . . . which would take about 18 per cent of payroll, or about twenty billion dollars (including health insurance and present levies for old-age insurance and unemployment compensation). Of course it would be taxation, not insurance.

The various proposals for aid to education are vaguely stated, but I would guess they might amount to a billion dollars a year. The housing program might cost 200 million. From the message we cannot judge the estimate of the additional public works, but the reclamation program is to be expanded, although the Republican Congress in 1947 appropriated more money than has ever been appropriated before in a single year.

In some manner not defined, the average income of farmers is to be raised well above that which exists at present. Any such agricultural program as the President seems to envision will certainly take cash from the Federal Treasury in large hunks. More money is asked for the school-lunch program, the electrification program, the soil conservation program and adequate diets for every American family.

Military Training Cost Cited]

Then, in the field of foreign affairs, we come to the Marshall Plan involving about three billion dollars a year more than we are now spending, but apparently included in this budget. The President states that we must maintain strong armed forces, and must add to our present system at least compulsory universal military training.

The cost of that is estimated anywhere from two billion to four billion dollars.

The President's air commission is about to recommend an

increase of two billion dollars a year in the expenditures for our Air Force. If war with Russia is our present concern, then certainly the Air Force is going to play a much more effective part both in defending this country and attacking Russia than universal military training.

Altogether, I would estimate that if we follow the President's recommendations, we would spend almost at once ten billion dollars a year more than we are now spending; with later increases to come. Where is this money coming from? We raise today about twenty billion dollars from the personal income tax. If we want to get the money from that personal tax, we will have to increase it by about 50 per cent.

Since you can't increase by 50 per cent the taxes of the wealthy, who pay 80 per cent already, most of the burden will have to fall on the lower and midde income groups. If the money is collected from more payroll taxes it will certainly fall on the lower incomes. If more business taxes and taxes on corporations are levied, they are paid in the last analysis by individuals, through higher prices or otherwise.

So in one way or another the sixty million workers in this country are going to pay those additional taxes, either directly or through further increases in prices.

"Something for Nothing"]

In short, the President is simply following the old New Deal principle of promising the people something for nothing. No one has ever found out how that can be done. I do not mean to say that all the features of the President's program are to be condemned. I only point out that taken together they add up to national bankruptcy.

The President in some parts of his message compares the condition of our people favorably with 1938, incidentally in the midst of a New Deal depression. At other points he pictures the condition of our people as about equal to what prevails in Russia. What have we got for all the New Deal spending of the past fifteen years, except taxes and rising prices and war?

Now the President talks about a new ten-year plan, doubling Joe Stalin's bid. What reason have we to think that the social welfare of our people would improve any more in the next ten

years than it has in the last fifteen years? The other feature of
the message which stands out is the New Deal request for more
power and more interference with the daily lives of the people.

The message asks again for rationing, for price control, for
wage control and for complete power to allocate the products
of industry.

It asks again the power to draft 1,200,000 boys a year out of
their homes and schools and trades and professions into military
training.

"Government Medicine" Hit]

It asks again for power to socialize and nationalize medicine.
Under the President's health program, $3,000,000,000 or $4,000,-
000,000 would pour into Washington in payroll taxes or other
taxes to be used by a Washington bureau to pay all the doctors
in the United States to give free medical service to all the people
in the United States. That means, in effect, that all the doctors
would become employes of the Federal Government.

It means that the Government by regulation would determine
when any family could have a doctor come to his home and
when they would have to go to the clinic or the hospital,
whether they could have X-ray treatments or special medicine,
and the whole character of their medical treatment. Certainly,
nothing could more intrude into the freedom of the American
family than Government medicine of this kind.

Throughout the message all the emphasis is on action by the
Federal Government. Not a word is said anywhere of preserving
the power of the state and local communities to improve their
own affairs or direct their own education, health, welfare or housing. The message follows the standard New Deal line that places
all power in Washington bureaus.

If we destroy the independence of our communities, I don't
believe we can retain any popular freedom in a country the size
of the United States. Again, I do not mean to condemn all of
the projects. I only point out that, taken together, they will add
up to a totalitarian state.

The ten-year Truman plan would leave about as much freedom in this country as Stalin's five-year plan has left in Russia.

Not only do control measures destroy freedom but they don't get the results.

President Truman, himself, said that rationing and price control are police state methods. Such methods won't work in the United States in peacetime as we saw under OPA. Black markets spring up over night.

If these controls could be enforced they would stifle production as they have in Europe and did here—and more production is the ultimate solution. Freedom and free competition made America the greatest producer in the world; and have made it possible for us to help Europe.

The President shows no sense of the real causes of inflation. Prices go up when there is more money to buy things than there are things to buy. We are producing more today than ever before, but the Government has created still more paper dollars. The ultimate solution of inflation is to increase production and that is what controls have always prevented. Then, while you are increasing production, you have to cut down spending, and that is what price control has always encouraged.

The President doesn't say a word about the need for economy. He claims credit for cutting the budget from $63,000,000,000 in the fiscal year 1946 when we were engaged in war against Japan, to $38,000,000,000 two years later when we are in peace. Not much credit in that. In 1948 we are still spending four times what was ever spent before the war.

The first step to stop spending is for the Government to stop spending. That will set an example and enable it to get some cooperation from the people so that they can spend less and save more. The biggest inflationary element has been the export of goods and services in 1947 up to $18,000,000,000, against only $8,000,000,000 of imports. Ten billion dollars came in here, mostly loaned by us, to compete with our citizens for goods and services produced here.

Of course prices have gone up. Of course wheat is at $3 a bushel. The President had full power to limit exports, but he hasn't used the power and he doesn't say a word about using it in his message.

Furthermore, the Administration let bank loans increase in a year by $5,000,000,000, creating that many more paper dollars, and failed to use the powers it always had to restrict bank credit. The President doesn't say a word about any of these American methods of preventing inflation.

Taxes Called Third of Income]

Outside of controls, his only suggestion is that taxes must remain high. Our tax burden today is about $40,000,000,000. With the state and local taxes, it amounts to about 30 per cent of our national income. This cost of government is a burden on the other 70 per cent of the productive workers. The tax burden is passed on for the most part into higher prices paid by every consumer for the food, clothing and shoes that he buys.

Less Government spending and less taxation are the most obvious of the methods of dealing with the price situation. The President recognizes that taxes are unbearably high and proposes a credit of $40 to each individual taxpayer plus $40 for each dependent. This will take about 11,000,000 taxpayers off the rolls altogether.

It is equivalent to a $200 additional exemption for persons in the low-income groups and less than $50 additional exemption for those in the higher groups.

It is about as discriminatory a proposal as could be made, and if followed to its logical conclusion will ultimately exempt a large proportion of all income and shift all taxes into a very small proportion of the population. Up to now we have gone on the theory that each citizen owes an obligation to his Government to contribute according to his means.

Business Tax Rise Opposed]

The President says a straight tax reduction would be inflationary, but if so his proposal is equally inflationary at this crucial time because it takes effect at once, whereas the proposed increase in corporation taxes won't be paid until 1949. In any event it is the total tax burden which increases prices, and that the President refuses to lower.

Of course the increase in corporation taxes from 38 per cent to 50 per cent is another discouragement to any increase in production needed for full employment and to lower prices.

New enterprises are less likely to be started if persons feel that the Government is going to take half the possible profits. Of course many new enterprises fail and the people who start them lose all the money they have put in. It would be "heads you win, tails I lose."

In one place in his message the President says: "We are today far short of the industrial capacity we need for a growing future. At least 50 billion dollars should be invested by industry to improve and expand our productive facilities over the next few years." In his mid-year economic report last July the President said: "High corporate profits have provided funds for a substantial proportion of the heavy volume of business investment during the first half of 1947."

Now does the President expect business to make this great investment of $50,000,000,000 if taxes take away the profits and make it unprofitable for new money to go into business? It is estimated today that it costs $6,000 of new investment to create one new job in industry. If we want to keep full employment going, that investment must continue. I suppose it is smart politics to take money out of corporation profits and divide it out among the voters at $40 a head, but sometimes I doubt whether smart politics is smart.

Twice last year, President Truman vetoed tax reduction bills on the pretense that they would increase inflation. Now in a message in which he says inflation is worse, he asks for tax reduction. Probably you will get tax reduction now, but what about the reduction you were entitled to last year and didn't get?

The President has followed the prediction of every member of Congress, newspaper correspondent and radio commentator. They all said that Truman vetoed the tax bills last year because of Republican sponsorship and that he would try to get credit this year—election year—for cutting taxes. It looks to me like playing politics with your money.

The Republican Congress proposes to go on with its program. It has consistently given the President all the powers he needs to stop inflation by American methods. We have given him everything except the OPA and wage-fixing and rationing, police-state methods. All the important powers he has had ever since the war, but hasn't used them. It doesn't look as if he wanted to reduce prices. Whenever any food price starts going down, or even threatens to go down, some Government department steps in and starts buying to keep up the price.

GOP Efforts Promised]

We will make every effort to cut Government expenditures, and really cut all taxes and the tax burden, and cut them for good.

We will scrutinize every expenditure, including the Marshall Plan, so that it may include nothing which is not absolutely necessary.

We will proceed with a program of social welfare in health, education and housing and social security. But our program will be based on state and local administration and control, and Federal aid in reasonable sums will be limited to those fields where the states and communities can adequately do the job which ought to be done, for the benefit of those of our population who cannot earn their own way.

We will insist upon sound fiscal policies to keep the economic machine running at full speed to provide employment and prosperity on a permanent basis. We will work out our program of progress along those American lines, within the principles of freedom and justice, which we followed for 150 years, and which have made this country the happiest on the face of the globe.

10

Lower Taxes and Reduced Government Spending

Dwight D. Eisenhower's Budget Message of 1954

Dwight D. Eisenhower (1890-   ) graduated from the United States Military Academy in 1915. After a career as a professional soldier in the peacetime regular army, he was appointed Allied Commander-in-Chief, North Africa, in 1942 and Commanding General of the Allied Powers, European Theater of Operations, in 1943. Upon the retirement of General of the Army George C. Marshall, in 1945, Eisenhower became Army Chief of Staff. From 1948 to 1952 he was officially president of Columbia University. In 1950 he was appointed Supreme Commander, Allied Powers in Europe, within the framework of the North Atlantic Treaty Organization. In 1952 the Republican Party nominated him as its presidential candidate, and by defeating Adlai Stevenson in the campaign he became the first Republican President since Herbert Hoover. He served two terms as President.

No document so well describes the scope of the activity of the Federal government as its annual budget. The President's budget message to Congress provides a succinct summary of his Administration's fiscal philosophy, the state of the economy, planned expenditures in foreign, defense, and domestic programs, and proposals to meet the required expenditures. It would be well to keep in mind the fact that during the 1920s the nation's expenditures were rarely more than $3 billion annually, and that they varied between $3½ and $9 billion in the 1930s. Walter Lippmann stated in 1960 that throughout the six-year period President Eisenhower was faithful to the basic principles of his budget of 1954.

For additional reading, see Merlo J. Pusey, *Eisenhower the President* (New York, 1956); Marquis Childs, *Eisenhower: Captive Hero* (New York, 1958); John K. Galbraith, *The Affluent Society* (Boston, 1958). In reading this document, note (1) the basic principles underlying Eisenhower's economic philosophy; (2) the principal spe-

Annual Budget Message to Congress: Fiscal Year 1955, January 21, 1954. *Public Papers of the Presidents, Dwight D. Eisenhower, 1954*, pp. 79-90.

cific recommendations included in the budget message; and (3) contrasts with President Kennedy's budget message of 1962 in respect to basic philosophy and recommendations. [16]

Annual Budget Message to the Congress:]
Fiscal Year 1955. January 21, 1954]

To THE CONGRESS OF THE UNITED STATES: I AM transmitting herewith the budget of the United States for the fiscal year ending June 30, 1955. . . .

When this administration took office on January 20 of last year one of its first concerns was the budget for the 1954 fiscal year, which had been sent to the Congress on January 9, 1953, by the previous administration. With the cooperation of the Congress that budget promptly was revised and reduced. This new budget is the first prepared entirely by this administration.

It provides adequately, in my judgment, for the national defense and the international responsibilities of the Nation—responsibilities which we must undertake as a leader of the free world. On the success of this leadership depends our national security and prosperity. The budget also provides adequately for the current needs of the Government and for constructive forward steps in our domestic responsibilities and programs.

The recommended budget continues the strengthening of our military posture; our progress in the development and production of atomic weapons; the expansion of our system of continental defense; assistance in the development of the military strength of friendly nations; and programs for rapid mobilization if an emergency should arise.

Authority is recommended for new and advanced work on the peacetime uses of atomic energy in the earnest hope that present international relations can be improved and the wonders of nuclear power can be turned gradually to the development of a more abundant life for ourselves and all mankind.

The budget contains provisions for legislative recommendations for expanding the coverage and increasing the benefits of our social security system; for promoting better housing conditions and more widespread home ownership in the Nation; for improving our system of education; for conserving our natural resources; for helping prevent the ravages of floods and soil erosion; for encouraging the expansion of adequate health and hospital care for our people; and for other constructive domestic purposes designed to strengthen the foundations of a stable and prosperous economy.

This budget continues the progress that has been made during the past year in reducing both requests for new appropriations and Government expenditures. The reductions in expenditures already accomplished, together with those now proposed, justify the tax reductions which took effect January I and the further tax revisions I am recommending. These lower taxes will encourage continued high capital investment and consumer purchases. Despite the substantial loss of revenue caused by these tax reductions, we have moved closer to a balanced budget.

One of the first problems of this administration was to bring the budget under better control. That was substantially accomplished in the revision of the original budget document for the fiscal year 1954. Now an amount approximately equal to the savings made in this new budget is being returned to the public in tax reductions and tax revisions. This amount substantially exceeds the estimated budget deficit.

In preparing this budget the administration has directed its attention to essential activities and programs rather than to those which some might consider desirable and appropriate, at this time, for the Federal Government to undertake. It assumes fairly stable conditions, internally and externally, during the period it covers. It allows for the continuing heavy demands of the national security programs on the budget. But as we continue to reduce and eliminate the less desirable or the unnecessary Government expenditures, it will become possible to turn to other purposes which are the most desirable in terms of their benefits to all the people.

This budget marks the beginning of a movement to shift to State and local governments and to private enterprise Federal activities which can be more appropriately and more efficiently carried on in that way. The lending activities of the Reconstruction Finance Corporation; the services provided by the Inland

Waterways Corporation; certain agricultural activities; and some aspects of our health, education, and welfare programs are examples of this type of action. In those cases where Federal participation is necessary, the effort of this administration is to develop partnerships rather than an exclusive and often paternalistic position for the Federal Government.

This budget also benefits from material savings from the decreased costs of Federal operations resulting from our constant effort to improve the management of Government activities and to find better and less expensive ways of doing the things which must be done by the Federal Government. . . .

General budget policy.—This administration is dedicated to greater efficiency and economy in meeting the Nation's security requirements and the necessary and valid functions of the Government.

The current estimates of the 1954 budget show that the requests for new appropriations were reduced about 12.5 billion dollars, new obligational authority was reduced more than 11 billion dollars, and expenditures were reduced 7 billion dollars below the totals estimated in the 1954 budget document of the previous administration.

Similar reductions continue in the budget recommended for the fiscal year 1955. Recommended new obligational authority is 4.4 billion dollars less than the current estimate for the fiscal year 1954, 15.5 billion dollars less than recommended for that year in the 1954 budget document, and 23.9 billion dollars less than in 1953. Estimated expenditures for the fiscal year 1955 are 5.3 billion dollars less than the current estimate for the fiscal year 1954, 12.3 billion dollars less than recommended in the 1954 budget document, and 8.4 billion dollars less than in 1953.

Thus, new obligational authority has been reduced 15.5 billion dollars and estimated expenditures have been reduced 12.3 billion dollars since this administration took office.

These reductions justified lower taxes. Without tax reductions, a budget surplus was in sight for the fiscal year 1955.

So that most of the new savings could be passed along to the taxpayers of the Nation as a whole, with beneficial effects on our entire economy, I believed it best to adopt a course leading toward the twin goals of a balanced budget and tax reductions.

The reductions in 1954 expenditures were devoted to reducing the large deficit forecast in the 1954 budget document. The anticipated savings in 1955 budget expenditures already have been reflected in the tax reductions of January 1 of this year and are also reflected in the tax revisions I am recommending in this message.

Together these tax reductions will total nearly 5 billion dollars.

We will still have a budgetary deficit of slightly less than 3 billion dollars for the fiscal year 1955, as now estimated. But we will continue determined efforts for economy to reduce that deficit during the 1955 fiscal year.

Furthermore, despite the loss of cash revenue from the tax reductions and revisions, the total cash transactions of the Government with the public are now estimated to show a small cash surplus for the fiscal year 1955.

Budget totals, fiscal year 1954.—The actual budget deficit for the fiscal year 1953 was 9.4 billion dollars. The budget deficit for the fiscal year 1954, indicated in the 1954 budget document, was 9.9 billion dollars. The current estimates of the budget for that year show a budgetary deficit of 3.3 billion dollars.

Total Government cash transactions with the public include the receipts and payments of the social security and other trust funds which are not considered part of the budget. In 1953 the excess of cash payments to the public over receipts from the public was 5.3 billion dollars. The 1954 budget document estimated an excess of cash payments of 6.6 billion dollars. Present estimates indicate an excess of cash payments over receipts in 1954 of more than 200 million dollars, a reduction of 6.4 billion dollars in the cash deficit originally estimated. . . .

Budget expenditures.—Total budget expenditures in the fiscal year 1955 are estimated at 65.6 billion dollars.

	Expenditures (in billions)
Fiscal year:	
1952	$65.4
1953	74.0
1954:	
As estimated, January 9, 1953	77.9
Revised estimate	70.9
1955 estimate	65.6

Proposed expenditure programs for 1955 fall in three broad categories: national security, major programs relatively uncontrollable under existing and proposed legislation, and all other Government programs.

Expenditures for major national security programs—for the military functions of the Department of Defense, the mutual military program, atomic energy, and stockpiling of strategic materials—dominate the budget and are estimated at 44.9 billion dollars in the fiscal year 1955. This compares with a presently estimated 48.7 billion dollars in 1954 and 50.3 billion dollars in 1953. These amounts are about the same percentage of total budget expenditures in each of the 3 years.

Closely related to these major security programs are other activities for national security included elsewhere in the budget. Our foreign economic assistance and information programs are particularly essential to deter aggression and strengthen the world forces for peace.

Proposed reductions in major national security expenditures in 1955 represent the largest single element of reduction from the current year's level of expenditures. I emphasize, however, that these savings result from revisions in programs, from shifts in emphasis, from better balanced procurement, and from improved management and operations. Our security is being strengthened—not weakened. Further, while expenditures for some programs in this category will be reduced, others will be increased.

Of the four major national security programs, proposed 1955 expenditures for the Atomic Energy Commission and for the mutual military program will be at the highest levels since the initiation of the two programs.

Within the Department of Defense the fiscal year 1955 expenditures on behalf of our airpower will be the largest since World War II. Allocations of expenditures for our continental defense program will be greater than in any previous year.

Expenditures for stockpiling—the fourth of the principal programs in the major national security category—will be less than in the fiscal year 1954, as a result of approaching fulfillment of stockpile requirements in certain categories and of lower world market prices for materials still required for the stockpile.

Budget expenditures for certain Government activities are, by law, relatively nondiscretionary, and depend largely on factors outside the annual budgetary process. While relatively few in number these represent a large amount of dollars and the budget each year has to provide funds for them. For example, once the laws are placed on the statute books, grants to States for many purposes depend upon the extent to which States take advantage of Federal grant-in-aid programs; veterans' pensions depend upon the number of qualified veteran applicants; farm price supports depend upon the size of crops and the demand for supported commodities; and interest payments on the national debt depend upon the amount of the debt and the rate of interest.

In the fiscal year 1955 it is estimated that budget expenditures of 14.1 billion dollars will be required to support these programs. This amount is about the same as presently estimated for 1954 and almost 800 million dollars less than similar expenditures in the fiscal year 1953.

Budget expenditures for other Government activities, which contain more elements controllable through the budget process, are reduced an estimated 2.2 billion dollars below the fiscal year 1953 and 1.5 billion dollars below the present estimate for 1954. This is a reduction, over the two fiscal years, of about 25 percent in the cost of these numerous day-to-day operations of the Government. These activities cover, in number, a large majority of the items in the budget, although the amount involved is about one-tenth of total budget expenditures.

Some substantial reductions in this category will result from a lessened postal deficit and management and program savings in many other departments. On the other hand, estimated expenditures for the Tennessee Valley Authority, urban development and redevelopment, college housing loans, the National Science Foundation, fish and wildlife resources, the school lunch program, and several other programs of domestic importance will be the largest in our history.

Budget receipts and taxes.—Budget receipts under existing and proposed legislation are estimated to be 62.7 billion dollars in the fiscal year 1955. This is 4.9 billion dollars less than presently estimated 1954 receipts; 1.9 billion dollars less than 1953, and 1.3 billion dollars more than 1952.

Total Government expenditures and taxes are now so high that we must choose our path carefully between inadequate revenues on the one hand and repressive taxation on the other. I am anxious to have taxes reduced as fast as that can be done without building up inflationary deficits. It is the determined purpose of this administration to make further reductions in taxes as rapidly as justified by prospective revenues and reductions in expenditures. The objective will be to return to the people, to spend for themselves and in their own way, the largest possible share of the money that the Government has been spending for them.

The start toward tax reductions is justified only because of success in reducing expenditures and improving the budgetary outlook. That outlook permits me to make some proposals for tax reform and reductions for millions of taxpayers at this time which represent much-needed improvements in our tax system. These proposals are directed toward removing the most serious tax hardships and tax complications, and reducing the tax barriers to continued economic growth. The proposals will encourage the initiative and investment which stimulate production and productivity and create bigger payrolls and more and better jobs. The details of these proposals are many and represent much cooperative work by the House Ways and Means Committee and its staff and the Treasury Department. In part II of my budget message, I list and describe 25 important tax revisions.

I do not believe that the budgetary situation will permit further reductions of taxes at this time. Hence, I repeat my recommendations of last May that the reductions in the general corporate income tax be deferred for 1 year; that the excise tax rates, scheduled to be reduced on April 1, including those on liquor, tobacco, automobiles, and gasoline, be continued at present rates; and that any adjustments in the other excise taxes be such as to maintain the total yield which we are now receiving from this source.

Debt management.—A sound dollar is the cornerstone of financing policy under this administration. The problem of debt management is not only one of offering securities for cash or refunding which the market will take, but of appraising the economic situation and adapting financing plans to it, so that as far as possible debt management does not contribute to either inflation or deflation.

This means close cooperation with the Federal Reserve System, whose duty it is under the law to administer the money supply, with these same objectives in view.

Nearly three-quarters of the debt we inherited a year ago matures within less than 5 years or is redeemable at the holder's option. Too large a proportion is in the hands of banks. This is the result of financing over a period of years too largely by short term issues at artificially low interest rates maintained by Federal Reserve support. These policies contributed to cheapening the dollar.

A start has been made in lengthening the maturities of the debt, as well as obtaining a wider distribution among individuals and other nonbank investors. In our 1953 debt operations, maturities were lengthened in 5 out of 9 times.

There is every reason to look forward with confidence to this country's ability to put its financial house in better order without serious disruption of credits or markets. The stream of the Nation's savings is huge, larger than ever before; the financial system is sound. With a reasonable assurance of sound money of stable buying power there is no better investment than securities of the United States Government.

The national debt is now close to the legal limit of 275 billion dollars. In view of the wide swings in receipts and expenditures and their unpredictability, it is not prudent to operate the huge business of the United States Government in such a straitjacket as the present debt limit.

These difficulties will become worse as we move forward in the year. We shall be close to the debt limit and our cash balances will be dangerously low on several occasions in the first half of the calendar year.

In the second half of the calendar year, when tax receipts are seasonally low, there will be no way of operating within the present debt limit.

For these reasons, I renew my request to the Congress to raise the debt limit.

Proposed legislation.—Legislative proposals are reflected in separate messages or are included in the appropriate sections of part II of this message.

A summary of the budgetary impact of the legislative program also is given in part II [not reproduced].

In summary, I emphasize that this budget carries out the policy of this administration to move toward reduced taxes and reduced Government spending as rapidly as our national security and well-being will permit.

By using necessity—rather than mere desirability—as the test for our expenditures, we will reduce the share of the national income which is spent by the Government. We are convinced that more progress and sounder progress will be made over the years as the largest possible share of our national income is left with individual citizens to make their own countless decisions as to what they will spend, what they will buy, and what they will save and invest. Government must play a vital role in maintaining economic growth and stability. But I believe that our development, since the early days of the Republic, has been based on the fact that we left a great share of our national income to be used by a provident people with a will to venture. Their actions have stimulated the American genius for creative initiative and thus multiplied our productivity.

This budget proposes that such progressive economic growth will be fostered by continuing emphasis on efficiency and economy in Government, reduced Government expenditures, reduced taxes, and a reduced deficit. The reduced request for new obligational authority promises further that, barring unforeseen circumstances, the budgets I shall recommend in the future will be directed toward the same objectives.

11

Spokesmen for the Negro Revolution

James Baldwin's "Stranger in the Village"

James Baldwin (1924-   ) was born in Harlem. His father was
at times a factory worker, more often than not unemployed, at other
times "a fanatical lay preacher." His mother was a remarkable woman
who successfully raised nine children in spite of poverty and discrimination in the Harlem slums. Baldwin completed high school in 1942,
but went to work in the factories after the death of his father in
1943. He was not happy in this work and he was consumed with
hatred for white men. Even in elementary school he enjoyed writing.
In 1946, he published a book review, and shortly thereafter he decided
to devote full time to his writing. In 1948 he went into exile in Paris,
and remained there for nine years, returning to the United States in
1957. Baldwin has contributed numerous articles to periodicals. His
first book, *Go Tell It on the Mountain*, published in 1953, won him a
reputation as one of the most brilliant and sensitive writers of his
day. For further reading, see James Baldwin, *Notes of a Native Son*
(Boston, 1955).

The article printed here was published while the *Brown* v. *Board
of Education* [of Topeka] was being argued before the Supreme
Court. It not only provides a good example of Baldwin's direct, moving literary style, but also provides a unique statement of the way a
sensitive Negro with experience both at home and in Europe viewed
the plight of his race. In reading this essay, note (1) Baldwin's reaction to his initial reception in the Swiss village; (2) his interpretation of the attitude of the white man toward the black man; (3) the
importance of the institution of slavery in making the American Negro
problem unique; (4) Baldwin's interpretation of the significance of
the concept of white supremacy.

James Baldwin, "Stranger in the Village," *Harper's Magazine*, Vol. CC, No.
    VII (October 1953), pp. 42-48. Reprinted by permission of the Bea-
    con Press and of John Farquharson Ltd. (London, England); copy-
    right 1955 by James Baldwin.

181]

I]

Fʀᴏᴍ ᴀʟʟ ᴀᴠᴀɪʟᴀʙʟᴇ ᴇᴠɪᴅᴇɴᴄᴇ ɴᴏ ʙʟᴀᴄᴋ ᴍᴀɴ
had ever set foot in this tiny Swiss village before I
came. I was told before arriving that I would probably be a
"sight" for the village; I took this to mean that people of my
complexion were rarely seen in Switzerland, and also that city
people are always something of a "sight" outside of the city. It
did not occur to me—possibly because I am an American—that
there could be people anywhere who had never seen a Negro.

It is a fact which cannot be explained on the basis of the
inaccessibility of the village. The village is very high, but it is
only four hours from Milan and three hours from Lausanne. It
is true that it is virtually unknown. Few people making plans
for a holiday would elect to come here. On the other hand, the
villagers are able, presumably, to come and go as they please—
which they do: to another town at the foot of the mountain,
with a population of approximately five thousand, the nearest
place to see a movie or go to the bank. In the village there is
no movie house, no bank, no library, no theater; very few radios,
one jeep, one station wagon; and, at the moment, one type-
writer, mine, an invention which the woman next door to me
here had never seen. There are about six hundred people living
here, all Catholic—I conclude this from the fact that the Catholic
church is open all year round, whereas the Protestant chapel,
set off on a hill a little removed from the village, is open only in
the summertime when the tourists arrive. There are four or five
hotels, all closed now, and four or five *bistros,* of which, however, only two do any business during the winter. These two do
not do a great deal, for life in the village seems to end around
nine or ten o'clock. There are a few stores, butcher, baker, *épi-
cerie,* a hardware store, and a money-changer—who cannot
change travelers' checks, but must send them down to the bank,
an operation which takes two or three days. There is something
called the *Ballet Haus,* closed in the winter and used for God
knows what, certainly not ballet, during the summer. There
seems to be only one schoolhouse in the village, and this for the
quite young children; I suppose this to mean that their older
brothers and sisters at some point descend from these mountains

in order to complete their education—possibly, again, to the town just below. The landscape is absolutely forbidding, mountains towering on all four sides, ice and snow as far as the eye can reach. In this white wilderness, men and women and children move all day, carrying washing, wood, buckets of milk or water, sometimes skiing on Sunday afternoons. All week long boys and young men are to be seen shoveling snow off the rooftops, or dragging wood down from the forest in sleds.

The village's only real attraction, which explains the tourist season, is the hot spring water. A disquietingly high proportion of these tourists are cripples, or semi-cripples, who come year after year—from other parts of Switzerland, usually—to take the waters. This lends the village, at the height of the season, a rather terrifying air of sanctity, as though it were a lesser Lourdes. There is often something beautiful, there is always something awful, in the spectacle of a person who has lost one of his faculties, a faculty he never questioned until it was gone, and who struggles to recover it. Yet people remain people, on crutches or indeed on deathbeds; and wherever I passed, the first summer I was here, among the native villagers or among the lame, a wind passed with me—of astonishment, curiosity, amusement, and outrage. That first summer I stayed two weeks and never intended to return. But I did return in the winter, to work; the village offers, obviously, no distraction whatever and has the further advantage of being extremely cheap. Now it is winter again, a year later, and I am here again. Everyone in the village knows my name, though they scarcely ever use it, knows that I come from America—though, this, apparently, they will never really believe: black men come from Africa—and everyone knows that I am the friend of the son of a woman who was born here, and that I am staying in their chalet. But I remain as much a stranger today as I was the first day I arrived, and the children shout *Neger! Neger!* as I walk along the streets.

It must be admitted that in the beginning I was far too shocked to have any real reaction. In so far as I reacted at all, I reacted by trying to be pleasant—it being a great part of the American Negro's education (long before he goes to school) that he must make people "like" him. This smile-and-the-world-

smiles-with-you routine worked about as well in this situation
as it had in the situation for which it was designed, which is to
say that it did not work at all. No one, after all, can be liked
whose human weight and complexity cannot be, or has not
been, admitted. My smile was simply another unheard-of phenomenon which allowed them to see my teeth—they did not,
really, see my smile and I began to think that, should I take to
snarling, no one would notice any difference. All of the physical
characteristics of the Negro which had caused me, in America,
a very different and almost forgotten pain were nothing less than
miraculous—or infernal—in the eyes of the village people. Some
thought my hair was the color of tar, that it had the texture of
wire, or the texture of cotton. It was jocularly suggested that I
might let it all grow long and make myself a winter coat. If I
sat in the sun for more than five minutes some daring creature
was certain to come along and gingerly put his fingers on my
hair, as though he were afraid of an electric shock, or put his
hand on my hand, astonished that the color did not rub off. In all
of this, in which it must be conceded there was the charm of
genuine wonder and in which there was certainly no element of
intentional unkindness, there was yet no suggestion that I was
human: I was simply a living wonder.

I knew that they did not mean to be unkind, and I know it
now; it is necessary, nevertheless, for me to repeat this to myself
each time that I walk out of the chalet. The children who shout
Neger! have no way of knowing the echoes this sound raises in
me. They are brimming with good humor and the more daring
swell with pride when I stop to speak with them. Just the same,
there are days when I cannot pause and smile, when I have no
heart to play with them; when, indeed, I mutter sourly to myself, exactly as I muttered on the streets of a city these children
have never seen, when I was no bigger than these children are
now: *Your* mother *was a nigger.* Joyce is right about history
being a nightmare—but it may be the nightmare from which
no one *can* awaken. People are trapped in history and history is
trapped in them.

II]

There is a custom in the village—I am told it is repeated in
many villages—of "buying" African natives for the purpose of

converting them to Christianity. There stands in the church all year round a small box with a slot for money, decorated with a black figurine, and into this box the villagers drop their francs. During the *carnaval* which precedes Lent, two village children have their faces blackened—out of which bloodless darkness their blue eyes shine like ice—and fantastic horsehair wigs are placed on their blond heads; thus disguised, they solicit among the villagers for money for the missionaries in Africa. Between the box in the church and the blackened children, the village "bought" last year six or eight African natives. This was reported to me with pride by the wife of one of the *bistro* owners and I was careful to express astonishment and pleasure at the solicitude shown by the village for the souls of black folk. The *bistro* owner's wife beamed with a pleasure far more genuine than my own and seemed to feel that I might now breathe more easily concerning the souls of at least six of my kinsmen.

I tried not to think of these so lately baptized kinsmen, of the price paid for them, or the peculiar price they themselves would pay, and said nothing about my father, who having taken his own conversion too literally never, at bottom, forgave the white world (which he described as heathen) for having saddled him with a Christ in whom, to judge at least from their treatment of him, they themselves no longer believed. I thought of white men arriving for the first time in an African village, strangers there, as I am a stranger here, and tried to imagine the astounded populace touching their hair and marveling at the color of their skin. But there is a great difference between being the first white man to be seen by Africans and being the first black man to be seen by whites. The white man takes the astonishment as tribute, for he arrives to conquer and to convert the natives, whose inferiority in relation to himself is not even to be questioned; whereas I, without a thought of conquest, find myself among a people whose culture controls me, has even, in a sense, created me, people who have cost me more in anguish and rage than they will ever know, who yet do not even know of my existence. The astonishment with which I might have greeted them, should they have stumbled into my African village a few hundred years ago, might have rejoiced their hearts. But the astonishment with which they greet me today can only poison mine.

And this is so despite everything I may do to feel differently, despite my friendly conversations with the *bistro* owner's wife, despite their three-year-old son who has at least become my friend, despite the *saluts* and *bonsoirs* which I exchange with people as I walk, despite the fact that I know that no individual can be taken to task for what history is doing, or has done. I say that the culture of these people controls me—but they can scarcely be held responsible for European culture. America comes out of Europe, but these people have never seen America, nor have most of them seen more of Europe than the hamlet at the foot of their mountain. Yet, they move with an authority which I shall never have; and they regard me, quite rightly, not only as a stranger in their village but as a suspect latecomer, bearing no credentials, to everything they have—however unconsciously—inherited.

For this village, even were it incomparably more remote and incredibly more primitive, is the West, the West onto which I have been so strangely grafted. These people cannot be, from the point of view of power, strangers anywhere in the world; they have made the modern world, in effect, even if they do not know it. The most illiterate among them is related, in a way that I am not, to Dante, Shakespeare, Michelangelo, Aeschylus, Da Vinci, Rembrandt, and Racine; the cathedral at Chartres says something to them which it cannot say to me, as indeed would New York's Empire State Building, should anyone here ever see it. Out of their hymns and dances come Beethoven and Bach. Go back a few centuries and they are in their full glory— but I am in Africa, watching the conquerors arrive.

The rage of the disesteemed is personally fruitless, but it is also absolutely inevitable; this rage, so generally discounted, so little understood even among the people whose daily bread it is, is one of the things that makes history. Rage can only with difficulty, and never entirely, be brought under the domination of the intelligence and is therefore not susceptible to any arguments whatever. This is a fact which ordinary representatives of the *Herrenvolk*, having never felt this rage and being unable to imagine it, quite fail to understand. Also, rage cannot be hidden, it can only be dissembled. This dissembling deludes the thoughtless, and strengthens rage, and adds to rage, contempt. There are, no doubt, as many ways of coping with the resulting complex of tensions as there are black men in the world, but no black man can hope ever to be entirely liberated from this internal warfare—rage, dissembling, and contempt having inevitably accompanied his first realization of the power of white men. What is crucial here is that, since white men represent in the black man's world so heavy a weight, white men have for black men a reality which is far from being reciprocal; and hence all black men have toward all white men an attitude which is designed, really, either to rob the white man of the jewel of his naïveté, or else to make it cost him dear.

The black man insists, by whatever means he finds at his disposal, that the white man cease to regard him as an exotic rarity and recognize him as a human being. This is a very charged and difficult moment, for there is a great deal of will power involved in the white man's naïveté. Most people are not naturally reflective any more than they are naturally malicious, and the white man prefers to keep the black man at a certain human remove because it is easier for him thus to preserve his simplicity and avoid being called to account for crimes committed by his forefathers, or his neighbors. He is inescapably aware, nevertheless, that he is in a better position in the world than black men are, nor can he quite put to death the suspicion that he is hated by black men therefore. He does not wish to be hated, neither does he wish to change places, and at this point in his uneasiness he can scarcely avoid having recourse to those legends which white men have created about black men, the most usual effect of which is that the white man finds himself enmeshed, so to speak, in his own language which describes hell, as well as the attributes which lead one to hell, as being as black as night.

Every legend, moreover, contains its residuum of truth, and the root function of language is to control the universe by describing it. It is of quite considerable significance that black men remain, in the imagination, and in overwhelming numbers in fact, beyond the disciplines of salvation; and this despite the fact that the West has been "buying" African natives for centuries. There is, I should hazard, an instantaneous necessity to be divorced from this so visibly unsaved stranger, in whose heart, moreover, one cannot guess what dreams of vengeance are being nourished; and, at the same time, there are few things on earth more attractive than the idea of the unspeakable liberty which is allowed the unredeemed. When, beneath the black mask, a human being begins to make himself felt one cannot escape a certain awful wonder as to what kind of human being it is. What one's imagination makes of other people is dictated, of course, by the laws of one's own personality and it is one of the ironies of black-white relations that, by means of what the white man imagines the black man to be, the black man is enabled to know who the white man is.

I have said, for example, that I am as much a stranger in this village today as I was the first summer I arrived, but this is not quite true. The villagers wonder less about the texture of my hair than they did then, and wonder rather more about me. And the fact that their wonder now exists on another level is reflected in their attitudes and in their eyes. There are the children who make those delightful, hilarious, sometimes astonishingly grave overtures of friendship in the unpredictable fashion of children; other children, having been taught that the devil is a black man, scream in genuine anguish as I approach. Some of the older women never pass without a friendly greeting, never pass, indeed, if it seems that they will be able to engage me in conversation; other women look down or look away or rather contemptuously smirk. Some of the men drink with me and suggest that I learn how to ski—partly, I gather, because they cannot imagine what I would look like on skis—and want to know if I am married, and ask questions about by *métier*. But some of the men have accused *le sale nègre*—behind my back—of stealing wood and there is already in the eyes of some of them that peculiar, intent, paranoiac malevolence which one sometimes surprises in the eyes of American white men when, out walking with their Sunday girl, they see a Negro male approach.

There is a dreadful abyss between the streets of this village and the streets of the city in which I was born, between the children who shout *Neger!* today and those who shouted *Nigger!* yesterday—the abyss is experience, the American experience. The syllable hurled behind me today expresses, above all, wonder: I am a stranger here. But I am not a stranger in America and the same syllable riding on the American air expresses the war my presence has occasioned in the American soul.

III]

For this village brings home to me this fact: that there was a day, and not really a very distant day, when Americans were scarcely Americans at all but discontented Europeans, facing a great unconquered continent and strolling, say, into a market-place and seeing black men for the first time. The shock this spectacle afforded is suggested, surely, by the promptness with which they decided that these black men were not really men but cattle. It is true that the necessity on the part of the settlers of the New World of reconciling their moral assumptions with the fact—and the necessity—of slavery enhanced immensely the charm of this idea, and it is also true that this idea expresses, with a truly American bluntness, the attitude which to varying extents all masters have had toward all slaves.

But between all former slaves and slaveowners and the drama which begins for Americans over three hundred years ago at Jamestown, there are at least two differences to be observed. The American Negro slave could not suppose, for one thing, as slaves in past epochs had supposed and often done, that he would ever be able to wrest the power from his master's hands. This was a supposition which the modern era, which was to bring about such vast changes in the aims and dimensions of power, put to death; it only begins, in unprecedented fashion, and with dreadful implications, to be resurrected today. But even had this supposition persisted with undiminished force, the American Negro slave could not have used it to lend his condition dignity, for the reason that this supposition rests on another: that the slave in exile yet remains related to his past, has some means—if only in memory—of revering and sustaining the forms of his former life, is able, in short, to maintain his identity.

This was not the case with the American Negro slave. He is unique among the black men of the world in that his past was taken from him, almost literally, at one blow. One wonders what on earth the first slave found to say to the first dark child he bore. I am told that there are Haitians able to trace their ancestry back to African kings, but any American Negro wishing to go back so far will find his journey through time abruptly arrested by the signature on the bill of sale which served as the entrance paper for his ancestor. At the time—to say nothing of the circumstances—of the enslavement of the captive black man who was to become the American Negro, there was not the remotest possibility that he would ever take power from his master's hands. There was no reason to suppose that his situation would ever change, nor was there, shortly, anything to indicate that his situation had ever been different. It was his necessity, in the words of E. Franklin Frazier, to find a "motive for living under American culture or die." The identity of the American Negro comes out of this extreme situation, and the evolution of this identity was a source of the most intolerable anxiety in the minds and the lives of his masters.

For the history of the American Negro is unique also in this: that the question of his humanity, and of his rights therefore as a human being, became a burning one for several generations of Americans, so burning a question that it ultimately became one of those used to divide the nation. It is out of this argument that the venom of the epithet *Nigger!* is derived. It is an argument which Europe has never had, and hence Europe quite sincerely fails to understand how or why the argument arose in the first place, why its effects are so frequently disastrous and always so unpredictable, why it refuses until today to be entirely settled. Europe's black possessions remained—and do remain—in Europe's colonies, at which remove they represented no threat whatever to European identity. If they posed any problem at all for the European conscience, it was a problem which remained comfortingly abstract: in effect, the black man, *as a man,* did not exist for Europe. But in America, even as a slave, he was an inescapable part of the general social fabric and no American could escape having an attitude toward him. Americans attempt until today to make an abstraction of the Negro, but the very nature of these abstractions reveals the tremendous effects the presence of the Negro has had on the American character.

When one considers the history of the Negro in America it is of the greatest importance to recognize that the moral beliefs of a person, or a people, are never really as tenuous as life—which is not moral—very often causes them to appear; these create for them a frame of reference and a necessary hope, the hope being that when life has done its worst they will be enabled to rise above themselves and to triumph over life. Life would scarcely be bearable if this hope did not exist. Again, even when the worst has been said, to betray a belief is not by any means to have put oneself beyond its power; the betrayal of a belief is not the same thing as ceasing to believe. If this were not so there would be no moral standards in the world at all. Yet one must also recognize that morality is based on ideas and that all ideas are dangerous—dangerous because ideas can only lead to action and where the action leads no man can say. And dangerous in this respect: that confronted with the impossibility of remaining faithful to one's beliefs, and the equal impossibility of becoming free of them, one can be driven to the most inhuman excesses. The ideas on which American beliefs are based are not, though Americans often seem to think so, ideas which originated in America. They came out of Europe. And the establishment of democracy on the American continent was scarcely as radical a break with the past as was the necessity, which Americans faced, of broadening this concept to include black men.

This was, literally, a hard necessity. It was impossible, for one thing, for Americans to abandon their beliefs, not only because these beliefs alone seemed able to justify the sacrifices they had endured and the blood that they had spilled, but also because these beliefs afforded them their only bulwark against a moral chaos as absolute as the physical chaos of the continent it was their destiny to conquer. But in the situation in which Americans found themselves, these beliefs threatened an idea which, whether or not one likes to think so, is the very warp and woof of the heritage of the West, the idea of white supremacy.

Americans have made themselves notorious by the shrillness and the brutality with which they have insisted on this idea, but they did not invent it; and it has escaped the world's notice that those very excesses of which Americans have been guilty imply a certain, unprecedented uneasiness over the idea's life and power, if not, indeed, the idea's validity. The idea of white supremacy rests simply on the fact that white men are the creators of civilization (the present civilization, which is the only one that matters; all previous civilizations are simply "contributions" to our own) and are therefore civilization's guardians and defenders. Thus it was impossible for Americans to accept the black man as one of themselves, for to do so was to jeopardize their status as white men. But not so to accept him was to deny his human reality, his human weight and complexity, and the strain of denying the overwhelmingly undeniable forced Americans into rationalizations so fantastic that they approached the pathological.

At the root of the American Negro problem is the necessity of the American white man to find a way of living with the Negro in order to be able to live with himself. And the history of this problem can be reduced to the means used by Americans—lynch law and law, segregation and legal acceptance, terrorization and concession—either to come to terms with this necessity, or to find a way around it, or (most usually) to find a way of doing both these things at once. The resulting spectacle, at once foolish and dreadful, led someone to make the quite accurate observation that "the Negro-in-America is a form of insanity which overtakes white men."

In this long battle, a battle by no means finished, the unforeseeable effects of which will be felt by many future generations, the white man's motive was the protection of his identity; the black man was motivated by the need to establish an identity. And despite the terrorization which the Negro in America endured and endures sporadically until today, despite the cruel and totally inescapable ambivalence of his status in his country, the battle for his identity has long ago been won. He is not a visitor to the West, but a citizen there, an American; as American as the Americans who despise him, the Americans who fear him, the Americans who love him—the Americans who became less than themselves, or rose to be greater than themselves by virtue of the fact that the challenge he represented was inescapable. He is perhaps the only black man in the world whose relationship to white men is more terrible, more subtle, and more meaningful than the relationship of bitter possessed to uncertain possessor. His survival depended, and his development depends, on his ability to turn his peculiar status in the Western world to his own advantage and, it may be, to the very great advantage of that world. It remains for him to fashion out of his experience that which will give him sustenance, and a voice.

The cathedral at Chartres, I have said, says something to the people of this village which it cannot say to me; but it is important to understand that this cathedral says something to me which it cannot say to them. Perhaps they are struck by the power of the spires, the glory of the windows; but they have known God, after all, longer than I have known him, and in a different way, and I am terrified by the slippery bottomless well to be found in the crypt, down which heretics were hurled to death, and by the obscene, inescapable gargoyles jutting out of the stone and seeming to say that God and the devil can never be divorced. I doubt that the villagers think of the devil when they face a cathedral because they have never been identified with the devil. But I must accept the status which myth, if nothing else, gives me in the West before I can hope to change the myth.

Yet, if the American Negro has arrived at his identity by virtue of the absoluteness of his estrangement from his past, American white men still nourish the illusion that there is some means of recovering the European innocence, of returning to a state in which black men do not exist. This is one of the greatest errors Americans can make. The identity they fought so hard to protect has, by virtue of that battle, undergone a change: Americans are as unlike any other white people in the world as it is possible to be. I do not think, for example, that it is too much to suggest that the American vision of the world—which allows so little reality, generally speaking, for any of the darker forces in human life, which tends until today to paint moral issues in glaring black and white—owes a great deal to the battle waged by Americans to maintain between themselves and black men a human separation which could not be bridged. It is only now beginning to be borne in on us—very faintly, it must be admitted, very slowly, and very much against our will—that this vision of the world is dangerously inaccurate; and perfectly useless. For it protects our moral high-mindedness at the terrible expense of weakening our grasp of reality. People who shut their eyes to reality simply invite their own destruction, and anyone who insists on remaining in a state of innocence long after that innocence is dead turns himself into a monster.

The time has come to realize that the interracial drama acted out on the American continent has not only created a new black man, it has created a new white man, too. No road whatever will lead Americans back to the simplicity of this European village where white men still have the luxury of looking on me as a stranger. I am not, really, a stranger any longer for any American alive. One of the things that distinguishes Americans from other people is that no other people has ever been so deeply involved in the lives of black men, and vice versa. This fact faced, with all its implications, it can be seen that the history of the American Negro problem is not merely shameful, it is also something of an achievement. For even when the worst has been said, it must also be added that the perpetual challenge posed by this problem was always, somehow, perpetually met. It is precisely this black-white experience which may prove of indispensable value to us in the world we face today. This world is white no longer, and it will never be white again.

12

The Supreme Court Rules on Segregation

Brown v. Board of Education
[of Topeka]

The decision of the Supreme Court in the cases *Brown* v. *Board of Education* (Kansas), *Briggs* v. *Elliott* (South Carolina), *Davis* v. *County School Board* (Virginia), and *Gebhart* v. *Belton* (Delaware) is one of the twentieth century's most historic. It struck at one of the foundation stones of racial segregation in the United States by declaring that the principle of "separate but equal" is not in accord with the Fourteenth Amendment. The decision indicates the origins of the "separate but equal" principle, and traces the gradual breakdown of that principle in constitutional law. Chief Justice Earl Warren, writing the decision for a unanimous court, not only approached the cases with an historical perspective but accepted findings of the social sciences as to the effect of segregation. For further reading see the reports of the United States Commission on Civil Rights for 1959, 1960, and 1961, published by the Government Printing Office. Book 2 ,of the report for 1961 is particularly useful. See also Albert P. Blaustein and Clarence Clyde Ferguson, Jr., *Desegregation and the Law: The Meaning and Effect of the School Segregation Cases*, Rev. ed. (New York, 1962).

In reading this decision note (1) the legal basis for school segregation prior to *Brown* v. *Board of Education;* (2) the legal grounds for requiring state graduate and professional schools to admit Negroes; and (3) the grounds for the present decision of the Court.

M̲R. CHIEF JUSTICE WARREN DELIVERED THE OPINION of the Court.

These cases come to us from the States of Kansas, South Caro-

347 *U.S. Reports*, 483-496. Argued December 9, 1952; reargued December 8, 1953; decided May 17, 1954. The footnotes are in the original decision of the Court.

lina, Virginia, and Delaware. They are premised on different facts and different local conditions, but a common legal question justifies their consideration together in this consolidated opinion.[1]

In each of the cases, minors of the Negro race, through their legal representatives, seek the aid of the courts in obtaining admission to the public schools of their community on a nonsegregated basis. In each instance, they had been denied admission to schools attended by white children under laws requiring or permitting segregation according to race. This segregation was alleged to deprive the plaintiffs of the equal protection of the

1. In the Kansas case, *Brown* v. *Board of Education,* the plaintiffs are Negro children of elementary school age residing in Topeka. They brought this action in the United States District Court for the District of Kansas to enjoin enforcement of a Kansas statute which permits, but does not require, cities of more than 15,000 population to maintain separate school facilities for Negro and white students. Kan. Gen. Stat. § 72-1724 (1949). Pursuant to that authority, the Topeka Board of Education elected to establish segregated elementary schools. Other public schools in the community, however, are operated on a nonsegregated basis. The three-judge District Court, convened under 28 U. S. C. §§ 2281 and 2284, found that segregation in public education has a detrimental effect upon Negro children, but denied relief on the ground that the Negro and white schools were substantially equal with respect to buildings, transportation, curricula, and educational qualifications of teachers. 98 F. Supp. 797. The case is here on direct appeal under 28 U. S. C. § 1253.

In the South Carolina case, *Briggs* v. *Elliott,* the plaintiffs are Negro children of both elementary and high school age residing in Clarendon County. They brought this action in the United States District Court for the Eastern District of South Carolina to enjoin enforcement of provisions in the state constitution and statutory code which require the segregation of Negroes and whites in public schools. S. C. Const., Art. XI, § 7; S. C. Code § 5377 (1942). The three-judge District Court, convened under 28 U. S. C. §§ 2281 and 2284, denied the requested relief. The court found that the Negro schools were inferior to the white schools and ordered the defendants to begin immediately to equalize the facilities. But the court sustained the validity of the contested provisions and denied the plaintiffs admission to the white schools during the equalization program. 98 F. Supp. 529. This Court vacated the District Court's judgment and remanded the case for the purpose of obtaining the court's views on a report filed by the defendants concerning the progress made in the equalization program. 342 U. S. 350. On remand, the District Court found that substantial equality had been achieved except for buildings and that the defendants were proceeding to rectify this inequality as well. 103 F. Supp. 920 The case is again here on direct appeal under 28 U. S. C. § 1253.

In the Virginia case, *Davis* v. *County School Board,* the plaintiffs are Negro children of high school age residing in Prince Edward County. They brought this action in the United States District Court for the Eastern District of Virginia to enjoin enforcement of provisions in the state constitution

laws under the Fourteenth Amendment. In each of the cases other than the Delaware case, a three-judge federal district court denied relief to the plaintiffs on the so-called "separate but equal" doctrine announced by this Court in *Plessy* v. *Ferguson,* 163 U. S. 537. Under that doctrine, equality of treatment is accorded when the races are provided substantially equal facilities, even though these facilities be separate. In the Delaware case, the Supreme Court of Delaware adhered to that doctrine, but ordered that the plaintiffs be admitted to the white schools because of their superiority to the Negro schools.

The plaintiffs contend that segregated public schools are not "equal" and cannot be made "equal," and that hence they are deprived of the equal protection of the laws. Because of the obvious importance of the question presented, the Court took juris-

---

and statutory code which require the segregation of Negroes and whites in public schools. Va. Const., § 140; Va. Code § 22-221 (1950). The three-judge District Court, convened under 28 U. S. C. §§ 2281 and 2284, denied the requested relief. The court found the Negro school inferior in physical plant, curricula, and transportation, and ordered the defendants forthwith to provide substantially equal curricula and transportation and to "proceed with all reasonable diligence and dispatch to remove" the inequality in physical plant. But, as in the South Carolina case, the court sustained the validity of the contested provisions and denied the plaintiffs admission to the white schools during the equalization program. 103 F. Supp. 337. The case is here on direct appeal under 28 U. S. C. § 1253.

In the Delaware case, *Gebhart* v. *Belton,* the plaintiffs are Negro children of both elementary and high school age residing in New Castle County. They brought this action in the Delaware Court of Chancery to enjoin enforcement of provisions in the state constitution and statutory code which require the segregation of Negroes and whites in public schools. Del. Const., Art. X, § 2; Del. Rev. Code § 2631 (1935). The Chancellor gave judgment for the plaintiffs and ordered their immediate admission to schools previously attended only by white children, on the ground that the Negro schools were inferior with respect to teacher training, pupil-teacher ratio, extracurricular activities, physical plant, and time and distance involved in travel. 87 A. 2d 862. The Chancellor also found that segregation itself results in an inferior education for Negro children (see note 10, *infra*), but did not rest his decision on that ground. *Id.,* at 865. The Chancellor's decree was affirmed by the Supreme Court of Delaware, which intimated, however, that the defendants might be able to obtain a modification of the decree after equalization of the Negro and white schools had been accomplished. 91 A. 2d 137, 152. The defendants, contending only that the Delaware courts had erred in ordering the immediate admission of the Negro plaintiffs to the white schools, applied to this Court for certiorari. The writ was granted, 344 U. S. 891. The plaintiffs, who were successful below, did not submit a cross-petition.

diction.[2] Argument was heard in the 1952 Term, and reargument was heard this Term on certain questions propounded by the Court.[3]

Reargument was largely devoted to the circumstances surrounding the adoption of the Fourteenth Amendment in 1868. It covered exhaustively consideration of the Amendment in Congress, ratification by the states, then existing practices in racial segregation, and the views of proponents and opponents of the Amendment. This discussion and our own investigation convince us that, although these sources cast some light, it is not enough to resolve the problem with which we are faced. At best, they are inconclusive. The most avid proponents of the post-War Amendments undoubtedly intended them to remove all legal distinctions among "all persons born or naturalized in the United States." Their opponents, just as certainly, were antagonistic to both the letter and the spirit of the Amendments and wished them to have the most limited effect. What others in Congress and the state legislatures had in mind cannot be determined with any degree of certainty.

An additional reason for the inconclusive nature of the Amendment's history, with respect to segregated schools, is the status of public education at that time.[4] In the South, the movement toward free common schools, supported by general taxation, had not yet taken hold. Education of white children was largely in

2. 344 U.S. 1, 141, 891.

3. 345 U.S. 972. The Attorney General of the United States participated both Terms as *amicus curiae.*

4. For a general study of the development of public education prior to the Amendment, see Butts and Cremin, A History of Education in American Culture (1953), Pts. I, II; Cubberley, Public Education in the United States (1934 ed.), cc. II-XII. School practices current at the time of the adoption of the Fourteenth Amendment are described in Butts and Cremin, *supra,* at 269-275; Cubberley, *supra,* at 288-339, 408-431; Knight, Public Education in the South (1922), cc. VIII, IX. See also H. Ex. Doc. No. 315, 41st Cong., 2d Sess. (1871). Although the demand for free public schools followed substantially the same pattern in both the North and the South, the development in the South did not begin to gain momentum until about 1850, some twenty years after that in the North. The reasons for the somewhat slower development in the South (e.g., the rural character of the South and the different regional attitudes toward state assistance) are well explained in Cubberley, *supra,* at 408-423. In the country as a whole, but particularly in the South, the War [1861-1865] virtually stopped all progress in public education. *Id.,* at 427-428. The low status of Negro education in all sections of the country, both before and immediately after the War, is de-

the hands of private groups. Education of Negroes was almost nonexistent, and practically all of the race were illiterate. In fact, any education of Negroes was forbidden by law in some states. Today, in contrast, many Negroes have achieved outstanding success in the arts and sciences as well as in the business and professional world. It is true that public school education at the time of the Amendment had advanced further in the North, but the effect of the Amendment on Northern States was generally ignored in the congressional debates. Even in the North, the conditions of public education did not approximate those existing today. The curriculum was usually rudimentary; ungraded schools were common in rural areas; the school term was but three months a year in many states; and compulsory school attendance was virtually unknown. As a consequence, it is not surprising that there should be so little in the history of the Fourteenth Amendment relating to its intended effect on public education.

In the first cases in this Court construing the Fourteenth Amendment, decided shortly after its adoption, the Court interpreted it as proscribing all state-imposed discriminations against the Negro race.[5] The doctrine of "separate but equal" did not

---

scribed in Beale, A History of Freedom of Teaching in American Schools (1941), 112-132, 175-195. Compulsory school attendance laws were not generally adopted until after the ratification of the Fourteenth Amendment, and it was not until 1918 that such laws were in force in all the states. Cubberley, *supra*, at 563-565.

   5. *Slaughter-House Cases,* 16 Wall. 36, 67-72 (1873); *Strauder* v. *West Virginia,* 100 U.S. 303, 307-308 (1880):

"It ordains that no State shall deprive any person of life, liberty, or property, without due process of law, or deny to any person within its jurisdiction the equal protection of the laws. What is this but declaring that the law in the States shall be the same for the black as for the white; that all persons, whether colored or white, shall stand equal before the laws of the States, and, in regard to the colored race, for whose protection the amendment was primarily designed, that no discrimination shall be made against them by law because of their color? The words of the amendment, it is true, are prohibitory, but they contain a necessary implication of a positive immunity, or right, most valuable to the colored race,—the right to exemption from unfriendly legislation against them distinctively as colored,—exemption from legal discriminations, implying inferiority in civil society, lessening the security of their enjoyment of the rights which others enjoy, and discriminations which are steps towards reducing them to the condition of a subject race."

See also *Virginia* v. *Rives,* 100 U.S. 313, 318 (1880); *Ex parte Virginia,* 100 U.S. 339, 344-345 (1880).

make its appearance in this Court until 1896 in the case of *Plessy* v. *Ferguson, supra,* involving not education but transportation.[6] American courts have since labored with the doctrine for over half a century. In this Court, there have been six cases involving the "separate but equal" doctrine in the field of public education.[7] In *Cumming* v. *County Board of Education,* 175 U. S. 528, and *Gong Lum* v. *Rice,* 275 U. S. 78, the validity of the doctrine itself was not challenged.[8] In more recent cases, all on the graduate school level, inequality was found in that specific benefits enjoyed by white students were denied to Negro students of the same educational qualifications. *Missouri ex rel. Gaines* v. *Canada,* 305 U.S. 337; *Sipuel* v. *Oklahoma,* 332 U. S. 631; *Sweatt* v. *Painter,* 339 U.S. 629; *McLaurin* v. *Oklahoma State Regents,* 339 U. S. 637. In none of these cases was it necessary to re-examine the doctrine to grant relief to the Negro plaintiff. And in *Sweatt* v. *Painter, supra,* the Court expressly reserved decision on the question whether *Plessy* v. *Ferguson* should be held inapplicable to public education.

In the instant cases, that question is directly presented. Here, unlike *Sweatt* v. *Painter,* there are findings below that the Negro and white schools involved have been equalized, or are being equalized, with respect to buildings, curricula, qualifications and salaries of teachers, and other "tangible" factors.[9] Our decision,

6. The doctrine apparently originated in *Roberts* v. *City of Boston,* 59 Mass. 198, 206 (1850), upholding school segregation against attack as being violative of a state constitutional guarantee of equality. Segregation in Boston public schools was eliminated in 1855. Mass. Acts 1855, c. 256. But elsewhere in the North segregation in public education has persisted in some communities until recent years. It is apparent that such segregation has long been a nationwide problem, not merely one of sectional concern.

7. See also *Berea College* v. *Kentucky,* 211 U.S. 45 (1908).

8. In the *Cumming* case, Negro taxpayers sought an injunction requiring the defendant school board to discontinue the operation of a high school for white children until the board resumed operation of a high school for Negro children. Similarly, in the *Gong Lum* case, the plaintiff, a child of Chinese descent, contended only that state authorities had misapplied the doctrine by classifying him with Negro children and requiring him to attend a Negro school.

9. In the Kansas case, the court below found substantial equality as to all such factors. 98 F. Supp. 797, 798. In the South Carolina case, the court below found that the defendants were proceeding "promptly and in good faith to comply with the court's decree." 103 F. Supp. 920, 921. In the

therefore, cannot turn on merely a comparison of these tangible factors in the Negro and white schools involved in each of the cases. We must look instead to the effect of segregation itself on public education.

In approaching this problem, we cannot turn the clock back to 1868 when the Amendment was adopted, or even to 1896 when *Plessy* v. *Ferguson* was written. We must consider public education in the light of its full development and its present place in American life throughout the Nation. Only in this way can it be determined if segregation in public schools deprives these plaintiffs of the equal protection of the laws.

Today, education is perhaps the most important function of state and local governments. Compulsory school attendance laws and the great expenditures for education both demonstrate our recognition of the importance of education to our democratic society. It is required in the performance of our most basic public responsibilities, even service in the armed forces. It is the very foundation of good citizenship. Today it is a principal instrument in awakening the child to cultural values, in preparing him for later professional training, and in helping him to adjust normally to his environment. In these days, it is doubtful that any child may reasonably be expected to succeed in life if he is denied the opportunity of an education. Such an opportunity, where the state has undertaken to provide it, is a right which must be made available to all on equal terms.

We come then to the question presented: Does segregation of children in public schools solely on the basis of race, even though the physical facilities and other "tangible" factors may be equal, deprive the children of the minority group of equal educational opportunities? We believe that it does.

In *Sweatt* v. *Painter, supra,* in finding that a segregated law school for Negroes could not provide them equal educational opportunities, this Court relied in large part on "those qualities

Virginia case, the court below noted that the equalization program was already "afoot and progressing" (103 F. Supp. 337, 341); since then, we have been advised, in the Virginia Attorney General's brief on reargument, that the program has now been completed. In the Delaware case, the court below similarly noted that the state's equalization program was well under way. 91 A. 2d 137, 149.

which are incapable of objective measurement but which make for greatness in a law school." In *McLaurin* v. *Oklahoma State Regents, supra,* the Court, in requiring that a Negro admitted to a white graduate school be treated like all other students, again resorted to intangible considerations: ". . . his ability to study, to engage in discussions and exchange views with other students, and, in general, to learn his profession." Such considerations apply with added force to children in grade and high schools. To separate them from others of similar age and qualifications solely because of their race generates a feeling of inferiority as to their status in the community that may affect their hearts and minds in a way unlikely ever to be undone. The effect of this separation on their educational opportunities was well stated by a finding in the Kansas case by a court which nevertheless felt compelled to rule against the Negro plaintiffs:

"Segregation of white and colored children in public schools has a detrimental effect upon the colored children. The impact is greater when it has the sanction of the law; for the policy of separating the races is usually interpreted as denoting the inferiority of the negro group. A sense of inferiority affects the motivation of a child to learn. Segregation with the sanction of law, therefore, has a tendency to [retard] the educational and mental development of negro children and to deprive them of some of the benefits they would receive in a racial[ly] integrated school system."[10]

Whatever may have been the extent of psychological knowledge at the time of *Plessy* v. *Ferguson,* this finding is amply supported by modern authority.[11] Any language in *Plessy* v. *Ferguson* contrary to this finding is rejected.

10. A similar finding was made in the Delaware case: "I conclude from the testimony that in our Delaware society, State-imposed segregation in education itself results in the Negro children, as a class, receiving educational opportunities which are substantially inferior to those available to white children otherwise similarly situated." 87 A. 2d 862, 865.

11. K. B. Clark, Effect of Prejudice and Discrimination on Personality Development (Midcentury White House Conference on Children and Youth, 1950); Witmer and Kotinsky, Personality in the Making (1952), c. VI; Deutscher and Chein, The Psychological Effects of Enforced Segregation: A Survey of Social Science Opinion, 26 J. Psychol. 259 (1948); Chein, What are the Psychological Effects of Segregation Under Conditions of Equal Facilities?, 3 Int. J. Opinion and Attitude Res. 229 (1949); Brameld, Educational Costs, in Discrimination and National Welfare (MacIver, ed., 1949), 44-48; Frazier, The Negro in the United States (1949), 674-681. And see generally Myrdal, An American Dilemma (1944).

We conclude that in the field of public education the doctrine of "separate but equal" has no place. Separate educational facilities are inherently unequal. Therefore, we hold that the plaintiffs and others similarly situated for whom the actions have been brought are by reason of the segregation complained of, deprived of the equal protection of the laws guaranteed by the Fourteenth Amendment. This disposition makes unnecessary any discussion whether such segregation also violates the Due Process Clause of the Fourteenth Amendment.[12]

Because these are class actions, because of the wide applicability of this decision, and because of the great variety of local conditions, the formulation of decrees in these cases presents problems of considerable complexity. On reargument, the consideration of appropriate relief was necessarily subordinated to the primary question—the constitutionality of segregation in public education. We have now announced that such segregation is a denial of the equal protection of the laws. In order that we may have the full assistance of the parties in formulating decrees, the cases will be restored to the docket, and the parties are requested to present further argument on Questions 4 and 5 previously propounded by the Court for the reargument this Term.[13] The Attorney General of the United States is again in-

12. See *Bolling* v. *Sharpe, post,* p. 497, concerning the Due Process Clause of the Fifth Amendment.

13. "4. Assuming it is decided that segregation in public schools violates the Fourteenth Amendment

"(a) would a decree necessarily follow providing that, within the limits set by normal geographic school districting, Negro children should forthwith be admitted to schools of their choice, or

"(b) may this Court, in the exercise of its equity powers, permit an effective gradual adjustment to be brought about from existing segregated systems to a system not based on color distinctions?

"5. On the assumption on which questions 4 (a) and (b) are based, and assuming further that this Court will exercise its equity powers to the end described in question 4 (b),

"(a) should this Court formulate detailed decrees in these cases;

"(b) if so, what specific issues should the decrees reach;

"(c) should this Court appoint a special master to hear evidence with a view to recommending specific terms for such decrees;

"(d) should this Court remand to the courts of first instance with directions to frame decrees in these cases, and if so what general directions should the decrees of this Court include and what procedures should the courts of first instance follow in arriving at the specific terms of more detailed decrees?"

vited to participate. The Attorneys General of the states requiring or permitting segregation in public education will also be permitted to appear as *amici curiae* upon request to do so by September 15, 1954, and submission of briefs by October 1, 1954.[14]

It is so ordered.

14. See Rule 42, Revised Rules of this Court (effective July 1, 1954).

13

United States Prestige Abroad
The U.S. Information Agency Report,
August 29, 1960

The following document is a partial text of a report by the United States Information Agency of August 29, 1960. The Eisenhower Administration had at first declined to make this report public when requested to do so by Democratic critics. In reading this document, note (1) what the report shows about the relative prestige of the United States and the Soviet Union in world opinion; (2) the bases for the judgments made; and (3) the reasons for changes in the relative position of the two powers. The report is important not only because of its factual content but because of its political implications in 1960. The reader might compare the controversy revolving around this report with the controversy over the relative striking power of the United States and the Soviet Union which developed during the presidential campaign year of 1964. For further reading see Richard Stebbins, *The United States in World Affairs, 1960* (Council on Foreign Relations, New York, 1961).

Free-World Views of the U.S.-U.S.S.R. Power Balance]

A. GENERAL TRENDS AND HIGHLIGHTS]

1. THE CONCEPT OF NATIONAL POWER IN INTERNA-tional relations is currently undergoing redefinition in the public mind. In this process, the elements that constitute power, the ways in which power is applied and the context in which power is envisaged and assessed are all being significantly revised and extended.

New York Times, November 2, 1960. Copyright by The New York Times. Reprinted by permission.

In this continuing flux, no clear and controlling concept, and no final verdict on power-in-being or on relative power positions holds decisive sway, although a number of the factors that influence popular judgment can be discerned, as well as the current general direction of those judgments.

2. Current views of relative U.S.-U.S.S.R. power have changed sharply since the advent of the first Sputnik and the development of intercontinental missile capabilities. Prior to these events, prevalent opinion was that the U.S. enjoyed clear preponderance of power.

The current consensus would appear to be that the U.S.S.R. now enjoys a rough but effective equivalence in strength over all. Behind in some fields, ahead in others, the U.S.S.R. is seen as capable of offering a credible competitive challenge to the U.S. in the major arenas of international rivalry.

3. The trend is adverse to the U.S. Despite some fluctuations, and area variations, impressions of Soviet power superiority or gains seem to be rising in public opinion rather than falling. Anticipations of what the trend in power will be—popular estimates of which nation will emerge generally strongest in a peaceful competition over the next few decades—in most available indicators favor the U.S.S.R.

4. In the critical areas of military strength and space achievements and a rate of economic growth capable of supporting them at a high level, popular opinion in most West European countries presumably the best informed and closely linked by interest and history, believes the U.S. to be inferior to the U.S.S.R., although more sophisticated opinion may perceive a rough balance. In these specific fields, too, the trend is adverse.

Elsewhere, most opinion is divided on military strength, with the predominant belief apparent that nuclear stalemate prevails.

However, in almost all areas, expectations appear to be that the U.S.S.R. will achieve military superiority, although there is probably no clear concept of what this superiority will consist of, or what its significance will be.

5. In most parts of the world, the U.S.S.R. is believed to lead the U.S. in space achievements. This impression, stemming from the first Sputnik and strengthened by its aftermath, appears to have sometimes a durability impervious to fact, sometimes a

volatility suggesting that it could be readily modified by sensational developments.

Given the present capabilities of both sides, it is probable that the most favorable verdict the U.S. can hope to elicit on its space performance will be the expectation of a see-saw pattern.

6. Virtually without exception, world opinion is now convinced that the U.S.S.R. has made tremendous economic progress over the past decade. So much, in fact, that the gap between it and the U.S., which is still acknowledged to have the world's most powerful economy, is rapidly being closed. Concurrent with the widely held view that the U.S.S.R.'s current rate of economic growth is substantially higher than that of the U.S., is the general tendency—even in highly industrialized Western Europe—to suspect that within the foreseeable future the U.S.S.R. might even surpass the U.S. in overall economic strength.

7. Popular acceptance of the idea that a "nuclear stalemate" obtains appears to be increasing; it may be the most widely held single view on relative U.S.-U.S.S.R. power. It does not necessarily conceive U.S.-U.S.S.R. strength as equal; it is based rather on the view that no margin of superiority is likely to be decisive in a nuclear war, since the side that initiated major hostilities would incur unacceptable retaliatory damage in turn.

This view is less a judgment on ratios of strength than a belief that strength is held in an equilibrium of deterrence, "the balance of terror."

The concept of such a deadlock seems to have rational and emotional attractiveness to foreign audiences: (1) Such a military stalemate appears to lessen the danger that either side would deliberately resort to force and is thus wishfully welcomed; (2) A balance of this kind appears to hold for third powers the prospect that their own international influence could assume expanded, perhaps decisive weight; (3) It permits readier maintenance or assumption of neutralist positions by eliminating the attraction of a possible victor—it is easier to be neutral if no one is going to win.

8. A nuclear stalemate carries for many the implication that the U.S.-U.S.S.R. rivalry will be resolved in alternative arenas. If major modern armaments are seen as unemployable to enforce settlement of the U.S.-U.S.S.R. competition, greater weight and

decisiveness are given to other aspects of strength—on the one hand, the political, economic, psychological, and ideological facets of a peaceful international competition; on the other, the ability successfully to fight a geographically limited war, a war with conventional weapons, or to intervene forcibly (directly or indirectly) in a local situation.

9. There appears to be a preponderance of belief that the U.S.S.R., rather than the U.S., would win a conventional war; there appears uncertainty whether wars could be confined to local areas or conventional weapons. In Western Europe, opinion seems convinced that any war between the major powers would be a nuclear war, and could not be localized; in areas where the interests of the greater powers do not appear so critically or manifestly engaged, the possibility of local and limited wars seems to have wider acceptance.

10. The sources of the public impression that the U.S.S.R. has closed or is closing the power gap appear to be primarily:

a. Widespread belief that the Soviets lead in space achievements, and that these can be equated directly with military capability, and to a lesser extent with overall scientific and technical development and with the efficacy of the Soviet system.

b. The greatly expanded international presence of the U.S.S.R., which has appeared in recent years to be exerting influence and leverage in areas which had hitherto been denied it or where it had hitherto been inactive.

c. The confident tone and aggressive posture of the U.S.S.R., which has appeared to be speaking and acting from assumed strength. This assumption has apparently been lent credibility less by Soviet propaganda efforts than by concrete Soviet actions or successes, and by the apparent corroboration given Soviet claims by Western reaction. U.S. expressions of public and official concern regarding the challenge of Soviet power appear to have been a significant element in validating the Soviet posture.

d. Doubts that the United States has succeeded in effectively organizing and focusing the resources of the Western alliance, or that the United States has shown itself fully effective in bringing its own power to bear on its objective.

e. Soviet foreign economic programs, that despite their comparatively restricted size have had high impact and visibility, through selective deployment and timing for maximum effect; these have helped to create the image of a productive and accelerating Soviet economy, especially in underdeveloped areas.

f. An impression of Soviet ruthlessness and fixity of purpose, combined with the impression that the Soviet people have greater faith in their principles, and are willing to work harder, than the people of the United States. This view has not served to raise [the] U.S.S.R. in general esteem over the United States, nor can it be equated with admiration for Communist institutions or doctrine, but presumably contributes to raising popular estimates of over-all Soviet capabilities.

g. In Asia particularly, the belief that Communist China, with its massive population, has shown tremendous economic growth and dynamism makes it appear a substantial increment to Communist bloc strength—a belief qualified, probably, by the sense that this strength is currently more potential than actual, and by some uncertainty about the ultimate correspondence of Communist Chinese and Soviet interests. In much of the Far East (notably excluding Japan) the impact of Soviet power is still relatively slight; Communist China is the basic power against which the United States is measured in Southeast Asia, and Soviet power is sometimes also viewed as a force to be measured against that of Communist China.

Western Europe]

Introduction]

The question "How do Western Europeans currently rank the United States and the Soviet Union on the international balance of power scale in view of their world-wide rivalry?" is not easily answered for two major reasons—both of which are highly subjective in character.

The first difficulty is inherent in the initial and personal decision regarding the relative weight to be assigned to each of the three major sectors of opinion, to political opinion as revealed in official government policy, parliamentary debates and public political speeches; newspaper opinion as reflected in editorials and feature commentaries; and man-in-the-street opinion as indicated by public opinion surveys.

However, given the kind of democratic political society that prevails throughout most of Western Europe, this appraisal arbitrarily assumes that political opinion is the most important, followed fairly close by press opinion and at some considerable distance by man-in-the-street opinion.

The second major difficulty stems from the lack of any commonly agreed on current yardsticks for measuring the relative power-standing vis-à-vis each other of such super-states as the United States and the Soviet Union. Although there is a fairly firm consensus as to what constitutes international power in the abstract—military strength, economic might, scientific-technological skill and moral stature—there is no corresponding agreement as to the relative importance of these various power-components within the context of the current U.S.-U.S.S.R. worldwide rivalry. For basic to any meaningful and realistic ordering is the subjective determination as to whether this rivalry will remain peaceful—i.e., confined to the struggle for the minds and stomachs of mankind—or whether it will eventually erupt into nuclear war. In either event, this appraisal again arbitrarily assumes that Western European opinion regards military strength—"Who can beat whom?"—and the will to use it as the acid tests of power in the current scientific nuclear-missile age, followed fairly closely by economic might and at some considerable distance by moral stature.

The Pre-Sputnik Image: Unchallenged U.S. Dominance]

From the vantage point of the present, it seems clear that "Sputnik I" and the cumulative American reaction to its manifold implications represent a major watershed in the Western European evaluation of the relative power standing of the United States and the Soviet Union. For, prior to the advent of the space or missile age in October, 1957, few Western Europeans seem to have entertained any real doubts about American military, scientific, economic and moral superiority vis-à-vis the U.S.S.R. and the American intention of using this superiority for the general good of mankind—at least for mankind in the free world.

The fact that the United States could expose the Soviet Union to nuclear destruction while the latter could not effectively retaliate in kind—the basis of the Dulles "massive retaliation" doctrine—was universally regarded as concrete evidence of American military superiority. A superiority, moreover, which most Western Europeans believed was implicitly acknowledged by the Soviet Union itself. For, following the formation in 1949 of the North Atlantic defense system based on U.S. nuclear might, there were no further direct Soviet challenges to the territorial status quo of Western Europe.

The fact that the United States had the highest standard of living of any nation in the world was viewed as indisputable proof of American economic superiority. A superiority, moreover, which was clearly demonstrated by the ease with which the United States carried the tremendous burden of the post-war economic reconstruction of Western Europe—the Marshall Plan —and furnished increasing amounts of economic and technical assistance to other needy regions.

The fact that on virtually all levels of American society there was mass ownership of products of American scientific-technological ingenuity—cars, radios, television sets, refrigerators, vacuum cleaners, washing machines, etc.—was generally regarded as incontrovertible proof of the validity of the traditional picture of American scientific-technological preeminence, a superiority, moreover, which had been clearly demonstrated in the development of the atomic and hydrogen bombs and in the means of delivering them to their intended targets.

The fact that the United States was an open and democratic society—one which was clearly dedicated in principle to the Western European liberal ideal of individual freedom, liberty and equality of opportunity—was strong evidence of the moral superiority of American society vis-à-vis its dictatorial and regimented Soviet counterpart. A superiority, moreover, which was clearly manifested in American goodwill and benevolence toward most nations in the difficult post-war era and in its assumption of the unsolicited role of defender of the free world against the march of international communism.

The Post-Sputnik Image: U.S. Dominance Seriously Questioned]

Under the cumulative impact of Soviet spectacular "firsts" in rocket development and the continuing chorus of sharp American self-criticism most Western Europeans have been shocked into a drastic—and perhaps excessive—revision of their pre-

Sputnik image of general Soviet inferiority to the United States. Accompanying this re-evaluation of the U.S.S.R. as a dynamic and powerful military-economic-and-scientific complex has been a concomitant re-examination of the continuing validity of the pre-Sputnik image of invincible American power and unquestioned world dominance.

Currently, most Western Europeans are convinced that the balance of military power no longer favors the United States as it formerly did. For, in their opinion, the Soviet leapfrog development of a nuclear intercontinental ballistic missile has cancelled out the pre-Sputnik American advantage of being able to rain nuclear destruction upon the Soviet Union while being virtually immune to a similar Soviet atack.

While sophisticated political and press opinion tends to regard the current military situation as one of nuclear stalemate in which neither of the two superpowers has any material advantage over the other, the more impressionistic popular opinion has seemingly concluded from Soviet boasts of superiority and American admissions of a temporary "missile gap" that the United States is not only currently militarily inferior to the U.S.S.R. but will continue to be so for the next decade or two as well.

Nevertheless, popular opinion is in complete accord with sophisticated opinion in holding that a major war between the U.S. and the U.S.S.R. is most unlikely in the present circumstances because, regardless of their relative military strengths, each still has the capability of inflicting terrible destruction upon the other.

In short, regardless of differences of opinion about the relative military strengths of the world's two super-states, there is universal acceptance of the Churchillian thesis that "mutuality of terror" is a major deterrent to war in the nuclear age.

Although convinced that the Soviet Union's recent success in redressing the military balance vis-à-vis the United States has paradoxically reduced the danger that either protagonist would deliberately resort to war as a means of resolving their differences, Western European opinion—at least on the more sophisticated political and press levels—is currently disturbed by two possible (albeit contradictory) implications of the post-Sputnik military situation.

First, the possibility of war by miscalculation—that is, the fear that war might inadvertently result from a Soviet miscalculation as to how far it can exploit the current nuclear stalemate for the attainment of limited objectives, such as the takeover of West Berlin, for instance.

And second, the possibility that Western Europe could no longer reckon unconditionally upon the protection of America's atomic shield in the event of limited conflicts—that is, the fear that the United States might consider the possible nuclear destruction of an American city (such as New York or Chicago or Los Angeles) as too high a price to pay for resolutely opposing a limited Soviet aggression such as the takeover of West Berlin or Helsinki, for example.

While Western European opinion still subscribes to the view that the United States is indubitably the world's economic leader ahead of the Soviet Union, its closest rival, of late increasing doubts—particularly on the more sophisticated political and press levels—have developed about the continuing supremacy of the American economy. Contributing to these growing reservations have been four major developments.

First, the general agreement that the Soviet Union's boasts of tremendous economic strides in the post-war era have a firm foundation in fact, as evidenced by such objective standards as the visible improvement in its level of living, its deep and continuing penetration of the aluminum, asbestos and oil export markets (to mention just a few) and its increasing foreign aid programs such as the ambitious Aswan Dam project on the Nile.

Second, the widespread currency and authenticity that American reports, both official and private, have given to the U.S.S.R.'s claim that its economy is growing at an appreciably faster rate than that of the United States and that the gap between the two is being rapidly closed—a claim which Western Europeans find easy to accept (even without American confirmation) in view of their own superior rate of economic growth over the last decade.

Third, the visible faltering of the American economy on at least four major occasions in the last fifteen years, most particularly the 1957-58 recession and the current economic difficulties.

And fourth, the apparent concern of the United States—as indicated by its current export drive and sponsorship of the still-to-be-born Organization of Economic Cooperation and Development—that it can no longer singlehandedly carry the increasing burden of economic assistance to the developing nations of the world in direct competition with the U.S.S.R.

The pre-Sputnik Western European image of the United States as the *scientific-technological* nation in the world has likewise been sharply eroded of late under the cumulative impact of the Soviet Union's spectacular success with outerspace satellites—largely because of the widespread layman's tendency to equate them with a high degree of scientific-technological attainment in general.

Although the almost universal acceptance of Soviet superiority in rocketry has resulted in an across-the-board upgrading of Soviet science and technology, Western European opinion is still inclined to believe that the United States leads the U.S.S.R. in the application of science for the general welfare of mankind. . . .

While the *moral* stature of the United States as a nation dedicated to freedom and liberty remains as high as ever, a number of developments have combined of late to induce in Western European opinion—particularly on the sophisticated political and press levels—increasing doubts about the continuing American ability to provide the kind of imaginative and responsive leadership required by changing world conditions, such as the shift in Soviet strategy from the crude "cold-war" philosophy of Stalin to the more subtle challenge posed by Khrushchev's "peaceful but competitive coexistence" philosophy.

A highly selective listing of the major events leading to this Western European questioning of American leadership during the last two and one-half years would of necessity include the following: the alleged tardy American recognition of the military and psychological challenge posed by the Soviet Union's spectacular series of "firsts" in outer-space developments, the alleged hiatuses in the conduct of American foreign policy occasioned by internal bickering, the illness of high U.S. officials and elections; the alleged amateurish bungling which led to the Soviet torpedoing of the much-heralded Paris summit conference and the Geneva disarmament talks; the alleged failure to prevent the division of Western Europe into two potentially rival economic groupings; and the alleged inability of the Eisenhower Administration to exercise effective and unified control over the complex governmental machinery concerned with foreign affairs.

Conclusions]

Three major conclusions are suggested by the preceding analysis of current Western European opinion of the relative power standing of the United States and the Soviet Union.

First, that the past few years have witnesed a sharp deterioration in the pre-Sputnik Western European image of American military, economic, scientific and moral superiority vis-à-vis the U.S.S.R.

Second, that during this same period Western European opinion has drastically revised its pre-Sputnik view of the U.S.S.R. as a generally backward nation to the current image of a modern dynamic and powerful military-economic-and-scientific complex —one, moreover, which has already taken giant strides towards redressing the balance with the United States.

And third, that Western European opinion is inclined to the "safe" view that the United States and the U.S.S.R. will become progressively more equal in over-all strength over the course of time, with neither having any appreciable military or economic or scientific advantage over the other.

14

Poisoning the World with Pesticides

Rachel L. Carson's *Silent Spring*

Rachel L. Carson (1907-1964) entered the Pennsylvania College for Women as an undergraduate, apparently intending to make writing a career. However, there her knack for writing became combined with an interest in science. She became a science major and three years after graduation in 1929 received a master's degree in zoology at Johns Hopkins. She taught zoology at the University of Maryland for five years, did additional research at the Marine Biological Laboratory at Woods Hole, Massachusetts, and in 1936 began a long career as aquatic biologist with the U.S. Bureau of Fisheries, later the U.S. Fish and Wildlife Service. This agency's principal aim was the conservation of the nation's wildlife, an aim close to Miss Carson's heart, and she herself wrote many of the official publications of the agency. In the meantime, however, she made available her literary skill to a larger public. In 1941 appeared her beautifully written *Under the Sea Wind,* and ten years later the best seller, *The Sea Around Us.* In these and other writings the case for conservation was implicit. In 1962, however, in a series of articles in *The New Yorker,* later incorporated with amplification in a book, *Silent Spring,* she took off her party gloves and shocked many readers with a brilliantly expressed attack upon post-World War II insecticides, fungicides, and herbicides.

The book is undoubtedly one of the most controversial of the postwar period. Her critics claim that she has drawn "unwarranted conclusions" and has ignored the benefits of the "pesticides." "Even before her book came out," according to the *Saturday Review,* "agricultural concerns, agitated as a hornet's nest hit by a DDT bomb, had set the wheels of counterattack in motion," but, the *Review* added, "thus far no one has been able to refute Miss Carson's facts and case histories." In any case, she succeeded in focusing attention, as had the early twentieth century muckrakers, at practices which at the very least called for exposure and further study.

In reading the following chapter from *Silent Spring* note (1) the threats to human health which Miss Carson describes; (2) her analysis of the functions of the Food and Drug Administration; and (3) the solutions that she suggests.

Beyond the Dreams of the Borgias]

THE CONTAMINATION OF OUR WORLD IS NOT ALONE a matter of mass spraying. Indeed, for most of us this is of less importance than the innumerable small-scale exposures to which we are subjected day by day, year after year. Like the constant dripping of water that in turn wears away the hardest stone, this birth-to-death contact with dangerous chemicals may in the end prove disastrous. Each of these recurrent exposures, no matter how slight, contributes to the progressive buildup of chemicals in our bodies and so to cumulative poisoning. Probably no person is immune to contact with this spreading contamination unless he lives in the most isolated situation imaginable. Lulled by the soft sell and the hidden persuader, the average citizen is seldom aware of the deadly materials with which he is surrounding himself; indeed, he may not realize he is using them at all.

So thoroughly has the age of poisons become established that anyone may walk into a store and, without questions being asked, buy substances of far greater death-dealing power than the medicinal drug for which he may be required to sign a "poison book" in the pharmacy next door. A few minutes' research in any supermarket is enough to alarm the most stouthearted customer—provided, that it, he has even a rudimentary knowledge of the chemicals presented for his choice.

If a huge skull and crossbones were suspended above the insecticide department the customer might at least enter it with the respect normally accorded death-dealing materials. But instead the display is homey and cheerful, and, with the pickles and olives across the aisle and the bath and laundry soaps adjoining, the rows upon rows of insecticides are displayed.

Within easy reach of a child's exploring hand are chemicals in *glass* containers. If dropped to the floor by a child or careless adult everyone nearby could be splashed with the same chemical that has sent spraymen using it into convulsions. These hazards of course follow the purchaser right into his home. A can of a mothproofing material containing DDD [dichloro-diphenyl-dichloroethane], for example, carries in very fine print the warning that its contents are under pressure and that it may burst if exposed to heat or open flame. A common insecticide for household use, including assorted uses in the kitchen, is chlordane. Yet the Food and Drug Administration's chief pharmacologist has declared the hazard of living in a house sprayed with chlordane to be "very great." Other household preparations contain the even more toxic dieldrin.

Use of poisons in the kitchen is made both attractive and easy. Kitchen shelf paper, white or tinted to match one's color scheme, may be impregnated with insecticide, not merely on one but on both sides. Manufacturers offer us do-it-yourself booklets on how to kill bugs. With push-button ease, one may send a fog of dieldrin into the most inaccessible nooks and crannies of cabinets, corners, and baseboards.

If we are troubled by mosquitoes, chiggers, or other insect pests on our persons we have a choice of innumerable lotions, creams, and sprays for application to clothing or skin. Although we are warned that some of these will dissolve varnish, paint, and synthetic fabrics, we are presumably to infer that the human skin is impervious to chemicals. To make certain that we shall at all times be prepared to repel insects, an exclusive New York store advertises a pocket-sized insecticide dispenser, suitable for the purse or for beach, golf, or fishing gear.

We can polish our floors with a wax guaranteed to kill any insect that walks over it. We can hang strips impregnated with the chemical lindane in our closets and garment bags or place them in our bureau drawers for a half year's freedom from worry over moth damage. The advertisements contain no suggestion that lindane is dangerous. Neither do the ads for an electronic device that dispenses lindane fumes—we are told that it is safe and odorless. Yet the truth of the matter is that the American Medical Association considers lindane vaporizers so dangerous that it conducted an extended campaign against them in its *Journal.*

The Department of Agriculture, in a *Home and Garden Bulletin,* advises us to spray our clothing with oil solutions of DDT [dichloro-diphenyl-trichloroethane], dieldrin, chlordane, or any of several other moth killers. If excessive spraying results in a white deposit of insecticide on the fabric, this may be removed by brushing, the Department says, omitting to caution us to be careful where and how the brushing is done. All these matters attended to, we may round out our day with insecticides by going to sleep under a mothproof blanket impregnated with dieldrin.

Gardening is now firmly linked with the super poisons. Every hardware store, garden-supply shop, and supermarket has rows of insecticides for every conceivable horticultural situation. Those who fail to make wide use of this array of lethal sprays and dusts are by implication remiss, for almost every newspaper's garden page and the majority of the gardening magazines take their use for granted.

So extensively are even the rapidly lethal organic phosphorus insecticides applied to lawns and ornamental plants that in 1960 the Florida State Board of Health found it necessary to forbid the commercial use of pesticides in residential areas by anyone who had not first obtained a permit and met certain requirements. A number of deaths from parathion had occurred in Florida before this regulation was adopted.

Little is done, however, to warn the gardener or homeowner that he is handling extremely dangerous materials. On the contrary, a constant stream of new gadgets make it easier to use poisons on lawn and garden—and increase the gardener's contact with them. One may get a jar-type attachment for the garden hose, for example, by which such extremely dangerous chemicals as chlordane or dieldrin are applied as one waters the lawn. Such a device is not only a hazard to the person using the hose; it is also a public menace. The *New York Times* found it necessary to issue a warning on its garden page to the effect that unless special protective devices were installed poisons might get into the water supply by back siphonage. Considering the number of such devices that are in use, and the scarcity of warnings such as this, do we need to wonder why our public waters are contaminated?

As an example of what may happen to the gardener himself, we might look at the case of a physician—an enthusiastic spare-time gardener—who began using DDT and then malathion on his shrubs and lawn, making regular weekly applications. Sometimes he applied the chemicals with a hand spray, sometimes with an attachment to his hose. In doing so, his skin and clothing were often soaked with spray. After about a year of this sort of thing, he suddenly collapsed and was hospitalized. Examination of a biopsy specimen of fat showed an accumulation of 23 parts per million of DDT. There was extensive nerve damage, which his physicians regarded as permanent. As time went on he lost weight, suffered extreme fatigue, and experienced a peculiar muscular weakness, a characteristic effect of malathion. All of these persisting effects were severe enough to make it difficult for the physician to carry on his practice.

Besides the once innocuous garden hose, power mowers also have been fitted with devices for the dissemination of pesticides, attachments that will dispense a cloud of vapor as the homeowner goes about the task of mowing his lawn. So to the potentially dangerous fumes from gasoline are added the finely divided particles of whatever insecticide the probably unsuspecting suburbanite has chosen to distribute, raising the level of air pollution above his own grounds to something few cities could equal.

Yet little is said about the hazards of the fad of gardening by poisons, or of insecticides used in the home; warnings on labels are printed so inconspicuously in small type that few take the trouble to read or follow them. An industrial firm recently undertook to find out just *how* few. Its survey indicated that fewer than fifteen people out of a hundred of those using insecticide aerosols and sprays are even aware of the warnings on the containers.

The mores of suburbia now dictate that crabgrass must go at whatever cost. Sacks containing chemicals designed to rid the lawn of such despised vegetation have become almost a status symbol. These weed-killing chemicals are sold under brand names that never suggest their identity or nature. To learn that they contain chlordane or dieldrin one must read exceedingly fine print placed on the least conspicuous part of the sack. The descriptive literature that may be picked up in any hardware- or garden-supply store seldom if ever reveals the true hazard involved in handling or applying the material. Instead, the typical illustration portrays a happy family scene, father and son smilingly preparing to apply the chemical to the lawn, small children tumbling over the grass with a dog.

The question of chemical residues on the food we eat is a hotly debated issue. The existence of such residues is either played down by the industry as unimportant or is flatly denied. Simultaneously, there is a strong tendency to brand as fanatics or cultists all who are so perverse as to demand that their food be free of insect poisons. In all this cloud of controversy, what are the actual facts?

It has been medically established that, as common sense would tell us, persons who lived and died before the dawn of the DDT era (about 1942) contained no trace of DDT or any similar material in their tissues. . . . [S]amples of body fat collected from the general population between 1954 and 1956 average from 5.3 to 7.4 parts per million of DDT. There is some evidence that the average level has risen since then to a consistently higher figure, and individuals with occupational or other special exposures to insecticides of course store even more.

Among the general population with no known gross exposures to insecticides it may be assumed that much of the DDT stored in fat deposits has entered the body in food. To test this assumption, a scientific team from the United States Public Health Service sampled restaurant and institutional meals. *Every meal sampled contained DDT*. From this the investigators concluded, reasonably enough, that "few if any foods can be relied upon to be entirely free of DDT."

The quantities in such meals may be enormous. In a separate Public Health Service study, analysis of prison meals disclosed such items as stewed dried fruit containing 69.6 parts per million and bread containing 100.9 parts per million of DDT!

In the diet of the average home, meats and any products

derived from animal fats contain the heaviest residues of chlorinated hydrocarbons. This is because these chemicals are soluble in fat. Residues on fruits and vegetables tend to be somewhat less. These are little affected by washing—the only remedy is to remove and discard all outside leaves of such vegetables as lettuce or cabbage, to peel fruit and to use no skins or outer covering whatever. Cooking does not destroy residues.

Milk is one of the few foods in which no pesticide residues are permitted by Food and Drug Administration regulations. In actual fact, however, residues turn up whenever a check is made. They are heaviest in butter and other manufactured dairy products. A check of 461 samples of such products in 1960 showed that a third contained residues, a situation which the Food and Drug Administration characterized as "far from encouraging."

To find a diet free from DDT and related chemicals, it seems one must go to a remote and primitive land, still lacking the amenities of civilization. Such a land appears to exist, at least marginally, on the far Arctic shores of Alaska—although even there one may see the approaching shadow. When scientists investigated the native diet of the Eskimos in this region it was found to be free from insecticides. The fresh and dried fish; the fat, oil. or meat from beaver, beluga, caribou, moose, oogruk, polar bear, and walrus; cranberries, salmonberries and wild rhubarb all had so far escaped contamination. There was only one exception—two white owls from Point Hope carried small amounts of DDT, perhaps acquired in the course of some migratory journey.

When some of the Eskimos themselves were checked by analysis of fat samples, small residues of DDT were found (0 to 1.9 parts per million). The reason for this was clear. The fat samples were taken from people who had left their native villages to enter the United States Public Health Service Hospital in Anchorage for surgery. There the ways of civilization prevailed, and the meals in this hospital were found to contain as much DDT as those in the most populous city. For their brief stay in civilization the Eskimos were rewarded with a taint of poison.

The fact that every meal we eat carries its load of chlorinated hydrocarbons is the inevitable consequence of the almost universal spraying or dusting of agricultural crops with these poisons. If the farmer scrupulously follows the instructions on the labels, his use of agricultural chemicals will produce no residues larger than are permitted by the Food and Drug Administration. Leaving aside for the moment the question whether these legal residues are as "safe" as they are represented to be, there remains the well-known fact that farmers very frequently exceed the prescribed dosages, use the chemical too close to the time of harvest, use several insecticides where one would do, and in other ways display the common human failure to read the fine print.

Even the chemical industry recognizes the frequent misuse of insecticides and the need for education of farmers. One of its leading trade journals recently declared that "many users do not seem to understand that they may exceed insecticide tolerances if they use higher dosages than recommended. And haphazard use of insecticides on many crops may be based on farmers' whims."

The files of the Food and Drug Administration contain records of a disturbing number of such violations. A few examples will serve to illustrate the disregard of directions: a lettuce farmer who applied not one but eight different insecticides to his crop within a short time of harvest, a shipper who had used the deadly parathion on celery in an amount five times the recommended maximum, growers using endrin—most toxic of all the chlorinated hydrocarbons—on lettuce although no residue was allowable, spinach sprayed with DDT a week before harvest.

There are also cases of chance or accidental contamination. Large lots of green coffee in burlap bags have become contaminated while being transported by vessels also carrying a cargo of insecticides. Packaged foods in warehouses are subjected to repeated aerosol treatments with DDT, lindane, and other insecticides, which may penetrate the packaging materials and occur in measurable quantities on the contained foods. The longer the food remains in storage, the greater the danger of contamination.

To the question "But doesn't the government protect us from

such things?" the answer is, "Only to a limited extent." The activities of the Food and Drug Administration in the field of consumer protection against pesticides are severely limited by two facts. The first is that it has jurisdiction only over foods shipped in interstate commerce; foods grown and marketed within a state are entirely outside its sphere of authority, no matter what the violation. The second and critically limiting fact is the small number of inspectors on its staff—fewer than 600 men for all its varied work. According to a Food and Drug official, only an infinitesimal part of the crop products moving in interstate commerce—far less than 1 per cent—can be checked with existing facilities, and this is not enough to have statistical significance. As for food produced and sold within a state, the situation is even worse, for most states have woefully inadequate law in this field.

The system by which the Food and Drug Administration establishes maximum permissible limits of contamination, called "tolerances," has obvious defects. Under the conditions prevailing it provides mere paper security and promotes a completely unjustified impression that safe limits have been established and are being adhered to. As to the safety of allowing a sprinkling of poisons on our food—a little on this, a little on that—many people contend, with highly persuasive reasons, that no poison is safe or desirable on food. In setting a tolerance level the Food and Drug Administration reviews tests of the poison on laboratory animals and then establishes a maximum level of contamination that is much less than required to produce symptoms in the test animal. This system, which is supposed to ensure safety, ignores a number of important facts. A laboratory animal, living under controlled and highly artificial conditions, consuming a given amount of a specific chemical, is very different from a human being whose exposures to pesticides are not only multiple but for the most part unknown, unmeasurable, and uncontrollable. Even if 7 parts per million of DDT on the lettuce in his luncheon salad were "safe," the meal includes other foods, each with allowable residues, and the pesticides on his food are, as we have seen, only a part, and possibly a small part, of his total exposure. This piling up of chemicals from many different sources creates a total exposure that cannot be measured. It is meaningless, therefore, to talk about the "safety" of any specific amount of residue.

And there are other defects. Tolerances have sometimes been established against the better judgment of Food and Drug Administration scientists . . . or they have been established on the basis of inadequate knowledge of the chemical concerned. Better information has led to later reduction or withdrawal of the tolerance, but only after the public has been exposed to admittedly dangerous levels of the chemical for months or years. This happened when heptachlor was given a tolerance that later had to be revoked. For some chemicals no practical field method of analysis exists before a chemical is registered for use. Inspectors are therefore frustrated in their search for residues. This difficulty greatly hampered the work on the "cranberry chemical," aminotriazole. Analytical methods are lacking, too, for certain fungicides in common use for the treatment of seeds—seeds which if unused at the end of the planting season, may very well find their way into human food.

In effect, then, to establish tolerances is to authorize contamination of public food supplies with poisonous chemicals in order that the farmer and the processor may enjoy the benefit of cheaper production—then to penalize the consumer by taxing him to maintain a policing agency to make certain that he shall not get a lethal dose. But to do the policing job properly would cost money beyond any legislator's courage to appropriate, given the present volume and toxicity of agricultural chemicals. So in the end the luckless consumer pays his taxes but gets his poisons regardless.

What is the solution? The first necessity is the elimination of tolerances on the chlorinated hydrocarbons, the organic phosphorus group, and other highly toxic chemicals. It will immediately be objected that this will place an intolerable burden on the farmer. But if, as is now the presumable goal, it is possible to use chemicals in such a way that they leave a residue of only 7 parts per million (the tolerance for DDT), or of 1 part per million (the tolerance for parathion), or even of only 0.1 part per million as is required for dieldrin on a great variety of fruits and vegetables, then why is it not possible, with only a little more care, to prevent the occurence of any residues at all? This, in fact, is what is required for some chemicals such as heptachlor, endrin, and dieldin on certain crops. If it is considered practical in these instances, why not for all?

But this is not a complete or final solution, for a zero tolerance on paper is of little value. At present, as we have seen, more than 99 per cent of the interstate food shipments slip by without inspection. A vigilant and aggressive Food and Drug Administration, with a greatly increased force of inspectors, is another urgent need.

This system, however—deliberately poisoning our food, then policing the result—is too reminiscent of Lewis Carroll's White Knight who thought of "a plan to dye one's whiskers green, and always use so large a fan that they could not be seen." The ultimate answer is to use less toxic chemicals so that the public hazard from their misuse is greatly reduced. Such chemicals already exist: the pyrethrins, rotenone, ryania, and others derived from plant substances. Synthetic substitutes for the pyrethrins have recently been developed so that an otherwise critical shortage can be averted. Public education as to the nature of the chemicals offered for sale is sadly needed. The average purchaser is completely bewildered by the array of available insecticides, fungicides, and weed killers, and has no way of knowing which are the deadly ones, which reasonably safe.

In addition to making this change to less dangerous agricultural pesticides, we should diligently explore the possibilities of non-chemical methods. Agricultural use of insect diseases, caused by a bacterium highly specific for certain types of insects, is already being tried in California, and more extended tests of this method are under way. A great many other possibilities exist for effective insect control by methods that will leave no residues on food. . . . Until a large-scale conversion to these methods has been made, we shall have little relief from a situation that, by any common-sense standards, is intolerable. As matters stand now, we are in little better position than the guests of the Borgias.

15

Computers and Automation as a Way of Life

Donald N. Michael's *Cybernation: The Silent Conquest*

This document consists of selections from a report published by the Center for the Study of Democratic Institutions, which in turn is supported by the Fund for the Republic. The Center is especially interested in "the emerging power of nongovernmental institutions." When the report was written, its author, Donald N. Michael, was director of planning and programs of the Peace Research Institute in Washington, D.C. He has been associated with the Brookings Institution, UNESCO, The Department of Defense, and the National Aeronautics and Space Administration. The extent to which "Cybernation," a term that refers to automation and computers, has become a part of our society is perhaps not sufficiently recognized by the average layman. For further reading see *The Annals of the American Academy of Political and Social Science* (Vol. 340), March 1962); and Norbert Wiener, *The Human Use of Human Beings: Cybernetics and Society*, 2d ed. (New York, 1956). In reading this document, note (1) the advantages and disadvantages of cybernation; (2) whether the author has suggested the dangers of relying too much on the conclusions of the computers; (3) the author's analysis of the problem of unemployment as it relates to cybernation; and (4) what solutions he suggests.

Introduction]

BOTH OPTIMISTS AND PESSIMISTS OFTEN CLAIM THAT automation is simply the latest stage in the evolution of technological means for removing the burdens of work. The assertion is misleading. There is a very good possibility that

Donald N. Michael, *Cybernation: The Silent Conquest*, Center for the Study of Democratic Institutions, Santa Barbara, c. 1962 by the Fund for the Republic Inc. By permission.

227]

automation is so different in degree as to be a profound difference in kind, and that it will pose unique problems for society, challenging our basic values and the ways in which we express and enforce them.*

In order to understand what both the differences and the problems are and, even more, will be, we have to know something of the nature and use of automation and computers. There are two important classes of devices. One class, usually referred to when one speaks of "automation," is made up of devices that automatically perform sensing and motor tasks, replacing or improving on human capacities for performing these functions. The second class, usually referred to when one speaks of "computers," is composed of devices that perform, very rapidly, routine or complex logical and decision-making tasks, replacing or improving on human capacities for performing these functions. . . .

The two classes of devices overlap. At one pole are the automatic producers of material objects and, at the other, the sophisticated analyzers and interpreters of complex data. In the middle zone are the mixed systems, in which computers control complicated processes, such as the operations of an oil refinery, on the basis of interpretations that they make of data automatically fed to them about the environment. Also in this middle zone are those routine, automatic, data-processing activities which provide men with the bases for controlling, or at least understanding, what is happening to a particular environment. Processing of social security data and making straightforward tabulations of census information are examples of these activities.†

*This paper makes the following assumptions in looking on the next twenty years or so: 1) international relations will derive from the same general conditions that pertain today; 2) the weapons systems industries will continue to support a major share of our economy; 3) major discoveries will be made and applied in other technologies, including psychology and medicine; 4) trends in megalopolis living and in population growth will continue; 5) no major shifts in underlying social attitudes and in public and private goals will take place. [Footnote in original.]

†In order to eliminate the awkwardness of repeating the words "automation" and "computers" each time we wish to refer to both at the same time, and in order to avoid the semantic difficulties involved in using one term or the other to mean both ends of the continuum, we invent the term "cybernation" to refer to *both* automation and computers. The word is legitimate at least to the extent that it derives from "cybernetics," a term invented by

Cybernated systems perform with a precision and a rapidity unmatched in humans. They also perform in ways that would be impractical or impossible for humans to duplicate. They can be built to detect and correct errors in their own performance and to indicate to men which of their components are producing the error. They can make judgments on the basis of instructions programmed into them. They can remember and search their memories for appropriate data, which either has been programmed into them along with their instructions or has been acquired in the process of manipulating new data. Thus, they can learn on the basis of past experience with their environment. They can receive information in more codes and sensory modes than men can. They are beginning to perceive and to recognize.

As a result of these characteristics, automation is being used to make and roll steel, mine coal, manufacture engine blocks, weave cloth, sort and grade everything from oranges to bank checks. . . .

At the other end of the continuum, computers are being used rather regularly to analyze market portfolios for brokers; compute the best combination of crops and livestock for given farm conditions; design and "fly" under typical and extreme conditions rockets and airplanes before they are built; design, in terms of cost and traffic-flow characteristics, the appropriate angles and grades for complex traffic interchanges; keep up-to-date inventory records and print new stock orders as automatically computed rates of sales and inventory status indicate. Computers have also been programmed to write mediocre TV dramas (by manipulating segments of the plot), write music, translate tolerably if not perfectly from one language to another, and simulate some logical brain processes (so that the machine goes about solving puzzles—and making mistakes in the process—in the ways people do.) Also, computers are programmed to play elaborate "games" by themselves or in collaboration with human beings. Among other reasons, these games are played to understand and plan more efficiently for the conduct of wars and the

---

Norbert Wiener to mean the processes of communication and control in man and machines. He derived it from the Greek word for "steersman." The theory and practice of cybernetics underlie all systematic design and application of automation and computers. [Footnote in original.]

procedures for industrial and business aggrandizement. Through such games, involving a vast number of variables, and contingencies within which these variables act and interact, the best or most likely solutions to complex problems are obtained.

The utility and the applicability of computers are being continually enhanced. For example, after a few hours of training, non-specialists can operate the smaller computers without the aid of programmers simply by plugging in pre-recorded instruction tapes that tell the computer how to do specific tasks. Instruction-tape libraries can supply pre-programmed computer directions for everything from finding the cube root of a number to designing a bridge. When the machine is through with one task, its circuits can be easily cleared so that a new set of pre-programmed instructions can be plugged in by its businessman operator.

But the capabilities of computers already extend well beyond even these applications. Much successful work has been done on computers that can program themselves. For example, they are beginning to operate the way man appears to when he is exploring ways of solving a novel problem. That is, they apply and then modify, as appropriate, previous experiences with and methods of solution for what appear to be related problems. Some of the machines show originality and unpredictability.

Another example of a machine the behavior of which is not completely controllable or predictable is the Perceptron, designed by Dr. Frank Rosenblatt. This machine can learn to recognize what it has seen before and to teach itself generalizations about what it recognizes. It can also learn to discriminate, and thereby to identify shapes similar to those it has seen before. Future versions will hear as well as see. It is not possible to predict the degree and quality of recognition that the machine will display as it is learning. It is designed to learn and discriminate in the same way that it is believed man may learn and discriminate; it has its own pace and style of learning, of refining its discriminations, and of making mistakes in the process.

It is no fantasy, then, to be concerned with the implications of the thinking machines. There is every reason to believe that within the next two decades machines will be available outside the laboratory that will do a credible job of original thinking, certainly as good thinking as that expected of most middle-level people who are supposed to "use their minds." There is no basis for knowing where this process will stop, nor, as Wiener has pointed out, is there any comfort in the assertion that, since man built the machine, he will always be smarter or more capable than it is. . . .

The Advantages of Cybernation]

IN RECENT YEARS DETERIORATING SALES PROSPECTS, rising production costs, increased foreign competition, and lower profits have led business management to turn to our national talent for technological invention as the most plausible means of reducing costs and increasing productivity, whether the product is an engine block or tables of sales figures. And the government, faced with the need to process and understand rapidly increasing masses of numerical facts about the state of the nation and the world, is already using 524 computers and is the major customer for more of them.

What are the advantages of cybernated systems that make government and private enterprise turn to them to solve problems?

In the first place, in a competitive society a successfully cybernated organization often has economic advantages over a competitor using people instead of machines. . . .

Not only must many organizations automate to compete, but the same principle probably holds for competing nations. We are by no means the only semi-cybernated society. Europe and Russia are well under way, and their machines and products compete with ours here and in the world market. The U.S.S.R. is making an all-out effort to cybernate as much of its planning-economic-industrial operation as it can.

In the second place, reducing the number of personnel in an organization reduces the magnitude of management's human relations tasks, whether these be coping with over-long coffee breaks, union negotiations, human errors, or indifference.

In the third place, cybernation permits much greater rationalization of managerial activities. The computers can produce information about what is happening now, as well as continuously up-dated information about what will be the probable consequences of specific decisions based on present and extrapolated circumstances. The results are available in a multitude of detailed or simplified displays in the form of words, tables of figures, patterns of light, growth and decay curves, dial readings, etc. In many situations, built-in feedback monitors the developing situation and deals with routine changes, errors, and needs with little or no intervention by human beings. This frees management for attention to more basic duties. . . .

Freeing management from petty distractions in these ways permits more precise and better substantiated decisions, whether they have to do with business strategy, government economic policy, equipment system planning, or military strategy and tactics. Thus, management in business or government can have much better control both over the system as it operates and over the introduction of changes into future operations. Indeed, the changes themselves may be planned in conformity with, and guided by, a strategy that is derived from a computer analysis of the future environment.

In the fourth place, cybernation allows government and industry much greater freedom in locating their facilities efficiently in relation to the accessibility of raw products, markets, transportation, and needed (or cheaper) human and material resources. Distance is no longer a barrier to control and coordination. The computers that control automated processes need not be near the factories nor the data-processing computers near their sources of information or users if other considerations are more pressing. Widely dispersed installations can be coordinated and controlled from still another place, and the dispersed units can interact with each other and affect one another's performance as easily, in many cases, as if they were all in the same place.

In the fifth place, some degree of cybernation is necessary to meet the needs of our larger population and to maintain or increase the rate of growth of the Gross National Product. An estimated 80,000,000 persons will be added to our population in the next twenty years. Beyond increases in productivity per man hour to be expected from the projected 20 per cent growth in the labor force during this same period, productive growth will have to be provided by machines.

If the criteria are control, understanding, and profits, there are strong reasons why government and business should want to, and indeed would have to, expand cybernation as rapidly as they can. The versatility of computers and automation is becoming better understood all the time by those who use them, even though, as with the human brain, most present users are far from applying their full potential. Cheap and general purpose computers or modular components applicable to many types of automatic production and decision-making are now being manufactured. . . .

The Problems of Cybernation]
Unemployment and Employment]

Blue-Collar Adults. "In the highly automated chemical industry, the number of production jobs has fallen 3% since 1956 while output has soared 27%. Though steel capacity has increased 20% since 1955, the number of men needed to operate the industry's plants—even at full capacity—has dropped 17,000. Auto employment slid from a peak of 746,000 in boom 1955 to 614,000 in November. . . . Since the meat industry's 1956 employment peak, 28,000 workers have lost their jobs despite a production increase of 3%. Bakery jobs have been in a steady decline from 174,000 in 1954 to 163,000 last year. On the farm one man can grow enough to feed 24 people; back in 1949 he could feed only 15."[9]

Further insight into the problem of declining employment for the blue-collar workers comes from union statements to the effect that the number of these employees in manufacturing has been reduced by 1,500,000 in the last six years. As one example from the service industries, automatic elevators have already displaced 40,000 operators in New York.

9. "The Automation Jobless . . . Not Fired, Just Not Hired," *Time*, LXXVII (February 24, 1961) 69. [Reference in original. Other numbered footnotes have been omitted.]

Another disturbing aspect of the blue-collar displacement problem is its impact on employment opportunities for Negroes. There is already an increasingly lopsided Negro-to-white unemployment ratio as the dock, factory, and mine operations where Negroes have hitherto found their steadiest employment are cybernated. This, plus the handicaps of bias in hiring and lack of educational opportunity, leaves Negroes very few chances to gain new skills and new jobs. Continued widespread and disproportionate firings of Negroes, if accompanied by ineffectual re-employment methods, may well produce a situation that will increase disenchantment abroad and encourage discontent and violence here.

Service Industries. It is commonly argued that, with the growth of population, there will always be more need for people in the service industries. The assumption is that these industries will be able to absorb the displaced, retrained blue-collar labor force; that automation will not seriously displace people who perform service functions; and that the demand for engineers and scientists will be so great as to provide employment for any number of the young pepole who graduate with engineering training. (Indeed, some of this demand is expected to arise from the needs of cybernetic systems themselves.)

It is all very well to speak glowingly of the coming growth in the service industries and the vast opportunities for well-paid jobs and job-upgrading that these activities will provide as blue-collar opportunities diminish. But is the future as bright and as simple as this speculation implies? In the first place, service activities will also tend to displace workers by becoming self-service, by becoming cybernated, and by being eliminated. Consider the following data: The U.S. Census Bureau was able to use fifty statisticians in 1960 to do the tabulations that required 4,100 in 1950. Even where people are not being fired, service industries can now carry on a vastly greater amount of business without hiring additional personnel; for example, a 50 per cent increase in the Bell System's volume of calls in the last ten years with only a 10 per cent increase in personnel.

Automation frequently permits the mass production of both cheap items and items of adequate to superior quality. It frequently uses methods of fabrication that make replacement of part or all of the item more efficient or less bother than repairing it. As automation results in more leisure time, certainly some of this time will be used by more and more do-it-yourselfers to replace worn-out or faulty components in home appliances that are now repaired by paid service personnel. Nor is it clear that repairing computers will be big business. Computer design is in the direction of microminiaturized components: when there is a failure in the system, the malfunctioning part is simply unplugged or pulled out, much as a drawer from a bureau, and replaced by a new unit. Routine procedures determine which component is malfunctioning, so routine that the larger computers now indicate where their own troubles are, so routine that small computers could be built to troubleshoot others. This does not mean that clever maintenance and repair people will be completely unnecessary, but it does mean that a much more careful estimate is required of the probable need for these skills in home-repair work or in computer-repair work.

Drip-dry clothes, synthetic fabrics, plus self-service dry and wet cleaning facilities, probably will outmode this type of service activity.

Identification by fingerprints, instantly checked against an up-to-date nation-wide credit rating (performed by a central computer facility), could eliminate all service activities associated with processing based on identification (for example, bank tellers). A computer that can identify fingerprints does not yet exist, but there is no reason to believe it will not be invented in the next two decades.

If people cost more than machines—either in money or because of the managerial effort involved—there will be growing incentives to replace them in one way or another in most service activities where they perform routine, predefined tasks. It is possible, of course, that eventually people will not cost more than machines, because there may be so many of them competing for jobs, including a growing number of working women. But will service people be this cheap? As union strength is weakened or threatened through reductions in blue-collar membership, unions will try, as they have already begun to do, to organize the white-collar worker and other service personnel more completely in order to help them to protect their jobs from managements willing to hire those who, having no other work to turn to, would work for less money. Former blue-collar workers who, through retraining, will join the ranks of the service group may help to produce an atmosphere conductive to such union-izing. But how many service organizations will accept the com-plications of union negotiations, strikes, personnel services, and higher wages in preference to investing in cybernation?

It is possible that as automation and computers are applied more widely an attitude of indifference to personalized service will gradually develop. People will not demand it and organiza-tions will not provide it. The family doctor is disappearing; clerks of all sorts in stores of all sorts are disappearing as well. . . . People either get used to this or, as in the case of the self-service supermarket, seem to prefer it. . . .

The greater the indifference to personalized service by both buyers and sellers, the greater the opportunity, of course, to remove human judgments from the system. Cybernation may well encourage further reductions in opportunities for service jobs.

Middle Management. The blue-collar worker and the rel-atively menial service worker will not be the only employment victims of cybernation. . . .

As cybernation moves into the areas now dominated by mid-dle management in government and in business—and this move is already beginning—growing numbers of middle managers will find themselves displaced. Perhaps the bulk of displaced mem-bers of the blue-collar and service work force might be trained "up" or "over" to other jobs with, generally speaking, little or no decline in status. But the middle manager presents a special and poignant problem. Where can he go? To firms that are not as yet assigning routine liaison, analysis, and minor executive tasks to machines? This may take care of some of the best of the displaced managers and junior executives, but if these firms are to have a future, the chances are that they will have to computer-ize eventually in order to compete. To the government? Again, some could join it, but the style and format of governmental operations may require readjustments that many junior execu-tives would be unable to make. And, in any case, government too, as we have seen, is turning to computers, and it is entirely possible that much of the work of *its* middle management will also be absorbed by the computers. Up into top management? A few, of course, but necessarily only a few. Into the service end of the organization, such as sales? Some here, certainly, if they have the talent for such work. If computers and automation lead to an even greater efflorescence of marginally differentiated articles and services, there will be a correspondingly greater emphasis on sales in an effort to compete successfully. But can this be an outlet for a truly significant portion of the displaced? And at what salary? Overseas appointments in nations not yet using cybernation at the management level? Again, for a few, but only for those with the special ability to fit into a different culture at the corresponding level from which they came.

Middle management is the group in the society with the most intensive emotional drive for success and status. Their family and social life is molded by these needs, as the endless literature on life in suburbia and exurbia demonstrate. They stand to be deeply disturbed by the threat and fact of their replacement by machines. One wonders what the threat will do to the ambitions of those who will be students and who, as followers of one of the persuasive American dreams, will have aspired to the role of middle manager "on the way up."

With the demise or downgrading of this group, changes in consumption levels and patterns can also be expected. These people, although they are not the only consumers of products of the sort advertised in *The New Yorker, Holiday,* and the like, are certainly among the largest of such consumers. They are the style-setters, the innovators, and the experimenters with new, quality products. With their loss of status and the loss of their buying power, one can imagine changes in advertising, or at least changes in the "taste" that this advertising tries to generate. It is possible that the new middle élite, the engineers, operations researchers, and systems analysts, will simply absorb the standards of the group they will have replaced. But they may be different enough in outlook and motives to have different styles in consumption.

Overworked Professionals. There are service jobs, of course, that require judgment about people by people. (We are not

including here the "personalized service" type of salesmanship.)
The shortage of people with these talents is evidenced by the
60-hour and more work-weeks of many professionals. But these
people are the products of special education, special motives,
and special attitudes that are not shared to any great degree by
those who turn to blue-collar or routine service tasks. Increasing
the proportion of citizens with this sort of professional com-
petence would require systematic changes in attitudes, motives,
and levels of education, not to mention more teachers, a professional service already in short supply. . . .

Even if the teachers and the appropriate attitudes already
existed, service needs at the professional level might not be great
enough to absorb a large share of the potentially unemployed.
Much of the work that now takes up the time of many professionals, such as doctors and lawyers, could be done by computers
—just as much of the time of teachers is now taken up by teaching what could be done as well by machines.

The development of procedures for medical diagnosis by machine is proceeding well. A completely automatic analysis of
data can produce just as good a diagnosis of brain malfunction
as that done by a highly trained doctor. Cybernated diagnosis
will be used in conjunction with improved multi-purpose anti-
biotics and with microminiaturized, highly sensitive, and accurate
telemetering equipment (which can be swallowed, imbedded
in the body, or affixed to it) in order to detect, perhaps at
a distance, significant symptoms. All of these developments are
likely to change the nature of a doctor's time-consuming tasks.
In the field of law successful codification, so that searches and
evaluations can be automatic, as well as changes in legal procedures, will probably make the lawyer's work substantially
different from what it is today, at least in terms of how he
allocates his time.

Computers probably will perform tasks like these because
the shortage of professionals will be more acute at the time the
computers acquire the necessary capabilities. By then, speeded-
up data processing and interpretation will be necessary if professional services are to be rendered with any adequacy. Once
the computers are in operation, the need for additional professional people may be only moderate, and those who are needed

will have to be of very high calibre indeed. Probably only a small percentage of the population will have the natural endowments to meet such high requirements. A tour of the strongholds of science and engineering and conversations with productive scientists and engineers already lead to the conclusion that much of what now appears to be creative, barrier-breaking "research and development" is in fact routine work done by mediocre scientists and engineers. We lose sight of the fact that not everybody with dirty hands or a white coat is an Einstein or a Steinmetz. Many first-class scientists in universities will testify that one consequence of the increasingly large federal funds for research is that many more mediocre scientists doing mediocre work are being supported. No doubt for some time to come good use can be made by good professionals of battalions of mediocre professionals. But battalions are not armies. And sooner or later one general of science or engineering will be able to fight this war for knowledge more effectively with more push-buttons than with more intellectual foot-soldiers.

Untrained Adolescents. "Altogether the United States will need 13,500,000 more jobs in the Sixties merely to keep abreast of the expected growth in the labor force. This means an average of 25,000 new jobs each week, on top of those required to drain the reservoir of present unemployment and to replace jobs made superfluous by improved technology. In the last year, despite the slackness of employment opportunities, 2,500,000 more people came into the job scramble than left it through death, age, sickness or voluntary withdrawal. This was more than double the 835,000 average annual growth in the working population in the last ten years. By the end of this decade, 3,000,000 youngsters will be starting their quest for jobs each year, as against 2,000,000 now. This almost automatically guarantees trouble in getting the over-all unemployment rate down to 4 per cent because the proportion of idleness among teen-age workers is always far higher than it is among their elders."[15]

The Labor Department estimates that 26,000,000 adolescents

15. A. H. Raskin, "Hard-Core Unemployment a Rising National Problem," *New York Times*, April 6, 1961, p. 18. [Reference in original. See footnote 9 above.]

will seek work in the Sixties. If present performance is any in-
dicator, in the decade ahead 30 per cent of adolescents will
continue to drop out before completing high school and many
who could go to college won't. The unemployment rate for
such drop-outs is about 30 per cent now. Robert E. Iffert, of the
Department of Health, Education, and Welfare, concluded in a
1958 study that approximately one-fourth of the students who
enter college leave after their freshman year never to return.
Figures compiled since then lead him to conclude that there has
been no significant change, in spite of the National Defense
Education Act, which was supposed to help reduce this figure.

If some figures recently given by James B. Conant turn out to
be typical, at least one situation is much more serious than the
average would imply. He found that in one of our largest cities,
in an almost exclusively Negro slum of 125,000, 70 per cent of
the boys and girls between 16 and 21 were out of school and
unemployed. In another city, in an almost exclusively Negro
slum, in the same age group, 48 per cent of the high school graduates were unemployed and 63 per cent of the high school drop-
outs were unemployed. These adolescents would in the normal
course join the untrained or poorly trained work force, a work
force that will be more and more the repository of untrainable
or untrained people displaced from their jobs by cybernation.
These adolescents will have the following choices: they can stay
in school, for which they are unsuited either by motivation or by
intelligence; they can seek training that will raise them out of the
untrained work force; they can compete in the growing manpower pool of those seeking relatively unskilled jobs; or they can
loaf.

If they loaf, almost inevitably they are going to become delin-
quent. Thus, without adequate occupational outlets for these
youths, cybernation may contribute substantially to further social disruption. . . .

Persuading drop-outs to stay in school will not be easy.
Teachers will not be easy to recruit unless they are well paid.
There is already a shortage of teachers. And let no one suggest
that an easy source of teachers would be displaced workers.
There is no reason to believe that they have the verbal and so-
cial facility to teach, and most of them would have nothing to

teach but skills that have become obsolete. Some, of course, might be taught to teach, though this would add obvious complications to the whole effort.

Knowing what to teach will depend on knowing what types of jobs are likely to exist when the student finishes his training. This will require knowledge about the trends and plans of local industry, if that is where the youths are to work (and if that is where industry plans to stay!), and of industries in other localities, if the youths are willing to move. Such knowledge often does not exist in a rapidly changing world or, if it exists, may not be forthcoming from businesses more concerned with competition than with the frustrated "delinquents" of their community. As of now, in the words of Dr. Conant, "unemployment of youth is literally nobody's affair."

Some Proposed Solutions. Retraining is often proposed as if it were also the cure-all for coping with adults displaced by cybernation as well as young people. In some circumstances it has worked well for some people, especially with office personnel who have been displaced by data-processing computers and have learned other office jobs, including servicing the computers. But in other cases, especially with poorly educated blue-collar workers, retraining has not always been successful, nor have new jobs based on that retraining been available. . . .

The problem of retraining blue-collar workers is formidable enough. But, in view of the coming role of cybernation in the service industries, the retraining problem for service personnel seems insuperable. No one has seriously proposed what service tasks this working group could be retrained *for*—to say nothing of training them for jobs that would pay high enough wages to make them good consumers of the cornucopia of products manufactured by automation.

Another proposal for coping with the unemployment-via-cybernation problem is shorter hours for the same pay. This approach is intended to maintain the ability of workers to consume the products of cybernation and, in the case of blue-collar workers, to maintain the strength of unions. This would retain the consumer purchasing capacity for x workers in those situations where the nature of the cybernation process is such that x men would do essentially the same work as x plus y men used to do. But when the task itself is eliminated or new tasks are developed that need different talents, shorter shifts clearly will not solve the problem. The latter conditions are the more likely ones as cybernation becomes more sophisticated. . . .

An obvious solution to unemployment is a public works program. If our understanding of the direction of cybernation is correct, the government will probably be faced for the indefinite future with the need to support part of the population through public works. There is no dearth of public work to be done, and it is not impossible that so much would continue to be needed that an appropriately organized public works program could stimulate the economy to the point that a substantial portion of the work force could be re-absorbed into the private sector. That is, although the proportion of workers needed for any particular task will be reduced through the use of cybernation, the total number of tasks that need to be done could equal or exceed the absolute number of people available to do them. It is not known whether this situation would obtain for enough tasks in enough places so that the portion of the population working on public projects would be relatively small. However, if it should turn out that this felicitous state of affairs could be realized in principle, clearly it could only be realized and sustained if there were to be considerable and continuous centralized planning and control over financing, the choice of public projects, and the places where they were to be done. If, for whatever reasons, this situation could not be achieved, the public works payroll would remain very large indeed.

What would be the effects on the attitudes and aspirations of a society, and particularly of its leadership, when a significant part of it is overtly supported by governmental public works programs? ("Overtly" is used because much of the aerospace industry in particular and of the weapons systems industry in general is subsidized by the government right now: they literally live off cost plus fixed fee contracts, and there is no other comparable market for their products.) Whatever else the attitudes might be, they certainly would not be conducive to maintaining the spirit of a capitalistic economy. This shift in perspective may or may not be desirable, but those who think it would be undesirable should realize that encouraging the extension of cybernation, in the interests of free enterprise and better profits, may be self-defeating. . . .

Additional Leisure]

It is generally recognized that sooner or later automation and computers will mean shorter working hours and greater leisure for most if not all of the American people. It is also generally, if vaguely, recognized that there probably are problems connected with the use of leisure that will take time to work out.

Two stages need to be distinguished: the state of leisure over the next decade or two, when our society will still be in transition to a way of life based on the widespread application of cybernation; and the relatively stable state some time in the future when supposedly everybody will have more leisure time than today and enough security to enjoy it. The transitional stage is our chief concern, for the end is far enough off to make more than some general speculations about it footless. At this later time people's behavior and attitudes will be conditioned as much by presently unforeseeable social and technological developments as by the character and impact of cybernation itself.

During the transition there will be four different "leisure" classes: 1) the unemployed, 2) the low-salaried employees working short hours, 3) the adequately paid to high-salaried group working short hours, and 4) those with no more leisure than they now have—which in the case of many professionals means very few hours of leisure indeed.

Leisure Class One. Today, most of the unemployed are from low educational backgrounds where leisure has always been simply a respite from labor. No particular aspirations to or positive attitudes about the creative use of leisure characterize this group. Since their main concern is finding work and security, what they do with their leisure is a gratuitous question; whatever they do, it will hardly contribute to someone else's profits. . . .

As cybernation expands its domain, the unemployed "leisure" class will not consist only of blue-collar workers. The displaced service worker will also swell the ranks of the unemployed, as well as the relatively well-trained white-collar workers until they can find jobs or displace from jobs the less well-trained or less presentable, like the college graduate filling-station attendant of not so many years ago. It is doubtful that during their unemployed period these people will look upon that time as "leisure" time. For the poorly educated, watching television, gossiping, and puttering around the house will be low-cost time-fillers between unemployment checks; for the better educated, efforts at systematic self-improvement, perhaps, as well as reading, television, and gossip; for many, it will be time spent in making the agonizing shift in style of living required of the unemployed. These will be more or less individual tragedies representing at any given time a small portion of the work force of the nation, statistically speaking. They will be spread over the cities and suburbs of the nation, reflecting the consequences of actions taken by particular firms. If the spirit of the day grows more statistical than individualistic, as this paper suggests later that it well might, there is a real question of our capacity to make the necessary organized effort in order to anticipate and cope with these "individual" cases. . . .

One wonders, too, what women, with their growing tendency to work—to combat boredom as well as for money—will do as the barriers to work become higher, as menial white-collar jobs disappear under the impact of cybernation, and as the competition increases for the remaining jobs. If there are jobs, 6,000,000 more women are expected to be in the labor force in 1970 than were in it in 1960. Out of a total labor force of 87,000,000 at that time, 30,000,000 would be women. To the extent that women who want jobs to combat boredom will not be able to get them, there will be a growing leisure class that will be untrained for and does not want the added leisure. As for those women who have a source of adequate income but want jobs because they are bored, they will have less and less to do at home as automated procedures further routinize domestic chores.

Leisure Class Two. A different kind of leisure problem will exist for the low-income group working shorter hours. This group will be composed of people with the attitudes and behavior traditionally associated with this class, as well as some others who will have drifted into the group as a result of having been displaced by cybernation. What evidence there is indicates that now and probably for years to come, when members of this group have leisure time as a result of fewer working hours, the tendency will be to take another job. It is reasonable to believe that the general insecurity inevitably arising from changing work arrangements and the over-all threat of automation would encourage "moonlighting" rather than the use of free time for recreation. If these people cannot find second jobs, it is hard to imagine their doing anything different with their free time from what they do now, since they will not have the money, the motives, or the knowledge to search out different activities. . . .

Leisure Class Three. Workers with good or adequate income employed for shorter hours are the group usually thought of when one talks about the positive opportunities for using extra leisure in a cybernated world. Its members for the most part will be the professional, semi-professional, or skilled workers who will contribute enough in their social role to command a good salary but who will not be so rare as to be needed for 40 hours a week. These people already value learning and learning to learn. Given knowledge about, money for, and access to new leisure-time activities, they are likely to make use of them. They could help to do various desirable social service tasks in the community, tasks for which there is not enough money to attract paid personnel of high enough quality. They could help to teach, and, by virtue of their own intimate experiences with cybernation, they would be able to pass on the attitudes and knowledge that will be needed to live effectively in a cybernated world. It is likely, too, that this group will be the chief repository of creative, skilled manual talents. In a nation living off mass-produced, automatically produced products, there may be a real if limited demand for hand-made articles. (We may become again in part a nation of small shopkeepers and craftsmen.) In general, this group of people will probably produce and consume most of its own leisure-time activities.

Leisure Class Four. The fourth group consists of those who probably will have little or no more leisure time than they now have except to the extent permitted by additions to their ranks and by the services of cybernation. But extrapolations for the foreseeable future indicate insufficient increases in the class of presently overworked professionals and executives. Computers should be able to remove many of the more tedious aspects of their work in another few years, but for some time to come these people will continue to be overburdened. Some of this relatively small proportion of the population may manage to get down to a 40-hour week, and these lucky few should find no difficulty in using their leisure as productively and creatively as those in the third group.

Thus, during the transition period, it is the second group, the low-salaried workers who cannot or will not find another job, that presents the true leisure problem, as distinct from the unemployment problem. Here is where the multiple problems connected with private and public make-play efforts may prove very difficult indeed. We have some knowledge about relatively low-income workers who become voluntarily interested in adult education and adult play sessions, but we have had no real experience with the problems of how to stimulate the interests and change the attitudes of a large population that is forced to work shorter hours but is used to equating work and security, that will be bombarded with an advertising *geist* praising consumption and glamorous leisure, that will be bounded closely on one side by the unemployed and on the other by a relatively well-to-do community to which it cannot hope to aspire. Boredom may drive these people to seek new leisure-time activities if they are provided and do not cost much. But boredom combined with other factors may also make for frustration and aggression and all the social and political problems these qualities imply.

Decisions and Public Opinion]

Privileged Information. The government must turn to computers to handle many of its major problems simply because the data involved are so massive and the factors so complex that only machines can handle the material fast enough to allow

timely action based on understanding of the facts. In the nature
of the situation, the decisions made by the government with the
help of computers would be based in good part on computers
that have been programmed with more or less confidential information—and privileged access to information, at the time it
is needed, is a sufficient if not always necessary condition for
attaining and maintaining power. There may not be any easy
way to insure that decisions based on computers could not become a threat to democratic government. . . .

The Control of Cybernation]

Time and Planning]

Time is crucial in any plan to cope with cybernation. Ways of
ameliorating its adverse effects require thinking farther ahead
than we ever do. In a society in the process of becoming cybernated, education and training for work as well as education and
training for leisure must begin early in life. Shifts in behavior,
attitudes, and aspirations take a long time to mature. It will be
extraordinarily difficult to produce appropriate "culture-bearers,"
both parents and teachers, in sufficient numbers, distribution,
and quality in the relatively brief time available. It is hard to
see, for example, how Congress, composed in good part of older
men acting from traditional perspectives and operating by sen-
iority, could recognize soon enough and then legislate well
enough to produce the fundamental shifts needed to meet the
complexities of cybernation. It is hard to see how our style of
pragmatic making-do and frantic crash programs can radically
change in the next few years. This is especially hard to visualize
when the whole cybernation situation is such that we find it
impossible to determine the consequences of cybernation even
in the medium long run. The differences expressed in the public
statements of business and labor demonstrate that any reconciliation of interests will be a very long-range effort indeed. "Drastic" actions to forestall or eliminate the ill-effects of cybernation
will not be taken in time unless we change our operating style
drastically.

Among the many factors contributing to the stability of a social system are two intimately intertwined ones: the types of tasks that are performed; and the nature of the relationship between the attitudes of the members of the society toward these tasks and their opinions about the proper goals of the individual members of the society and the right ways of reaching them.

The long-range stability of the social system depends on a population of young people properly educated to enter the adult world of tasks and attitudes. Once, the pace of change was slow enough to permit a comfortable margin of compatibility between the adult world and the one children were trained to expect. This compatibility no longer exists. Now we have to ask: What should be the education of a population more and more enveloped in cybernation? What are the appropriate attitudes toward and training for participation in government, the use of leisure, standards of consumption, particular occupations?

Education must cope with the tranisional period when the disruption among different socio-economic and occupational groups will be the greatest; and the later, relatively stable period, if it ever comes to exist, when most people would have adequate income and shorter working hours. The problem involves looking ahead five, ten, twenty years to see what are likely to be the occupational and social needs and attitudes of those future periods; planning the intellectual and social education of each age group in the numbers needed; motivating young people to seek certain types of jobs and to adopt the desirable and necessary attitudes; providing enough suitable teachers; being able to alter all of these as the actualities in society and technology indicate; and directing the pattern of cybernation so that it fits with the expected kinds and distribution of abilities and attitudes produced by home and school. . . .

16

The New Frontier

John F. Kennedy (1917-1963), son of Joseph P. Kennedy, served as congressman from Massachusetts from 1947 to 1953, and was elected senator in 1952. His *Profiles in Courage* (1956) won a Pulitzer prize. He received the Purple Heart and the Navy and Marine Corps Medal for gallantry as a PT-boat commander during World War II. He was elected President of the United States in 1960. Cold biographical facts and a listing of legislative accomplishments do not explain the hold which President Kennedy was able to obtain on the hearts and aspirations of the American people and of countless others throughout the world. The outpouring of grief and sympathy which occurred after his assassination on November 22, 1963, provided dramatic evidence that, even more than the hard-headed qualities of political realism which he obviously possessed, he had come to symbolize youthful vigor and idealism. Perhaps his most eloquent expression of this quality was his Inaugural Address delivered on January 20, 1961, less than three years before his death.

In reading President Kennedy's Budget Message of 1962, note (1) the economic philosophy expressed; (2) the programs which constituted the New Frontier; (3) comparisons with the program of the Fair Deal as described in Truman's State of the Union Message of 1948 [8]; and (4) contrasts with Eisenhower's economic philosophy as expressed in his Budget Message of 1954 [10]. For further reading see *Economic Report of the President*, transmitted to Congress, January, 1962 (Washington, 1962); James M. Burns, *John Kennedy: A Political Profile* (New York, 1960); and Norman Mailer, *The Presidential Papers* (New York, 1963).

A. John F. Kennedy's Inaugural Address
January 20, 1961

VICE PRESIDENT JOHNSON, MR. SPEAKER, MR. CHIEF *Justice, President Eisenhower, Vice President Nixon, President Truman, Reverend Clergy, fellow citizens:* We observe today not a victory of party but a celebration of

Public Papers of the President of the United States: John F. Kennedy . . . January 20 to December 31, 1961 (Washington, 1962), pp. 1-3.

freedom—symbolizing an end as well as a beginning—signifying renewal as well as change. For I have sworn before you and Almighty God the same solemn oath our forebears prescribed nearly a century and three quarters ago.

The world is very different now. For man holds in his mortal hands the power to abolish all forms of human poverty and all forms of human life. And yet the same revolutionary beliefs for which our forebears fought are still at issue around the globe— the belief that the rights of man come not from the generosity of the state but from the hand of God.

We dare not forget today that we are the heirs of that first revolution. Let the word go forth from this time and place, to friend and foe alike, that the torch has been passed to a new generation of Americans—born in this century, tempered by war, disciplined by a hard and bitter peace, proud of our ancient heritage—and unwilling to witness or permit the slow undoing of those human rights to which this nation has always been committed today at home and around the world.

Let every nation know, whether it wishes us well or ill, that we shall pay any price, bear any burden, meet any hardship, support any friend, oppose any foe to assure the survival and the success of liberty.

This much we pledge—and more.

To those old allies whose cultural and spiritual origins we share, we pledge the loyalty of faithful friends. United, there is little we cannot do in a host of cooperative ventures. Divided, there is little we can do—for we dare not meet a powerful challenge at odds and split asunder.

To those new states whom we welcome to the ranks of the free, we pledge our word that one form of colonial control shall not have passed away merely to be replaced by a far more iron tyranny. We shall not always expect to find them supporting our view. But we shall always hope to find them strongly supporting their own freedom—and to remember that, in the past, those who foolishly sought power by riding the back of the tiger ended up inside.

To those peoples in the huts and villages of half the globe struggling to break the bonds of mass misery, we pledge our best efforts to help them help themselves, for whatever period is required—not because the communists may be doing it, not because we seek their votes, but because it is right. If a free society cannot help the many who are poor, it cannot save the few who are rich.

To our sister republics south of our border, we offer a special pledge—to convert our good words into good deeds—in a new alliance for progress—to assist free men and free governments in casting off the chains of poverty. But this peaceful revolution of hope cannot become the prey of hostile powers. Let all our neighbors know that we shall join with them to oppose aggression or subversion anywhere in the Americas. And let every other power know that this Hemisphere intends to remain the master of its own house.

To that world assembly of sovereign states, the United Nations, our last best hope in an age where the instruments of war have far outpaced the instruments of peace, we renew our pledge of support—to prevent it from becoming merely a forum for invective—to strengthen its shield of the new and the weak —and to enlarge the area in which its writ may run.

Finally, to those nations who would make themselves our adversary, we offer not a pledge but a request: that both sides begin anew the quest for peace, before the dark powers of destruction unleashed by science engulf all humanity in planned or accidental self-destruction.

We dare not tempt them with weakness. For only when our arms are sufficient beyond doubt can we be certain beyond doubt that they will never be employed.

But neither can two great and powerful groups of nations take comfort from our present course—both sides overburdened by the cost of modern weapons, both rightly alarmed by the steady spread of the deadly atom, yet both racing to alter that uncertain balance of terror that stays the hand of mankind's final war.

So let us begin anew—remembering on both sides that civility is not a sign of weakness, and sincerity is always subject to proof. Let us never negotiate out of fear. But let us never fear to negotiate.

Let both sides explore what problems unite us instead of belaboring those problems which divide us.

Let both sides, for the first time, formulate serious and precise proposals for the inspection and control of arms—and bring the absolute power to destroy other nations under the absolute control of all nations.

Let both sides seek to invoke the wonders of science instead of its terrors. Together let us explore the stars, conquer the deserts, eradicate disease, tap the ocean depths and encourage the arts and commerce.

Let both sides unite to heed in all corners of the earth the command of Isaiah—to "undo the heavy burdens . . . (and) let the oppressed go free."

And if a beach-head of cooperation may push back the jungle of suspicion, let both sides join in creating a new endeavor, not a new balance of power, but a new world of law, where the strong are just and the weak secure and the peace preserved.

All this will not be finished in the first one hundred days. Nor will it be finished in the first one thousand days, nor in the life of this Administration, nor even perhaps in our lifetime on this planet. But let us begin.

In your hands, my fellow citizens, more than mine, will rest the final success or failure of our course. Since this country was founded, each generation of Americans has been summoned to give testimony to its national loyalty. The graves of young Americans who answered the call to service surround the globe.

Now the trumpet summons us again—not as a call to bear arms, though arms we need—not as a call to battle, though embattled we are—but a call to bear the burden of a long twilight struggle, year in and year out, "rejoicing in hope, patient in tribulation"—a struggle against the common enemies of man: tyranny, poverty, disease and war itself.

Can we forge against these enemies a grand and global alliance, North and South, East and West, that can assure a more fruitful life for all mankind? Will you join in that historic effort?

In the long history of the world, only a few generations have been granted the role of defending freedom in its hour of maximum danger. I do not shrink from this responsibility—I welcome it. I do not believe that any of us would exchange places with any other people or any other generation. The energy, the faith, the devotion which we bring to this endeavor will light our country and all who serve it—and the glow from that fire can truly light the world.

And so, my fellow Americans: ask not what your country can do for you—ask what you can do for your country.

My fellow citizens of the world: ask not what America will do for you, but what together we can do for the freedom of man.

Finally, whether you are citizens of America or citizens of the world, ask of us here the same high standards of strength and sacrifice which we ask of you. With a good conscience our only sure reward, with history the final judge of our deeds, let us go forth to lead the land we love, asking His blessing and His help, but knowing that here on earth God's work must truly be our own.*

°NOTE [in original]: The President spoke at 12:52 p.m. from a platform erected at the east front of the Capitol. Immediately before the address the oath of office was administered by Chief Justice Warren.

The President's opening words "Reverend Clergy" referred to His Eminence Richard Cardinal Cushing, Archbishop of Boston; His Eminence Archbishop Iakovos, head of the Greek Archdiocese of North and South America; the Reverend Dr. John Barclay, pastor of the Central Christian Church, Austin, Tex.; and Rabbi Dr. Nelson Glueck, President of the Hebrew Union College, Cincinnati, Ohio.

B. John F. Kennedy's Budget Message of 1962
Fiscal Year 1963. January 18, 1962

To THE CONGRESS OF THE UNITED STATES: I PRESENT with this message my budget recommendations for the fiscal year 1963, beginning next July 1.

This is the first complete budget of this administration. It has been prepared with two main objectives in mind:

First, to carry forward efficiently the activities—ranging from defense to postal services, from oceanographic research to space exploration—which by national consensus have been assigned to the Federal Government to execute;

Second, to achieve a financial plan—a relationship between receipts and expenditures—which will contribute to economic

New York Times, January 19, 1962. Copyright by The New York Times. Reprinted by permission.

growth, high employment, and price stability in our national economy.

Budget expenditures for fiscal 1963 will total $92.5 billion under my recommendations—an increase of $3.4 billion over the amount estimated for the present fiscal year. More than three-quarters of the increase is accounted for by national security and space activities, and the bulk of the remainder by fixed interest charges.

Because of the increasing requirements for national security, I have applied strict standards of urgency in reviewing proposed expenditures in this budget. Many desirable new projects and activities are being deferred. I am, moreover, recommending legislation which will reduce certain budgetary outlays, such as the postal deficit and the cost of farm price and production adjustments.

It would not, of course, be sensible to defer expenditures which are of great significance to the growth and strength of the Nation. This budget therefore includes a number of increases in existing programs and some new proposals of high priority—such as improvements in education and scientific research, retraining the unemployed and providing young people with greater employment opportunities, and aid to urban mass transportation.

Budget receipts in fiscal year 1963 are estimated to total $93 billion, an increase of $10.9 billion over the recession-affected level of the present fiscal year. These receipts estimates are based on the expectation that the brisk recovery from last year's recession will continue through the coming year and beyond, carrying the gross national product during calendar 1962 to a record $570 billion.

The administrative budget for 1963 thus shows a modest surplus of about $500 million. Federal accounts on the basis of the consolidated cash statement—combining the administrative budget with other Federal activities, mainly the social security, highway, and other trust funds—show an estimated excess of receipts from the public of $1.8 billion over payments to the public. And in the terms in which our national income accounts are calculated—using accrued rather than cash receipts and expenditures, and including only transactions directly affecting production and income—the Federal surplus is estimated at $4.4 billion.

By all three measures in current use, therefore, the Federal Government is expected to operate in 1963 with some surplus. This is the policy which seems appropriate at the present time. The economy is moving strongly forward, with employment and incomes rising. The prospects are favorable for further rises in the coming year in private expenditures, both consumption and investment. To plan a deficit under such circumstances would increase the risk of inflationary pressures, damaging alike to our domestic economy and to our international balance of payments. On the other hand, we are still far short of full capacity use of plant and manpower. To plan a larger surplus would risk choking off economic recovery and contributing to a premature downturn.

Under present economic circumstances, therefore, a moderate surplus of the magnitude projected above is the best national policy, considering all of our needs and objectives.

Budget Expenditures]

The total of budget expenditures—estimated at $92.5 billion in fiscal 1963—is determined in large measure by the necessary but costly programs designed to achieve our national security and international objectives in the current world situation. Expenditures for national defense, international, and space programs account for more than three-fifths of total 1963 budget outlays, and for more than three-fourths of the estimated increase in expenditures in 1963 as compared to 1962. Indeed, apart from the expected increase in interest payments, expenditures for the so-called "domestic civil" functions of government have been held virtually stable between 1962 and 1963.

Within this total there are important shifts in direction and emphasis. Expenditures for agricultural programs, for the postal deficit, and for temporary extended unemployment compensation are expected to drop. The fact that funds for these purposes can be reduced permits us to make increases in other important areas—notably education, health, housing, and natural resource development—without raising significantly total expenditures for domestic civil functions.

National defense. This budget carries forward the policies instituted within the past 12 months to strengthen our military forces and to increase the flexibility with which they can be controlled and applied. The key elements in our defense program include: a strategic offensive force which would survive and respond overwhelmingly after a massive nuclear attack; a command and control system which would survive and direct the response; an improved anti-bomber defense system; a civil defense program which would help to protect an important proportion of our population from the perils of nuclear fallout; combat-ready limited war forces and the air and sealift needed to move them quickly to wherever they might have to be deployed; and special forces to help our allies cope with the threat of Communist-sponsored insurrection and subversion.

Increases in expenditures for the Nation's defense are largely responsible for the rise in the budget of this administration compared to that of its predecessor. For fiscal years 1962 and 1963, expenditures for the military functions of the Department of Defense are estimated at about $9 billion higher, and new obligational authority at $12 to $15 billion more, than would have been required to carry forward the program as it stood a year ago.

For the coming year, the budget provides for further significant increases in the capabilities of our strategic forces, including additional Minuteman missiles and Polaris submarines. These forces are large and versatile enough to survive any attack which could be launched against us today and strike back decisively. The programs proposed in this budget are designed to assure that we will continue to have this capability in the future. This assurance is based on an exhaustive analysis of all the available data on Soviet military forces and the strengths and vulnerabilities of our own forces under a wide range of possible contingencies.

To strengthen the defenses of the North American Continent, this budget proposes additional measures to increase the effectiveness of our anti-bomber defense system, continued efforts to improve our warning of ballistic missile attack, and further research and development at a maximum rate on anti-missile defense possibilities.

The budget for the current year provides for identifying and marking available civilian shelter space for approximately 50 million people. This phase of the civil defense program is proceeding ahead of schedule. For 1963, I am requesting nearly $700 million for civil defense activities of the Department of Defense, including $460 million for a new cost-sharing program with State and local governments and private organizations to provide shelters in selected community buildings, such as schools and hospitals.

Although a global nuclear war poses the gravest threat to our survival, it is not the most probable form of conflict as long as we maintain the forces needed to make a nuclear war disastrous to any foe. Military aggression on a lesser scale is far more likely. If we are to retain for ourselves a choice other than a nuclear holocaust or retreat, we must increase considerably our conventional forces. This is a task we share with our free world allies. . . .

International affairs and finance. A significant change has taken place in our international assistance programs in recent years. Military assistance expenditures are declining to an estimated $1.4 billion in 1963 compared with $2.2 billion 5 years earlier. The more industrialized European countries have almost completely taken over the cost of their own armament. In less developed countries, the military assistance program continues to provide essential maintenance, training, and selective modernization of equipment, with increased emphasis on internal security, including anti-guerilla warfare.

On the other hand, expenditures for economic and financial assistance to the developing nations of the world have been increasing and are estimated at $2.5 billion in 1963. These expenditures, largely in the form of loans, will rise further in later years as development loan commitments being made currently are drawn upon. A corresponding increase is taking place in the contributions of other industrialized countries.

The new Agency for International Development has been providing needed leadership in coordinating the various elements of our foreign aid programs throughout the world. A consistent effort is being made to relate military and economic assistance to the overall capabilities and needs of recipient countries to achieve economic growth and sustain adequate military strength. To make our assistance more effective, increasing emphasis is being placed on self-help measures and necessary reforms in these countries. The authority provided last year to make long-term loan commitments to developing countries will be of invaluable assistance to orderly long-range planning. Efforts will also be made to foster more effectively the contribution of private enterprise to development, though such means as investment guarantees and assistance for surveys of investment opportunities.

In August 1961, the United States formally joined with its neighbors to the south in the establishment of the Alliance for Progress, an historic cooperative effort to speed the economic and social development of the American Republics. For their part, the Latin American countries agreed to undertake a strenuous program of social and economic reform and development through this decade. As this program of reform and development proceeds, the United States is pledged to help. To this end, I am proposing a special long-term authorization for $3 billion of aid to the Alliance for Progress within the next 4 years. In addition, substantial continued development loans are expected from the Export-Import Bank and from U.S. funds being administered by the Inter-American Development Bank. These, together with the continued flow of agricultural commodities under the Food for Peace program, will mean support for the Alliance for Progress in 1963 subsequently exceeding $1 billion.

Space search and technology. Last year I proposed and the Congress agreed that this Nation should embark on a greater effort to explore and make use of the space environment. This greater effort will result in increased expenditures in 1962 and 1963, combined, of about $1.1 billion above what they would have been under the policies of the preceding administration; measured in terms of new obligational authority, the increase is $2.4 billion for the 2 years. With this increase in funds there has been a major stepup in the programs of the National Aeronautics and Space Administration in such fields as communications and meteorology and in the most dramatic effort of all

—mastery of space symbolized by an attempt to send a man to the moon and back safely to earth.

Action is being taken to develop the complex Apollo space-craft in which the manned lunar flights will be made, and to develop the large rockets required to boost the spacecraft to the moon. The techniques of manned space flight, particularly those of long-term flight and of rendezvous between two spacecraft in earth orbit, are being studied both in ground research and in new flight programs.

Our space program has far broader significance, however, than the achievement of manned space flight. The research effort connected with the space program—and particularly the tremendous technological advances necessary to permit space flight—will have great impact in increasing the rate of technical progress throughout the economy.

Domestic civil functions. Despite the necessary heavy emphasis we are giving to defense, international, and space activities, the budget reflects many important proposals to strengthen our national economy and society. It has been possible to include these proposals without any substantial increase in the total cost of domestic civil functions mainly because of proposed reductions in postal and agricultural expenditures. Some of the more important proposals in domestic civil programs are mentioned below.

Agriculture and agricultural resources. In the development of farm programs we are striving to make effective use of American agricultural abundance, to adjust farm production to bring it in line with domestic and export requirements, and to maintain and increase income for those who are engaged in farming. The steps taken thus far, including the temporary wheat and feed grain legislation enacted in the last session of the Congress, contributed significantly to the rise in farm income last year and to some reduction—the first in 9 years—in surplus stocks. However, new long-range legislation is needed to permit further adaptation of our farm programs to the rapidly increasing productive efficiency in agriculture and to avoid continuing high budgetary costs. The reduction in agricultural expenditures in this budget (from $6.3 billion in 1962 to $5.8 billion in 1963) reflects the proposals to this end which I shall be presenting to the Congress in a special message.

The 1963 budget also provides for expansion of the food stamp plan into additional pilot areas, and for a substantial increase in Rural Electrification Administration loan funds—to permit financing of additional generation and transmission facilities where that is necessary. The adequacy of the funds recommended will depend on the willingness of other power suppliers to meet the requirements of the rural electric cooperatives on a reasonable basis.

Natural resources. Estimated expenditures of $2.3 billion in this budget for the conservation and development of our natural resources are higher than in any previous year.

The 1963 budget makes provision for the Corps of Engineers, the Bureau of Reclamation, and the Tennessee Valley Authority to start construction on 43 new water resources projects with an estimated total Federal cost of $600 million. The longe-range programs for the national parks and forests are also being strengthened.

One of our most pressing problems is the adequate provision of outdoor recreational facilities to meet the needs of our expanding population. The Federal Government, State and local agencies, and private groups must all share in the solution. By the end of this month the comprehensive report of the Outdoor Recreation Resources Review Commission is expected to be available. The Secretary of the Interior, at my request, is preparing a plan for the Federal Government to meet its share of the responsibility for providing outdoor recreational opportunities, including those related to fish and wildlife.

Commerce and transportation. Budget expenditures for commerce and transportation programs are estimated to decline from $2.9 billion in 1962 to $2.5 billion in 1963. This decline reflects mainly a drop of $592 million for the postal service, based on my legislative proposal to increase postal rates to a level that will cover the costs of postal operations, except for those services properly charged to the general taxpayer.

Outlays for the Federal-aid highway program are financed almost entirely through the highway trust fund and are not included in the budget total. Combined, Federal budget and trust fund expenditures for commerce and transportation programs in 1963 will amount to almost $6 billion.

Substantially increased expenditures are provided in the 1963 budget for the new program to assist the redevelopment of areas with persistent unemployment and underemployment and for the expanding development and operation of the Federal airways system.

Housing and community development. The long strides forward in housing and community development programs authorized by the Housing Act of 1961 are making it possible to accelerate progress in renewing our cities, in financing needed public facilities, in preserving open space, and in supplying housing accommodations, both public and private, within the means of low- and middle-income families and elderly people. The major new proposal I expect to make in this field will extend the authority for Federal aids to urban mass transportation.

Health, labor, and welfare. Budget expenditures for health, labor, and welfare programs are estimated at $5.1 billion and trust fund expenditures at $21.6 billion in 1963. The budget includes increased funds for health research and for a major strengthening of the programs of the Public Health Service, the Office of Vocational Rehabilitation, and the Food and Drug Administration. The budget and trust accounts also reflect the legislative recommendations which are pending in the Congress to provide a substantial increase in aid for medical education and to enact health insurance for the aged through social security.

I have given particular attention in this budget to strengthening the labor and manpower functions of the Department of Labor and related agencies. In addition to increased funds for the United States Employment Service and for other existing Federal programs, the budget includes funds for the urgently needed legislation providing for Federal aid for training or retraining unemployed workers, and for the training of our

young people through an experimental youth employment opportunities program.

Many American families rely for help and for a new start in
life upon the public assistance programs. Yet these programs
frequently lack both the services and the means to discharge
their purpose constructively. This budget includes substantial
increases for public assistance. I am also proposing a significant
modernization and strengthening of the welfare programs to
emphasize those services which can help restore families to self-
sufficiency.

Education. Expenditures for existing and proposed education
programs are estimated to be $1.5 billion in 1963, an increase
of $327 million over 1962. A strong educational system provid-
ing ready access for all to high quality free public elementary
and secondary schools is indispensable in our democratic society. Moreover, able students should not be denied a higher
education because they cannot pay expenses or because their
community or State cannot afford to provide good college facilities. This budget therefore includes funds for the legislative
recommendations pending before the Congress to provide loans
for the construction of college academic facilities and funds for
college scholarships, and assistance to public elementary and
secondary education through grants for the construction of classrooms and for teachers' salaries. The budget also includes funds
for a new program of financial aid to improve the quality of
education by such means as teacher training institutes. Continuing our policy of building the research effort of the Nation,
funds are recommended for the National Science Foundation to
expand support for basic research and the construction of research facilities, particularly at colleges and universities, and to
strengthen programs in science education.

Veterans benefits and services. Our first concern in veteran
programs is that adequate benefits be provided for those disabled in the service of their country. The last increase in compensation rates for service-disabled veterans was enacted in
1957. To offset increases in the cost of living since that time, I
again recommend that the Congress enact legislation to estab-

lish higher rates, particularly for the severely disabled. The 1963 budget provides $64 million for this proposal.

New Obligational Authority]

Before Federal funds can be spent, the Congress must enact authority for each agency to incur financial obligations. For the current year, it now appears that $3.8 billion of new obligational authority over the amount already enacted will be required. Of this amount, $2 billion represents standby authority for lending in case of need to the International Monetary Fund—in accordance with the recently concluded agreement under which other countries will make available twice this amount of standby authority. This will make a total of $95.7 billion of new obligational authority for fiscal 1962.

For 1963, my recommendations for new obligational authority total $99.3 billion. This includes substantial sums needed for forward funding of programs—such as those of the Department of Defense and the National Aeronautics and Space Administration—under which commitments are made in one year and expenditures often occur in later years.

Budget Receipts]

The estimate of budget receipts for fiscal year 1963 rests on projections of economic recovery and growth which will be discussed in the Economic Report. In brief, the revenue estimates are based on the assumption that the gross national product will rise from $521 billion in the calendar year 1961 to $570 billion in calendar 1962. At this level of output, corporate profits in calendar 1962 would be about $56.5 billion and personal income about $448 billion. These figures do not reflect the additional stimulus which would be given to investment and incomes in the economy by the investment tax credit now pending before the Congress.

Since the spring of calendar year 1961, the average gain in gross national product has been about 2½% per quarter. The economic assumptions underlying the budget estimates will be realized with a somewhat more modest rate of gain of approximately 2% per quarter. This pace of advance would reduce the rate of unemployment to approximately 4% of the civilian labor force by the end of fiscal 1963. . . .

Tax reform proposals. Extensive and careful consideration has already been given to the proposals enumerated in my special tax message to the Congress last April. These tax reform proposals, as I noted last year, represent a first step in improving our tax system. The House Committee on Ways and Means has made action on a similar set of recommendations its first order of business this year. I hope they will be enacted early in this session. . . .

Extension of present tax rates. The budget outlook for 1963 requires that the present tax rates on corporation income and certain excises be extended for another year beyond their scheduled expiration date of June 30, 1962. Existing law calls for changes which would lower the general corporation income tax rate from 52% to 47%; reduce the excise rates on distilled spirits, beers, wines, cigarettes, passenger automobile parts and accessories; and allow the tax on general telephone services to expire. I recommend postponement of these changes for another year to prevent a revenue loss of $2.8 billion in 1963.

Transportation tax and user charges. Under existing law, the 10% tax on transportation of persons is scheduled for reduction to 5% on July 1, 1962. This tax poses special problems for common carriers which must compete with private automobiles not subject to the tax. At the same time it is clearly appropriate that passengers and shippers who benefit from special Government programs should bear a fair share of the costs of these programs.

Accordingly, I recommend that the present 10% tax as it applies to passenger transportation other than by air be repealed effective July 1, 1962. I also recommend enactment of new systems of user charges for commercial and general aviation and for transportation on inland waterways. . . .

Public Debt]

Changes in the public debt from year to year reflect mainly the amount of the budget surplus or deficit. With a budget surplus of $500 million proposed for 1963, the public debt on June 30, 1963, is expected to be $294.9 billion compared with $295.4 billion at the end of the current year.

The limit on the public debt now stands at $298 billion until June 30, 1962, after which the permanent ceiling of $285 billion again becomes effective. The present temporary limit was established last June before the Berlin situation required additional defense expenditures which used up the margin of flexibility included in the $298 billion limit. . . .

Despite the expectation of budget balance for fiscal 1963 as a whole, with the debt expected to return to the $295 billion level on June 30, 1963, seasonal requirements will temporarily raise the outstanding debt during the course of the year to nearly $305 billion. To make the usual allowance for a margin of flexibility in fiscal 1963, and to restore immediately needed flexibility for operations over the remainder of fiscal 1962, I urge prompt enactment of a temporary increase of the debt limit to $308 billion; to be available for the remainder of this year and throughout fiscal 1963.

Budget and Fiscal Policy]

Beyond the specific elements of budget expenditures and receipts, it is necessary to consider the relationship of the budget as a whole to the national economy. Three aspects of this relationship have been given particular attention in the preparation of this budget.

The budget and economic growth and stability. Our national economic policy is to achieve rapid economic progress for the Nation, with the benefits widely distributed among all parts of the population, to achieve and maintain levels of employment and output commensurate with our growing labor force and productive capacity, and at the same time to maintain reasonable price stability.

The Federal budget has a major role to play in achieving these objectives. Basic investments and services of large importance to the Nation are provided through the Government. Striking evidence of this contribution is that the Federal budget today supports about two-thirds of all the scientific research and development going forward in the Nation. The budget also supports education, transportation, and other developmental activities contributing to national growth.

Federal budget policy also has a major role to play in economic stabilization. This role was evident in fiscal years 1961 and 1962, when deficits were incurred in turning the business cycle from recession to recovery, as had been true in 1958-59 and in earlier recessions.

We do not expect another economic recession during the period covered by this budget. However, experience has taught us that periodic fluctuations in the economy cannot be completely avoided, and that Federal fiscal policy should work flexibly and promptly in such situations. For this, we need standby plans, the merits and mechanics of which have been explored ahead of time by the Congress and the administration.

Three proposals particularly merit congressional consideration at this time:

First, the President should be given standby discretionary authority, subject to congressional veto, to reduce personal income tax rates on clear evidence of economic need, for periods and by percentages set in the legislation.

Second, he should have standby power to initiate, when unemployment rises sharply, a temporary expansion in Federal and federally aided public works programs including authority for new Federal grants and loans for State and local capital improvements. The legislation providing for such an anti-recession program should ensure that projects to be financed will meet high-priority needs, will be started promptly and completed rapidly, and will result in a net addition to Federal, State, or local expenditures.

Third, legislation should be enacted to strengthen considerably the Federal-State unemployment insurance system, including a permanent system of extended unemployment benefits for workers with long work experience and in recession periods for all workers. These recommendations will be discussed in the Economic Report.

The budget and the balance of payments. In formulating this budget, careful consideration has been given to the impact on our international balance of payments of Federal expenditures abroad for defense, foreign assistance, and the conduct of foreign affairs. During the coming year, U.S. Government expenditures abroad are estimated to be $4.4 billion, compared with $4.6 billion in the current year, mainly for construction and procurement of goods and services for U.S. military and civilian operations abroad; military and civilian salaries; and the fraction of foreign assistance which does not directly finance U.S. exports. The 1963 estimate reflects many actions which have been taken to reduce the level of Government expenditures abroad. We are managing to strengthen our military defenses overseas without increasing our foreign exchange outlays, and with respect to economic aid we are stressing even further the procurement of American goods and services.

This budget also reflects other measures we are taking to improve the balance of payments, including tax measures to encourage the modernization of productive equipment and consequent increases in our competitive ability in world markets, stepped up export promotion activities, greater encouragement to foreign travel in the United States, and reduced tax inducements to invest in developed areas abroad rather than at home. To improve further our balance of payments position, we are continuing negotiations with other industrialized countries with the objective of increasing their purchases of defense material in the United States and their contributions to the economic advance of the developing countries.

Basic improvement in our balance of payments will depend primarily upon our ability to continue a high degree of overall price stability and to improve the competitive position of U.S. goods in world markets. The dynamic development and prospective expansion of the European Economic Community are resulting in fundamental changes in world commerce. This pattern of growth presents us with unparalleled export opportunity as well as a continuing challenge. We must meet these changes boldly, confident in our continuing ability to compete on the world markets and to participate in the enormous benefits to all concerned which accrue from the worldwide division of labor and expansion of trade. These are the objectives of the legislative recommendations concerning trade expansion which I shall be sending to the Congress shortly in a special message.

The budget and Federal capital outlays. In contrast with the practice of many businesses, State and local governments, and foreign governments, the budget of the U.S. Government lumps together expenditures for capital investment and for current operations. Nevertheless it is clearly of importance, in analyzing the significance of the Federal budget to the Nation, to recognize that the budget includes substantial expenditures for loans, public works, and other durable assets and capital items which will yield benefits in future years.

Furthermore, increasing attention has been given in recent years to the significance of "developmental" expenditures—outlays for education and training, and for research, which have the effect of adding to the Nation's level of knowledge and of skill, and thereby increase the capacity to produce a larger national output in future years. . . .

Efficiency and Economy in the Public Service]

The effort to increase the degree of effciency with which the public business is conducted requires constant and unremitting effort on many fronts. This budget reflects continuing improvement in many agencies in productivity per employee, brought about through better training, better supervision, more effective organization, and more efficient equipment.

The first requirement for efficiency and economy in Government is highly competent personnel. In this regard we face one very important problem on which I am placing a new recommendation before the Congress.

This is the urgent need to achieve a reform of white-collar salary systems to enable the Government to obtain and keep the high quality personnel essential for its complex and varied programs. Such a reform should bring career employee salaries at all except the very top career levels into reasonable comparability with private enterprise salaries for the same level of work, and provide salary structures with pay distinctions more adequately reflecting differences in degree of responsibility. These two fundamental standards have been widely supported in the past as proper objectives in determining Government salary structures and I now urge that they be given practical effect. . . .

Important steps to improve the military pay structure, particularly for higher ranking officers, have been taken in recent years, first in 1955 and, more significantly, in 1958. However, the adjustments now being recommended in civilian compensation require study of the possible need for further changes in military compensation. Consequently, I am directing that a thorough review be made which will permit an up-to-date appraisal of the many elements of military compensation and their relationship to the new proposed levels of civilian compensation to the new proposed levels of civilian compensation. There is one area, however, which has already been adequately reviewed. To reflect an acknowledged rise in housing costs, I am proposing legislation to provide selective increases in the basic allowance for quarters payable to military personnel. As in the case of the civilian pay adjustments, these increases should take effect January 1, 1963. . . .

Conclusion]

This budget represents a blending of many considerations which affect our national welfare. Choices among the conflicting claims on our resources have necessarily been heavily influenced by international developments that continue to threaten world peace. At the same time, the budget supports those activities that have great significance to the Nation's social and economic growth—the mainsprings of our national strength and leadership. In my judgment, this budget meets our national needs within a responsible fiscal framework—which is the test of the budget as an effective instrument of national policy. I recommend it to the Congress for action, in full confidence that it provides for the prudent use of our resources to serve the national interest.

17

Ten-Year Prospect in Space Exploration

Staff Report of the Select Committee on Astronautics and Space Exploration, 1959

The scientist must constantly caution the novice that leadership in science is not necessarily reflected by a nation's ability to put man in orbit or to reach the moon. More knowledge may be gained by the small satellite packed with scientific instruments than from the manned vehicle whirling through space at more than 17,000 miles an hour. In the last analysis, what provides leadership is basic research. At the same time, among the dramatic developments of the period 1945-62 have been the successes of the United States and the Soviet Union in sending men into space and the preparations of these two nations to send manned expeditions to the moon—or perhaps even to some of the planets. In 1959, the Select Committee on Astronautics and Space Exploration drew together in the following document the ideas of many scientists who were willing to suggest what might be possible in the next ten years in the field of space exploration. In reading the document, note (1) the seriousness with which the idea of space exploration was viewed; (2) the practical uses to which the conquest of space may be put; and (3) how many of the prophecies have already come true. For further reading, see *Space Handbook: Astronautics and Its Applications*, Staff Report of the Select Committee on Astronautics and Space Exploration (Washington, 1959).

Hᴇʀᴇ . . . ɪs ᴘʀᴇsᴇɴᴛᴇᴅ ᴛʜᴇ ᴛʜɪɴᴋɪɴɢ ᴏғ ᴘʀᴀᴄᴛɪᴄᴀʟ, dedicated, and knowledgeable men about the future development of space exploration.

The conquering of outer space is no longer fantasy. Today

The Next Ten Years in Space, 1959-1969. A Staff Report of the Select Committee on Astronautics and Space Exploration, Washington, 1959, pp. 3-15.

man-made satellites circle the globe at more than 17,000 miles an hour, to be followed in the near future by manned space stations, by lunar bases, by exploration of Venus, Mars, and Mercury. After that, in the more distant future, will come flights beyond the solar system, to other worlds, to other galaxies.

That is the consensus of those who proffered their views to the committee. There was some difference of opinion as to when these epochal events would occur, but there was little disagreement that they would, in the course of time, come to pass. For the most part, the outside time limit was set at 20 years.

Some authorities stressed that there were many things which should and could be done within the next 10 years, but whether they would be accomplished depended in good part on just how great an effort was expended by the people, the Congress, and the Government.

There were those who expressed confidence that the United States would soon take its rightful place in the forefront of space development. There were others who hoped for the best, but expressed alarm over a general feeling of complacency which they felt still existed.

The Moon]

When man first began to reason, he looked upon the Moon with awe. There were those who worshiped the Moon as a diety and over the ages many were sacrificed to appease it.

But as man's reasoning power increased and with it his knowledge of the universe, there came a longing to know what was on the Moon. Was there any life, even in a very primitive stage? Was there any air? What was obscured on the "other" side of the Moon?

Today, man looks to the Earth's natural satellite as once Christopher Columbus and the early explorers looked to the west, to new worlds to explore. We dream now of setting foot upon this object which whirls about the Earth some 240,000 miles distant.

It is noteworthy that not one authority questioned the possibility of man's reaching the Moon. The only question appeared to be when.

According to Dr. [Herbert F.] York, [Chief Scientist of the

Advanced Research Projects Agency] in views endorsed by Roy W. Johnson, and Rear Adm. John E. Clark, Director and Deputy Director of ARPA, respectively, man can first set foot upon the lunar dust in "just about 10 years (perhaps in as little as 7, if a very high priority were placed on this goal)."

The prediction that man may reach the Moon in 10 years is not confined to the military. "Certainly within 10 years manned flights around the Moon and return can be accomplished," said Donald W. Douglas, "and possibly during that time manned landings on the Moon and return will be possible."

Wernher von Braun, scientific chief of the Army Ballistic Missile Agency, also thinks this is possible.

"It is my opinion," he wrote the committee, "that manned flight around the Moon is possible within the next 8 to 10 years, and a 2-way flight to the Moon, including landing, a few years thereafter."

Dr. Fred L. Whipple, Director of the Smithsonian Astrophysical Laboratory, predicted that during the next decade "Equipment will have been safely landed on the Moon to set up a remote-controlled observatory" and "the back side of the Moon will have become as well known as the near side."

There were several who felt it would be the following decade (1969-79) before man first set foot upon the lunar terrain. Among these was Capt. R. C. Truax, of ARPA, who has devoted more than 20 years to rocketry, and who expressed belief that a circumlunar shot, to return a picture of the far side of the Moon, should be possible around 1968-69. He saw no reason why almost identical equipment, thrown into an orbit around the Moon, could not map the entire lunar surface "in fine detail."

"Such a feat," he stated, "will require several attempts, even with largely proven equipment, but should be possible before the end of the decade for a total added expenditure of less than the Vanguard program. [in the neighborhood of $111 million]."

"Manned circumlunar flight," continued Captain Truax, "falls into the same category of exploitations of military equipment for scientific and cultural purposes. The million-pound vehicle will be developed primarily to put large unmanned, and later manned, satellites into orbit. With minor modifications, the same vehicle can send a manned expedition round the Moon. Such a voyage would be a prelude to a manned lunar landing within the following decade."

In summing up, Truax listed these achievements as possible during the period 1959-69, at an estimated expenditure of $20 billion during the decade:

Numerous small unmanned single-purpose satellites, one large manned multipurpose space station, circumlunar instrumented flights, a soft-landing lunar craft instrumented to make numerous surface measurements critical to a later manned landing, and a manned circumlunar flight.

"These accomplishments," he stated, "are real and solid, though they are considerably below some glowing predictions."

Dr. S. Fred Singer, University of Maryland physicist, thought it probable that existing ICBM rocket development would make it possible "to design and operate a manned vehicle around the Moon which will again return to Earth."

"Judging from the probable state of ICBM rocket development," he stated, "it should be possible to design and operate a manned vehicle around the Moon which will again return to the Earth. This is probably the ultimate that can be done without new developments in rockets and, therefore, without large additional expenditures of money and effort. Such a project would * * * be * * * a real step in the direction of manned space travel."

Singer described how it would be done. He said:

"The vehicle would have to start from the Earth with about escape speed, 7 miles per second. Its occupant could operate a small 'vernier rocket' to put him on the correct precalculated orbit after the main rocket has burned out. Once in the correct orbit, no further adjustment will be necessary; the Moon's gravitational field will again 'reflect' the vehicle after it has passed around the far side."

Recovering the first astronaut would be a difficult task. "Probably the best method," Singer asserted, "is to use the Earth's atmosphere again to slow the vehicle down to satellite speed. By reentering fairly deeply on the first pass, enough energy would be expended so that the vehicle is thrown into an elliptic orbit, and as energy is expended on each pass, the ellipse shrinks quite rapidly into a circle. From there the reentry would proceed as in the case of a manned satellite." . . .

Mars and Venus]

Man's age-old dream of leaving the confines of the Earth has not been limited to reaching the Moon. The planets, especially Mars and Venus, have been perhaps even stronger magnets.

Ever since astronomers first reported "canals" and polar snow caps upon Mars, man has speculated about it. Is it a dead planet? Is it strewn with the remnants of ancient civilizations? Does life exist upon this world? For the first time now, a positive answer to this age-old riddle may lie ahead.

As for Venus, what mysteries lie behind its swirling clouds? Does it hide a lush tropical climate, as some believe, is it a watery waste, or is it a desert swept by duststorms?

The closest Mars will come to the Earth in the next decade will be approximately 35 million miles in 1971, the nearest approach since 1924. Venus is about 26 million miles from the Earth at its closest approach.

Dr. York foresees manned expeditions to these planets "a few years after 1968," but added that they could, perhaps, be made "in just about 10 years, if a very high priority were placed on this goal."

To von Braun "It seems unlikely that either Soviet or United States technology will be far enough advanced in the next 10 years to permit man's reaching the planets." But he declared that instrumented probes to Mars and Venus "are a certainty" within that period.

National Aeronautics and Space Administration scientists look to the "eventual establishment" of scientific bases on Mars and Venus, as well as the Moon. They do not predict just how soon, but they foresee during the next decade the mapping of the surfaces of the two planets by space probes, as well as attempts at "soft landings" of instrumented payloads "to determine many surface and atmospheric properties of these bodies and whether life in some form exists."

Although the civilian space agency did not anticipate that landings on Mars and Venus would occur by 1969, its scientists advised the committee that "an active program should be underway" by then for a manned expedition to circumnavigate Mars or Venus. This would be the prelude to a landing on the planets.

Krafft A. Ehricke, chief of astronautics for Convair, foresaw during the coming decade "Interplanetary space probes exploring the region between Mercury and Earth as well as between Earth and Mars and beyond in the asteroid belt between Mars and Jupiter."

"These probes can be of low-flight accuracy," declared Ehricke, "since they do not have to meet another body in space. They require no optical equipment and no navigation equipment. The messages which they transmit back to Earth on meteoritic material, interplanetary gas, electric and magnetic phenomena, etc., require low power. Therefore their overall weight can be comparatively small, between 200 and 1,000 pounds." He added that during the next 10 years there will be only 5 opportunities to launch a Mars probe and 7 occasions for a Venus probe. The best opportunity for a Venus probe will be in 1959 and 1967, while the most favorable opportunity for a Mars exploration would be provided in November 1962 and November 1964.

With the advent of the 1½-million-pound booster vehicle, on which plans are now underway, Ehricke said it will become possible to transmit a probe to the planet Jupiter, 387 million miles from the Earth at its closest approach.

Ehricke said the Jupiter probe is a difficult project which "may not be practical" until the end of the sixties. The vehicle would take a year to reach its destination, but would be of "considerable scientific interest."

George L. Haller, vice president of General Electric Co., proposed this 3-year program beginning with a Venus probe in 1959.

"(1) a Venus satellite;
(2) a Mars satellite;
(3) a close lunar satellite;
(4) a lunar soft landing;
(5) a trans-Mercury (solar) probe;
(6) a trans-Mars (outer planetary) probe;
(7) a Venus slow descent;
(8) a Mars soft landing."

Haller said that the missions to the planets could carry, as on the lunar probes, payloads of 50 to 250 pounds, sufficient to enable them to learn, among other things, "what the clouds that blanket Venus consist of, whether or not Venus rotates, and whether or not there is any form of life on Mars."

"A common error [in forecasting progress]," Haller also said, "is that of being too optimistic about what can be achieved in a few years and too cautious about the developments to be expected in 20 to 30 years * * *.

"Man's venture into space is the great enterprise of this century * * *. Tremendous progress has already been made. Yet in the light of what remains to be done, all that has been accomplished so far is not more than a tennis ball as viewed in relation to the Earth."

Andrew Haley, [President of the International Astronautical Federation,] said the coming decade "should see the successful launching of Mars, Venus, and Moon probes and the establishment of many heretofore undreamed of orbits."

But he maintained that the exploration of Mars and Venus by manned expeditions will probably have to wait until the development of "propulsion systems capable of delivering millions of pounds of thrust at speeds in the order of one-third the speed of light," about 62,000 miles a second.

He warned that the exploration of outer space will not be without its sacrifices in human lives.

"Biological hazards arising from travel in outer space will be diagnosed and largely overcome [but] the penalty for these investigations will be the sacrificing of numerous warm-blooded animals and, in time, of numerous human beings. The sacrifice of human beings will be roughly a little higher than was incident to man's conquest of the air."

Man in Space]

When will man fly in our space? His first sustained flight in outer space will probably be in a space vehicle which will orbit the Earth—and the consensus of some of the experts is that this event is not far distant. The biggest problem still to be overcome, apparently, before man can circle the globe as a human satellite, is bringing him back safely to the Earth.

Rear Adm. John T. Hayward, Research and Development Chief for the Navy, put it this way: "Perhaps the key to man in space, Moon flights, etc., can be stated as follows: manned space flight will be practicable when there is *reasonable* chance for survival and rescue." Hayward predicted that man will fly in space orbit within the decade.

At least one expert believes man will orbit the Earth in 1959 and that man will be a Soviet citizen.

"I believe," stated Frederick C. Durant III, former president of the International Astronautical Federation, "that the U.S.S.R. will continue to shock this country rudely, pressing their current advantageous lead. I believe they will send man into orbital flight and recover him several times during the next year."

What is the consensus of the experts as to when man will spring from a speed of something like 2,000 miles per hour (performed for a brief period of time in experimental planes, to something like the 18,000 miles per hour at which the average satellite orbits?

While, with the one exception already noted, none would predict the step would be taken in 1959, others felt it would be accomplished within a few years.

Aeronutronic Systems' scientists foresaw a manned satellite in orbit within a few years which would remain aloft for possibly months.

Dr. Eric Durand, Aeronutronics' head of space sciences, stated:

"The present Atlas booster is capable of putting a man in a satellite orbit for a limited period, and provide for his safe return. This capability will be improved with the Titan, particularly through the use of advanced propellants, such as fluorine-hydrazine or fluorine-ammonia in the second stage.

"The advent later of a 1-million-pound-thrust booster will make it possible to put a large satellite in orbit with a crew of 2 or more men, and durations measured in weeks and possibly months." Durand estimated the 1-million-pound-thrust booster would be operational by 1961.

Predictions varied among the other experts who gave the committee the benefit of their views as to when man would orbit the Earth. Some emphasized that this would merely be another step in the direction of controlled space flight, necessary before man could really explore outer space.

Brig. Gen. H. A. Boushey, Air Force Director of Advanced Technology, foresaw such quick advances in space technology that within 4 to 5 years orbital refueling or restaging will be underway. "By such means," he stated, "the severe heating and deceleration problems of reentry can be completely avoided. * * * I think the first manned, orbital restaging or refueling flight will be accomplished within 4 or 5 years, and I fully expect that the necessary priority and emphasis will be placed on this key phase of space exploration." He told the committee that by 1965 manned maintenance, repair, and resupply space vehicles will be in use for military, commercial, and scientific purposes.

Roy K. Knutson, chairman of North American Aviation's space committee, thought the "initial flights would probably consist of a single orbit of the Earth, [with] the environmental system * * * capable of sustaining life for at least 24 hours in order to provide for emergencies."

"The capsule," continued Knutson, "would be decelerated out of orbit by a retrorocket. Speed of descent would be checked by speed brakes and, later, a ribbon parachute. The point at which the retrorocket is fired would be carefully controlled so that the recovery trajectory would land the capsule on the North American Continent in daylight hours.

"A manned capsule will provide a rapid means of getting man into orbit and for studying physiological effects, such as weightlessness."

NASA scientists cautioned the committee that a manned vehicle cannot be placed in orbit about the Earth until three basic questions have been answered regarding (1) high-energy radiation, both primary and cosmic ray and the newer plasma type discovered in the IGY satellite series, (2) man's ability to withstand long periods of loneliness and strain while subjected to the strange environment of which weightlessness is the factor least evaluated, and (3) reentry into the atmosphere and safe landing. They added that the reliability of the launching rocket must also be increased before a manned capsule is used as a payload.

Space Stations—Controlled Flight]

The development of space stations and controlled space flight will follow successful manned orbit in the opinion of the astronautical authorities.

Many of the experts stressed the need for space stations in fixed positions in relation to the Earth, from which expeditions could be launched to the Moon and possibly beyond. Some regarded a space station as a necessary prerequisite to a successful assault upon the Moon. . . .

Near the end of the period 1959-69, Boushey foresaw the construction of a large space station. He said it will be assembled "section by section as the result of numerous individual firings from an equatorial launching site. Final joinup of these sections will be accomplished by piloted 'space tugs' which will operate in orbit during their entire useful life. In addition to the 'tugs,' manned resupply and maintenance spacecraft will shuttle from the Earth's Equator to the orbiting satellites. Of course, military spacecraft will police the near vicinity of the Earth to prevent the use of space for aggressive purposes."

With the development that will by now have taken place, said Boushey, "a piloted spacecraft, taking full advantage of outgoing and returning refueling in the equatorial orbit, will land on the Moon."

T. F. Morrow, vice president of Chrysler Corp., did not anticipate the construction of space stations until after the next decade, but predicted that "manned flights of limited duration will be commonplace. Flights will exceed the few minutes of the current planned programs and, toward the end of the decade, will include space trips encircling the Earth and the Moon. The means of establishing space platforms will be developed, but operations from space platforms are not contemplated in this period."

Morrow, whose firm is instrumental in the manufacture of the Army's Redstone missile, added however:

"The essential instruments of scientific investigation to make this space exploration fruitful are available now. The most difficult problem to be solved is attainment of safety and reliability. Our success in conquest of space will be measured, not in terms of brilliance of technical innovation, but in terms of attaining through sound basic concepts, product engineering, and manufacturing control an indispensable high degree of safety and reliability in large rocket vehicles as indicated by Redstone reliability of more than 90 percent."

Dr. Walter R. Dornberger, rocket expert for Bell Aircraft, viewed as one of the most important achievements of the next 10 years "The development of manned and unmanned space vehicles, maneuverable in space and able to rendezvous with permanent satellites or space systems."

The main area for space vehicles during the 1959-69 period, predicted Dornberger, "will be mainly up to 650 miles this side of the radiation cloud at operational times of up to 2 to 3 weeks."

The next decade, he said, will see the following developments: manned and automatic space astronomical observatories; manned space laboratories; manned and automatic filling, storage, supply and assembly space facilities; manned space maintenance and supply and rescue ships—all climaxed by the first manned flight to the Moon.

General Gavin said that "in the near future—when guidance devices permit—soft landings, rocket cargo and passenger transport will become feasible.

"We will probably reach the time," he predicted, "when we can consider rocket transport superior to airplane for anything over a thousand miles or so—just as we have long since reached a point of recognizing that planes are superior to automobiles for distances over a hundred miles."

Alexander Kartveli, vice president of Republic Aviation, predicted that by 1968, 3 years after man orbits the Moon, a space station will be established for staging flights to the Moon and planets.

"Manned space stations," he said, "have been suggested as a staging area for further exploration of space. The present man-in-space programs planned for the near future offer considerable hope that in a 10-year period the first operational space stations will have been placed in orbit."

He cautioned, however, that the launching of any manned

system "requires a period of testing with similar unmanned systems to assure reliability."

Communications, television, weather, astronomy]

Many space authorities believe that the first big economic payoff from advancement of astronautics will arise from the "fixing" of satellites in a 24-hour "stationary" orbit approximately 22,000 miles from the Earth.

Some felt it was the next big step in satellites and one which would affect the lives of the great mass of people on the Earth more than anything in the way of spectacular feats which might follow.

Arthur C. Clarke, English scientist and author, foresaw the day when stationary satellites would make television available to everyone on Earth. He declared that "Of all the applications of astronautics during the coming decade, I think the communications satellite the most important. * * * it is now widely conceded that this may be the only way of establishing a truly global TV service. The political, commercial, and cultural implications of this, however, do not yet seem so thoroughly appreciated.

"Living as I do in the Far East, I am constantly reminded of the struggle between the Western World and the U.S.S.R. for the uncommitted millions of Asia. The printed word plays only a small part in this battle for the minds of largely illiterate populations, and even radio is limited in range and impact.

"But when line-of-sight TV transmissions become possible from satellites directly overhead, the propaganda effect may be decisive, especially if it is coupled with a drive to produce simple and cheap battery-operated receivers.

"There could be few communities which would be unable to afford one set (in Ceylon there are dozens of radios blaring in every village) and when we consider the effect of TV upon our own ostensibly educated public, the impact upon the peoples of Asia and Africa may be overwhelming. It may well determine whether Russian or English is the main language of the future."

"The TV satellite is mightier than the ICBM," he concluded.

The possibilities of employing fixed satellites for weather observations have proven equally intriguing to space authorities. While none would predict that they would someday make of weather forecasting an exact science, the general belief was that a tremendous improvement would result.

Dr. F. W. Reichelderfer, Chief of the U.S. Weather Bureau, told the committee: "The development of meteorological satellites and the application of new observations and data from this source to the problems of meteorology offers promise of one of the most revolutionary advances in the history of the science. It should make possible the immediate detection of new storm formations—hurricanes, extratropical cyclones, etc.—any place over the globe. Its worldwide weather-observing potentialities are of utmost importance in human welfare relating to weather and climate."

It is generally agreed that billions of dollars would be saved and many deaths prevented if sudden onslaughts of bad weather could be predicted sufficiently in advance so that the necessary steps might be taken to protect people and industry.

Reichelderfer said the prospects of being freed from the various limitations which make accurate and advance weather forecasting difficult "is no longer just a dream of the meteorologist, and researcher."

"Earth satellites can serve as global weather-observing platforms," he said. "Studies clearly indicate that Earth satellites fitted with television cameras, radiometers, and radar could telemeter to ground stations sufficient data on the weather as seen by the satellites to make it possible for man to actually achieve weather surveillance and analysis on a global basis.

"Satellites could televise to Earth stations in considerable detail direct photographic observations of the cloud systems of the globe, particularly those associated with major storms. Similarly, the extent of polar ice caps and snow-covered surfaces bearing on processes in the atmosphere could be determined."

Admiral Hayward told the committee that "there is every reason to expect the development of a navigational satellite system that will provide the required accuracy to ensure the safe navigation of all ships of the world in all oceans of the world—

regardless of the weather. It may even be possible to extend this system to the safe navigation of aircraft on long extended flights. Additionally, such satellites could provide for the accurate measuring of the Earth, its islands and mountains."

Dr. Louis G. Dunn, president of Space Technology Laboratories, expressed optimism about communications satellites. "It is safe to predict," he said, "that this particular use of rocket vehicles will have more direct effect on the man in the street than any other development in space technology. He will now for the first time be able to see, as well as hear, an English cricket game, the shelling of Quemoy, the coronation of a Pope."

As for costs, Dr. Dunn says: "A careful analysis of the relative costs of satellites and of more conventional communication systems shows that even at today's costs the communications satellite cost less than the underseas telephone cable per cycle of band width and is comparable in cost with that of the overseas radio system."

The National Aeronautics and Space Administration also predicted many beneficial uses for satellites, including meteorology, communications, geodetics and navigation.

"A system of meteorological satellites," Dr. Glennan said, "will some day provide continuous worldwide observation of cloud cover, storms, heat input and other meteorological measurements which can be used for improved forecasting, and perhaps, at some future date, control of the weather."

Scientists of the Dow Chemical Co. predicted that in addition to satellites, nuclear-powered ramjets, flying continuously, will "undoubtedly" record the cloud cover and the upper atmospheric conditions at all points around the world to permit accurate short-range weather forecasting.

Ehricke saw instrumented satellites providing a global post office and television relay, improved weather and navigation aids, with the latter "acting like a radio star for ships in the case of overcast," and an early warning system against enemy attack, especially with long-range missiles.

L. Eugene Root, missiles expert for Lockheed Aircraft, predicted that distances of several hundred million miles will be spanned by pictures and other media. He commented that: "in the next decade, communications systems capable of spanning planetary distances of several hundred million miles, such as will be involved in planetary probes, solar probes and artificial asteroids, will be developed for transmission of complex data, including pictures."

Root described what he thought the next 10 years would bring in communications. "In addition to the frequency bands now in use, new systems using presently untapped portions of the entire frequency spectrum, from X-ray frequencies on up, will begin to be evolved for extraterrestial space-to-space transmission. Erectible or unfurlable antennas, dishes, and mirrors, possibly steerable and highly directive, will have been evolved for space vehicles and communications satellites. New methods of information coding and processing will permit compact reliable low-power drain communication links capable of handling much more complex information than at present."

Root predicted that astronomy, too, will greatly benefit from new developments. During the next decade "astronomical observations from space vehicles will be an accomplished fact (and) will revolutionize conventional astronomy."

He raised the possibility that future astronomical techniques may bring the answer to the evolution of the universe. Radio telescopes will look into space for much greater distances than is now possible. "If at these much greater distances the distribution of galaxies in space is much more dense, then we would have an argument for an evolutionary theory of the universe where galaxies are created once and for all and simply expand from some point in time. If, on the other hand, the distribution of galaxies remains uniform, we would have an argument for continuous creation of galaxies with no necessity for supposing creation at some finite time in the past."

This speculation was similar to that of Prof. A. C. B. Lovell, noted British astronomer, who has long believed that radio-telescopes may solve some of the main mysteries of the universe. Lovell suggests that any telescope, if carried in an Earth satellite, will reach space-time distances of much greater magnitude than is possible today and thus obtain information of the state of the universe as it existed billions of years ago.

Dr. Harold C. Weber, the Army's Chief Scientific Adviser, implies that it will be difficult to evaluate the magnitude of knowledge to be obtained from the study and exploration of outer space, although certainly it will be great.

Immediate results, he said, will include more accurate maps of the Earth to replace the surprisingly "inaccurate" maps we now have; worldwide communications "on a reliable scale" through the use of satellites; greatly increased amounts of information concerning weather and the formation of weather patterns which may result even in some slight control over weather; greatly increased knowledge concerning the composition "and probably the life history of the universe"; and "ability to perform quantitative experiments on a grand scale in outer space which will contribute new knowledge to our understanding of matter, energy and time. * * *"

Propulsion, the Key to Space Travel]

Since the time of Jules Verne men have envisioned journeys to distant worlds in interstellar space ships which cruise at fantastic speeds. More recently, science fiction has been replete with stories of space travel. In many such journeys the space voyager travels in comfortable craft, unencumbered by unusual or heavy garments until he prepares to leave his ship. He has at his command suitable propulsion systems, including auxiliary ones, which blast him from Earth swiftly and efficiently. He is generally at ease in his spaceship, protected by heat, air, light and other conveniences and necessities.

This view by science fiction assumes that a variety of serious technical problems have been solved, which often is not the case today.

Scientists have little doubt that these obstacles can be overcome. But how and when? Will nuclear power be available for propulsion and auxiliary uses before the next decade ends? Will ion rockets be practical? What of solar boiler rockets? Plasma jets? Photon rockets? Magnetic propulsion and braking? Solar sails?

The predictions and speculations embrace virtually all the levels of human imagination.

Technicians of the Thiokol Chemical Corp. said the problem of developing engines of very high thrust is responsible for a "serious lag in space technology in the United States." However, they thought that solid propellant engines developing 10 to 100 times a million-pound thrust "present only straight-forward engineering problems." Within 10 years they predict large solid propellant engines for the first stages of space vehicles capable of lifting gross loads of over 10 million pounds.

What is really needed, they say, "is a way to contain a fluid having a temperature of 10 million degrees Kelvin. Such a rocket would permit space travel with a fuel-mass ratio of about 2 pounds per ton at takeoff. Space travel could then be accomplished with all the comforts of a voyage on an ocean liner."

The company concluded that such achievements probably lie beyond the next decade but felt they could crystallize "if we, as a nation, want them enough to put forth the effort needed for their attainment."

Concerning the feasibility of nuclear propulsion for space vehicles, Chairman John A. McCone of the Atomic Energy Commission said that investigations over the past 3 years "have made us confident that nuclear energy will play a prominent role in the conquest of space." He pointed to projects Rover and SNAP as examples of experiments going on in this field. "Rover is concerned with the application of nuclear energy to rocket propulsion," he explained. "SNAP is concerned with the development of small, lightweight nuclear auxiliary-power units for use in space environment. Both radio-isotopic and reactor energy sources are being exploited for this application."

Assuming the necessary effort and support, McCone said the decade ahead should:

(1) Demonstrate by full-power ground test a nuclear rocket engine capable of boosting extremely large payloads into space. (2) Operate for many months an electricity-producing, satellite-borne, nuclear auxiliary power unit. (3) Develop and test nuclear electric drive units capable of providing propulsive power for space probes. (4) Develop and test units wihch will convert nuclearly developed heat directly into electricity without resort to rotating equipment.

Dr. T. C. Merkle, nuclear power expert at the University of California, suggested that there is not yet developed a "complete conceptual design" for the "space cruising" stage. Therefore, he said, from the propulsion standpoint it is necessary to develop some of the systems now being explored in a tentative manner to a high degree of practicality "before we can be truly said to be in the space age." He said nuclear energy will be necessary to accomplish these results and foresees in the next 10 years heat-exchanger rockets, mainly for booster use; light reliable reactor systems for space-station power-plants and, eventually, for use by landing parties on the Moon or planets; and ion rocket schemes to be used as the last stage of planetary probe vehicles.

Dr. Raemer E. Schreiber, Los Alamos scientist, said the actual operation of the experimental high temperature rocket reactor will probably take place this year. The reactor is known as KIWI-A and is a heat-exchanger device, blowing propellant gas through channels in solid fuel elements and exhausting it through a nozzle.

He emphasized that even though such reactors have "attractive performance for orbital missions and limited interplanetary exploration" they make use of only a small part of the nuclear potential.

"Basic studies are therefore being made on nonconventional reactor concepts in which the temperature and specific impulse of the system are much less limited by internal structural considerations. In addition, rather encouraging results have been obtained in the study of direct electrical power generation from fission heat. The generation of electricity by thermoelectric effect in metals has been known for many years, but is a relatively inefficient process. The similar effect in a gaseous plasma potentially has a much higher efficiency."

Schreiber disclosed that solar sailing has been investigated and shows some promise as a method of orbit-to-orbit propulsion. The technique would use pressure from the Sun's radiation to generate motion. "This is very minute, but is adequate for maneuvering a space craft into various Earth orbits and to do rather leisurely interplanetary exploration. A thin sail some 500 yards in diameter is needed for a space capsule weighing 500 pounds. * * * Control of orientation is accomplished by counter-rotating the sail and the payload and making use of the resultant gyroscopic action."

Dan A. Kimball, president of Aerojet Corp., thought that present propulsion systems developed for the military intercontinental ballistic missiles can be clustered to provide boost thrusts of from 1 to 1½ million pounds. Clustering existing powerplants beyond this level, he said, would be impractical from the standpoint of reliability and complexity. However, he thought single-engine thrust of this magnitude should be developed within 5 years. By clustering these more powerful engines, he continued, total thrusts of 10 to 15 million pounds might be achieved.

Missions beyond the next decade, in Kimball's view, will require still larger boost systems for which nuclear rockets may provide "significant advantages in reduced gross weight * * * and a single stage configuration." He pointed to charged colloidal propulsion systems as a means of vernier control and navigation in sustained space flight, and added "* * * our engineers visualize that a recombination power plant can also be developed. This powerplant would utilize energy available in the upper atmosphere and would be particularly suitable for manned flight in the regime of Mach 10 or more and at altitudes of 50 to 100 miles. To date, the studies and experimentation on these advanced propulsion systems show promising indications of their feasibility." . . .

18

The Cuban Missile Crisis and its Resolution

Khrushchev v. Kennedy in the Nuclear Age

On April 12, 1961, President Kennedy made the following statement in his press conference:

"There will not be under any conditions, an intervention in Cuba
by United States armed forces. This government will do everything
it possibly can . . . to make sure that there are no Americans involved
in any actions inside Cuba."

On April 17, 1961, a small anti-Castro force invaded Cuba. According to the *New York Times* (April 22, 1961) the United States Central Intelligence Agency "planned, coordinated and directed the
operations that ended in the defeat on a beachhead" in Cuba on
April 19th. Indeed on April 24, a spokesman for President Kennedy
stated forthrightly that the President "as President . . . bears full responsibility for the events having to do with the Cuban invasion."

On October 14, 1962, a U-2 high-flying reconnaissance plane carried out a mission over Cuba. On the following day, American intelligence officers concluded that the photographs taken by this plane
proved that Soviet medium-range ballistics missiles were being installed near San Cristobal. High-level conferences in the United States
immediately began and continued while additional intelligence was
gathered. A key to understanding the seriousness of the situation was

Exchange of Messages between Premier Khrushchev and President Ken-
    nedy, April 18, 1961, *New York Times,* April 19, 1961; President
    Kennedy's speech on Cuba to the American Society of Newspaper Edi-
    tors, April 20, 1961, *ibid.,* April 21, 1961,; President Kennedy's address
    to the nation outlining moves to be taken against the Soviet arms build-up
    in Cuba, October 22, 1962, *ibid.,* October 23, 1962; excerpts from
    Ambassador Adlai Stevenson's address to the United Nations on the
    Cuban crisis, October 23, 1962, *ibid.,* October 24, 1962. Copyright by
    The New York Times. Reprinted by permission. For further reading,
    see Robert F. Smith, *The United States and Cuba: Business and
    Diplomacy, 1917-1960* (New Haven, Conn., 1962); Tad Szulc and
    Karl E. Meyer, *The Cuban Invasion: The Chronicle of Disaster* (New
    York, 1962); and Roger Hillsman, "The Cuban Crisis: How Close
    We Were to War," *Look,* XXVIII (Aug. 25, 1964), pp. 17 *et. seq.*

that the Soviet Union's position continued to be that only defensive weapons were being sent to Cuba. If Russia should develop Cuba into a missile base, whatever advantage the United States might have had in nuclear striking power would have been seriously jeopardized. After considering several alternatives, President Kennedy decided on October 20 to impose a selective blockade against Cuba. The blockade was announced two days later. For a week, an air of extreme tension prevailed within the United States as the armed forces were alerted, and exceedingly delicate official and unofficial negotiations took place. On October 28, Premier Khrushchev announced that the work on the Cuban bases would be stopped, and the missiles returned to the Soviet Union. Looking back at the exciting series of events almost two years later, Roger Hilsman wrote: "The threat of nuclear war has not been eliminated from the world, nor is there yet a reconciliation between East and West. But if either of these objectives ever is attained, historians will probably mark the Cuban missile crisis of 1962 as the beginning."

The section below consists of four documents. In the first two (the exchange of messages between President Kennedy and Premier Khrushchev of April 18, 1961 and President Kennedy's speech to the newspaper editors on April 20, 1961), note the international manifestations of the Cuban fiasco of that year; in the last two (President Kennedy's address of October 22, 1962 outlining moves to be taken against the Soviet Arms buildup in Cuba and the section of Adlai Stevenson's address to the United Nations on October 23), note the explanations for the actions that led to one of the most important American diplomatic victories of the "Cold War."

A. Statement by Premier Khrushchev]

By The Associated Press]

MOSCOW, April 18, [1961]—Premier Khrushchev's message today to President Kennedy:

Mr. PRESIDENT, I ADDRESS THIS MESSAGE TO YOU AT an hour of anxiety fraught with danger to world peace. An armed aggression has begun against Cuba.

It is not a secret to anyone that the armed bands which invaded that country had been trained, equipped and armed in the United States of America. The planes which bomb Cuban cities belong to the United States of America, the bombs they drop have been made available by the American Government.

Here in the Soviet Union all this arouses a natural feeling of indignation on the part of the Soviet Government and Soviet people.

Once recently we exchanged views through our representatives. We spoke about the common desire of both sides to make joint efforts to improve relations between our countries and avert the danger of war.

Your statement of a few days ago to the effect that the United States would not take part in military operations against Cuba produced the impression that the top echelons of the United States are aware of the consequences of aggression against Cuba to world peace and to the United States itself.

How are we to understand what is really being done by the United States now that the attack on Cuba has become a fact?

Action Still Possible]

It is yet not too late to prevent the irreparable. The Government of the United States still can prevent the flames of war kindled by the interventionists on Cuba from spreading into a conflagration which it will be impossible to cope with.

I earnestly appeal to you, Mr. President, to call a halt to the aggression against the Republic of Cuba. The military techniques and the world political situation now are such that any so-called "small-war" can produce a chain reaction in all parts of the world.

As to the Soviet Union, there should be no misunderstanding of our position: we shall render the Cuban people and their Government all necessary assistance in beating back the armed attack on Cuba.

We are sincerely interested in a relaxation of international tension, but if others aggravate it, we shall reply in full measure. And, in general, it is hardly possible to handle matters in such a way as to settle the situation and extinguish the conflagration in one area and kindle a new conflagration in another.

I hope that the United States Government will take into account these considerations of ours, prompted as they are by the sole concern for preventing such steps which could lead the world to a military catastrophe.

B. The Answer by President Kennedy]

Special to "The New York Times."]

WASHINGTON, April 18—President Kennedy's answer to Premier Khrushchev:

MR. CHAIRMAN:

You are under a serious misapprehension in regard to events in Cuba. For months there has been evident and growing resistance to the Castro dictatorship.

More than 100,000 refugees have recently fled from Cuba into neighboring countries. Their urgent hope is naturally to assist their fellow Cubans in their struggle for freedom. Many of these refugees fought alongside Dr. Castro against the Batista dictatorship; among them are prominent leaders of his own original movement and government.

These are unmistakable signs that Cubans found intolerable the denial of democratic liberties and the subversion of the 26 of July Movement by an alien-dominated regime. It cannot be surprising that, as resistance within Cuba grows, refugees have been using whatever means are available to return and support their countrymen in the continuing struggle for freedom. Where people are denied the right of choice, recourse to such struggle is the only means of achieving their liberties.

I have previously stated and I repeat now that the United States intends no military intervention in Cuba. In the event of any military intervention by outside force we will immediately honor our obligations under the inter-American system to protect this hemisphere against external aggression.

The Spirit of Liberty]

While refraining from military intervention in Cuba, the people of the United States do not conceal their admiration for Cuban patriots who wish to see a democratic system in an independent Cuba. The United States Government can take no action to stifle the spirit of liberty.

I have taken careful note of your statement that the events

in Cuba might affect peace in all parts of the world. I trust that this does not mean that the Soviet Government, using the situation in Cuba as a pretext, is planning to inflame other areas of the world. I would like to think that your Government has too great a sense of responsibility to embark upon any enterprise so dangerous to general peace.

I agree with you as to the desirability of steps to improve the international atmosphere. I continue to hope that you will cooperate in opportunities now available to this end.

A prompt cease-fire and peaceful settlement of the dangerous situation in Laos, cooperation with the United Nations in the Congo and a speedy conclusion of an acceptable treaty for the banning of nuclear tests would be constructive steps in this direction.

The regime in Cuba could make a similar contribution by permitting the Cuban people freely to determine their own future by democratic processes and freely to cooperate with their Latin-American neighbors.

I believe, Mr. Chairman, that you should recognize that free peoples in all parts of the world do not accept the claim of historical inevitability for Communist revolution.

What your Government believes is its own business; what it does in the world is the world's business. The great revolution in the history of man, past, present and future, is the revolution of those detemined to be free.

C. Text of Address by President to U. S. Editors]
April 20, 1961]

Following is the text of President Kennedy's speech yesterday at the convention in Washington of the American Society of Newspaper Editors, as recorded by The New York Times.

THE PRESIDENT OF A GREAT DEMOCRACY SUCH AS OURS and the editors of great newspapers such as yours owe a common obligation to the people—an obligation to present the facts, to present them with candor and to present them in perspective.

It is with that obligation in mind that I have decided in the last twenty-four hours to discuss briefly at this time the recent events in Cuba.

On that unhappy island, as in so many other arenas of the contest for freedom, the news has grown worse instead of better.

I have emphasized before that this was a struggle of Cuban patriots against a Cuban dictator. While we could not be expected to hide our sympathies, we made it repeatedly clear that the armed forces of this country would not intervene in any way.

Any unilateral American intervention in the absence of an external attack upon ourselves or an ally would have been contrary to our traditions and to our international obligations. But let the record show that our restraint is not inexhaustible.

Should it ever appear that the inter-American doctrine of noninterference merely conceals or excuses a policy of non-action; if the nations of this hemisphere should fail to meet their commitments against outside Communist penetration, then I want it clearly understood that this Government will not hesitate in meeting its primary obligations, which are the security of our nation.

"Bloody Streets of Budapest"]

Should that time ever come, we do not intend to be lectured on intervention by those whose character was stamped for all time on the bloody streets of Budapest. Nor would we expect or accept the same outcome which this small band of gallant Cuban refugees must have known that they were chancing, determined as they were, against heavy odds, to pursue their courageous attempts to regain their island's freedom.

But Cuba is not an island unto itself, and our concern is not ended with mere expressions of nonintervention or regret. This is not the first time in either ancient or recent history that a small band of freedom fighters has engaged the armor of totalitarianism. It is not the first time that Communist tanks have rolled over gallant men and women fighting to redeem the independence of their homeland.

Nor is it by any means the final episode in the eternal struggle against tyranny anywhere on the face of the globe, including Cuba itself.

Mr. Castro has said that these were mercenaries. According to press reports, the final message to be relayed from the refugee forces on the beach came from the rebel commander when asked if he wished to be evacuated.

His answer was: "I will never leave this country."

That is not the reply of a mercenary. He has gone now to join in the mountains countless other guerrilla fighters who are equally determined that the dedication of those who gave their lives shall not be forgotten and that Cuba must not be abandoned to the Communists. And we do not intend to abandon it either.

Final Word Unspoken]

The Cuban people have not yet spoken their final piece, and I have no doubt that they and the Revolutionary Council, led by Dr. Cardona—and members of the families of the Revolutionary Council, I am informed by the doctor yesterday, are involved themselves in the island—will continue to speak out for a free and independent Cuba.

Meanwhile, we will not accept Mr. Castro's attempt to blame this nation for the hatred with which his one-time supporters now regard his repression. But there are from this sobering episode useful lessons for us all to learn. Some may be still obscure and await further information. Some are clear today.

First, it is clear that the forces of communism are not to be underestimated in Cuba or anywhere else in the world. The advantages of a police state, its use of mass terror and arrest to prevent the spread of free dissent, cannot be overlooked by those who expect the fall of every fanatic tyrant.

If the self-discipline of the free cannot match the iron discipline of the mailed fist in economic, political, scientific and all the other kinds of struggle as well as the military, then the peril to freedom will continue to rise.

Secondary, it is clear that this nation, in concert with all the free nations of this hemisphere, must take an ever closer and more realistic look at the menace of external Communist intervention and domination in Cuba.

The American people are not complacent about Iron Curtain tanks and planes less than ninety miles from their shore, but a nation of Cuba's size is less a threat to our survival than it is a base for subverting the survival of other free nations throughout the hemisphere.

It is not our interest or our security but theirs which is now today in the greater peril. It is for their sake as well as our own that we must show our will. The evidence is clear and the hour is late.

We and our Latin friends will have to face the fact that we cannot postpone any longer the real issue of survival of freedom in this hemisphere itself. On that issue, unlike perhaps some others, there can be no middle ground.

Together we must build a hemisphere where freedom can flourish and where any free nation under outside attack of any kind can be assured that all of our resources stand ready to respond to any request for assistance.

Third and finally, it is clearer than ever that we face a relentless struggle in every corner of the globe that goes far beyond the clash of armies or even nuclear armaments.

The armies are there and in large numbers. The nuclear armaments are there. But they serve primarily as the shield behind which subversion, infiltration and a host of other tactics steadily advance, picking off vulnerable areas, one by one, in situations which do not permit our own armed intervention.

Power is the hallmark of this offensive—power and discipline and defeat. The legitimate discontent of yearning people is exploited. The legitimate trappings of self-determination are employed, but once in power all talk of discontent is repressed. All self-determination disappears and the promise of a revolution of hope is betrayed, as in Cuba, into a reign of terror.

Those who, on instruction, staged automatic riots in the streets of free nations over the efforts of a small group of young Cubans to regain their freedom should recall the long roll-call of refugees who cannot now go back to Hungary, to North Korea, to North Vietnam, East Germany or to Poland, or to any of the other lands from which a steady stream of refugees poured forth in eloquent testimony to the cruel oppression now holding sway in their homeland.

We dare not fail to see the insidious nature of this new and deeper struggle. We dare not fail to grasp the new concept, the new tools, the new sense of urgency we will need to combat it, whether in Cuba or South Vietnam. And we dare not fail to realize that this struggle is taking place every day without fanfare in thousands of villages and markets day and night and in classrooms all over the globe.

The message of Cuba, of Laos, of the rising din of Communist voices in Asia and Latin America, these messages are all the same. The complacent, the self-indulgent, the soft societies, are about to be swept away with the debris of history. Only the strong, only the industrious, only the determined, only the courageous, only the visionary who determine the real nature of our struggle can possibly survive.

Traditional Outlook]

No greater task faces this country or this Administration, no other challenge is more deserving of our every effort and energy. Too long we have fixed our eyes on traditional military needs; on armies prepared to cross borders; on missiles poised for flight. Now it should be clear that this is no longer enough; that our security may be lost piece by piece, country by country, without the firing of a single missile or the crossing of a single border.

We intend to profit from this lesson. We intend to re-examine and reorient our forces of all kinds; our tactics and our institutions here in this community. We intend to intensify our efforts for a struggle in many ways more difficult than war, where disappointments will often accompany us.

For I am convinced that we in this country and in the free world possess the necessary resources and the skill and the added strength that comes from a belief in the freedom of man.

And I am equally convinced that history will record the fact that this bitter struggle reached its climax in the late Nineteen Fifties and the early Nineteen Sixties.

Let me then make clear as the President of the United States that I am determined upon our system's survival and success, regardless of the cost and regardless of the peril.

D. Text of Kennedy's Address Outlining
Cuban Missiles Situation

*WASHINGTON, Oct. 22 [1962] (AP)—Following is the pre-
pared text of President Kennedy's speech to the nation tonight:*[1]

Gᴏᴏᴅ ᴇᴠᴇɴɪɴɢ, ᴍʏ ꜰᴇʟʟᴏᴡ ᴄɪᴛɪᴢᴇɴs:
This Government, as promised, has maintained
the closest surveillance of the Soviet military build-up on the
island of Cuba.

Within the past week, unmistakable evidence has established
the fact that a series of offensive missile sites is now in preparation on that imprisoned island.

The purpose of these bases can be none other than to provide
a nuclear stike capability against the Western Hemisphere.

Upon receiving the first preliminary hard information of this
nature last Tuesday morning at 9 A.M. I directed that our surveillance be stepped up. And having now confirmed and completed our evaluation of the evidence and our decision on a
course of action, this Government feels obliged to report this
new crisis to you in full detail.

Two Types of Missile Sites]

The characteristics of these new missile sites indicate two distinct types of installations. Several of them include medium
range ballistic missiles, capable of carrying a nuclear warhead
for a distance of more than 1,000 nautical miles. Each of these
missiles, in short, is capable of striking Washington, D.C., the
Panama Canal, Cape Canaveral, Mexico City, or any other city
in the southeastern part of the United States, in Central America
or in the Caribbean area.

Additional sites not yet completed appear to be designed for
intermediate range ballistic missiles—capable of traveling more
than twice as far—and thus capable of striking most of the major
cities in the Western Hemisphere, ranging as far north as Hud-

1. From *The New York Times*, October 23, 1962.

son's Bay, Canada, and as far south as Lima, Peru. In addition, jet bombers, capable of carrying nuclear weapons, are now being uncrated and assembled on Cuba, while the necessary air bases are being prepared.

This urgent transformation of Cuba into an important strategic base—by the presence of these large, long-range and clearly offensive weapons of sudden mass destruction—constitutes an explicit threat to the peace and security of all the Americas, in flagrant and deliberate defiance of the Rio pact of 1947, the traditions of this nation and hemisphere, the joint resolution of the 87th Congress, the Charter of the United Nations, and my own public warnings to the Soviets on Sept. 4 and 13.

This action also contradicts the repeated assurances of Soviet spokesmen, both publicly and privately delivered, that the arms build-up in Cuba would retain its original defensive character, and that the Soviet Union had no need or desire to station strategic missiles on the territory of any other nation.

He Sees Advance Plan]

The size of this undertaking makes clear that it had been planned some months ago. Yet only last month, after I had made clear the distinction between any introduction of ground-to-ground missiles and the existence of defensive antiaircraft missiles, the Soviet Government publicly stated on Sept. 11 that "the armaments and military equipment sent to Cuba are designed exclusively for defensive purposes," that "there is no need for the Soviet Union to shift its weapons . . . for a retaliatory blow to any other country, for instance Cuba," and that "the Soviet Union has so powerful rockets to carry these nuclear warheads that there is no need to search for sites for them beyond the boundaries of the Soviet Union."

That statement was false.

Only last Thursday, as evidence of this rapid offensive build-up was already in my hand, Soviet Foreign Minister Gromyko told me in my office that he was instructed to make it clear once again, as he said his Government had already done, the Soviet assistance to Cuba "pursued solely the purpose of contributing to the defense capabilities of Cuba," that "training by Soviet specialists of Cuban nationals in handling defensive armaments was by no means offensive," and that "if it were otherwise, the Soviet Government would never become involved in rendering such assistance."

That statement also was false.

Neither the United States of America nor the world Community of nations can tolerate deliberate deception and offensive threats on the part of any nation, large or small.

We no longer live in a world where only the actual firing of weapons represents a sufficient challenge to a nation's security to constitute a maximum peril.

Nuclear weapons are so destructive, and ballistic missiles are so swift, that any substantially increased possibility of their use or any sudden change in their development may well be regarded as a definite threat to the peace.

For many years, both the Soviet Union and the United States —recognizing this fact—have deployed strategic nuclear weapons with great care, never upsetting the precarious status quo which ensured that these weapons would not be used in the absence of some vital challenge.

Our own strategic missiles have never been transferred to the territory of any other nation under a cloak of secrecy and deception; and our history—unlike that of the Soviets since World War II—demonstrates that we have no desire to dominate or conquer any other nation or impose our system upon its people.

Nevertheless, American citizens have become adjusted to living daily on the bull's eye of Soviet missiles located inside the U. S. S. R. or in submarines.

In that sense, missiles in Cuba add to an already clear and present danger—although, it should be noted, the nations of Latin America have never previously been subjected to a potential nuclear threat.

But this secret, swift and extraordinary build-up of Communist missiles—in an area well-known to have a special and historical relationship to the United States and the nations of the

Western Hemisphere, in violation of Soviet assurances, and in defiance of American and hemispheric policy—this sudden, clandestine decision to station strategic weapons for the first time outside of Soviet soil—is a deliberately provocative and unjustified change in the status quo which cannot be accepted by this country, if our courage and our commitments are ever to be trusted again by either friend or foe.

The 1930's taught us a clear lesson: Aggressive conduct, if allowed to grow unchecked and unchallenged, ultimately leads to war. This nation is opposed to war. We are also true to our word.

Our unswerving objective, therefore, must be to prevent the use of these missiles against this or any other country, and to secure their withdrawal or elimination from the Western Hemisphere.

Our policy has been one of patience and restraint, as befits a peaceful and powerful nation, which leads a worldwide alliance. We have been determined not to be diverted from our central concerns by mere irritants and fanatics.

He Outlines Steps]

But now further action is required—and it is under way; and these actions may only be the beginning. We will not prematurely or unnecessarily risk the costs of worldwide nuclear war in which even the fruits of victory would be ashes in our mouth —but neither will we shrink from that risk at any time it must be faced.

Acting, therefore, in the defense of our own security and that of the entire Western Hemisphere, and under the authority entrusted to me by the Constitution as endorsed by the resolution of the Congress, I have directed that the following initial steps be taken immediately:

First: To halt this offensive build-up, a strict quarantine on all offensive military equipment under shipment to Cuba is being initiated. All ships of any kind bound for Cuba, from whatever nation or port, will, if found to contain cargoes of offensive weapons, be turned back. This quarantine will be extended, if needed, to other types of cargo and carriers. We are not at this time, however, denying the necessities of life as the Soviet attempted to do in their Berlin blockade of 1948.

Second: I have directed the continued and increased surveillance of Cuba and its military build-up. The Foreign Ministers of the OAS in their communiqué of Oct. 6 rejected secrecy on such matters in this hemisphere. Should these offensive military preparations continue, thus increasing the threat to the hemisphere, further action will be justified. I have directed the armed forces to prepare for any eventualities; and I thrust that, in the interest of both the Cuban people and the Soviet technicians at these sites, the hazards to all concerned of continuing this threat will be recognized.

Third: It shall be the policy of this nation to regard any nuclear missile launched from Cuba against any nation in the Western Hemisphere as an attack by the Soviet Union on the United States requiring a full retaliatory response upon the Soviet Union.

Fourth: As a necessary military precaution, I have reinforced our base at Guantanamo, evacuated today the dependents of our personnel there and ordered additional military units to stand by on an alert basis.

Fifth: We are calling tonight for an immediate meeting of the organs of consultation under the Organization of American States, to consider this threat to hemispheric security and to invoke Articles 6 and 8 of the Rio treaty in support of all necessary action. The United Nations Charter allows for regional security arrangements—and the nations of this hemisphere decided long ago against the military presence of outside powers. Our other allies around the world have also been alerted.

Sixth: Under the Charter of the United Nations, we are asking tonight that an emergency meeting of the Security Council be convoked without delay to take action against this latest Soviet threat to world peace. Our resolution will call for the prompt dismantling and withdrawal of all offensive weapons in Cuba, under the supervision of UN observers, before the quarantine can be lifted.

Seventh and finally: I call upon Chairman Khrushchev to halt and eliminate this clandestine, reckless and provocative threat to world peace and to stable relations between our two nations. I call upon him further to abandon this course of world domination, and to join in an historic effort to end the perilous arms race and transform the history of man.

He has an opportunity now to move the world back from the abyss of destruction—by returning to his Government's own words that it had no need to station missiles outside its own territory, and withdrawing these weapons from Cuba—by refraining from any action which will widen or deepen the present crisis—and then by participating in a search for peaceful and permanent solutions.

This nation is prepared to present its case against this Soviet threat to peace, and our own proposals for a peaceful world, at any time and in any forum—in the O.A.S., in the United Nations, or in any other meeting that could be useful—without limiting our freedom of action.

We have in the past made strenuous efforts to limit the spread of nuclear weapons. We have proposed the elimination of all arms and military bases in a fair and effective disarmament treaty. We are prepared to discuss new proposals for the removal of tensions on both sides—including the possibilities of a genuinely independent Cuba, free to determine its own destiny. We have no wish to war with the Soviet Union—for we are a peaceful people who desire to live in peace with all other peoples.

Difficult with Intimidation]

But it is difficult to settle or even discuss these problems in an atmosphere of intimidation. That is why this latest Soviet threat —or any other threat which is made either independently or in response to our actions this week—must and will be met with determination. Any hostile move anywhere in the world against the safety of freedom of peoples to whom we are committed— including in particular the brave people of West Berlin—will be met by whatever action is needed.

Finally, I want to say a few words to the captive people of Cuba, to whom this speech is being directly carried by special radio facilities.

I speak to you as a friend, as one who knows of your deep attachment to your fatherlands, as one who shares your aspirations for liberty and justice for all. And I have watched with sorrow how your nationalist revolution was betrayed—and how your fatherland fell under foreign domination.

Now your leaders are no longer Cuban leaders inspired by Cuban ideals. They are puppets and agents of an international conspiracy which has turned Cuba against your friends and neighbors in the Americas—and turned it into the first Latin-American country to become a target for nuclear war—the first Latin-American country to have these weapons on its soil.

These new weapons are not in your interest. They can only undermine it. But this country has no wish to cause you to suffer or to impose any system upon you. We know your lives and land are being used as pawns by those who deny you freedom.

Many times in the past, the Cuban people have risen to throw out tyrants who destroyed their liberty, and I have no doubt that most Cubans today look forward to the time when they will be truly free—free from foreign domination. Free to choose their own leaders. Free to select their own system. Free to own their own land. Free to speak and write and worship without fear or degradation. And then shall Cuba be welcomed back to the society of free nations and to the associations of this hemisphere.

My fellow citizens: Let no one doubt that this is a difficult and dangerous effort on which we have set out. No one can foresee precisely what course it will take or what costs or casualties will be incurred. Many months of sacrifice and self-discipline lie ahead—months in which both our will and our patience will be tested—months in which many threats and denunciations will keep us aware of our danger. But the greatest danger of all would be to do nothing.

The path we have chosen for the present is full of hazards, as all paths are—but it is the one most consistent with our character and courage as a nation and our commitments around the world. The cost of freedom is always high—but Americans have always paid it. And one path we shall never choose is the path of surrender or submission.

Our goal is not the victory of might but the vindication of

right—not peace at the expense of freedom, but both peace and freedom, here in this hemisphere, and, we hope, around the world. God willing, that goal will be achieved.

E. Stevenson Address]

October 23, 1962[1]]

I HAVE ASKED FOR AN EMERGENCY MEETING OF THE Security Council to bring to your attention a grave threat to the Western Hemisphere and to the peace of the world.

Last night, the President of the United States reported the recent alarming military developments in Cuba.

The President announced the initiation of a strict quarantine on all offensive military weapons under shipment to Cuba. He did so because, in the view of my Government, the recent developments in Cuba—the importation of teh cold war into the heart of the Americas—constitute a threat to the peace of this hemisphere, and, indeed, to the peace of the world.

Seventeen years ago the representatives of fifty-one nations gathered in San Francisco to adopt the Charter of the United Nations.

Like many peoples, we welcomed the world of the Charter, for our society is based on principles of choice and consent.

We believe the principles of an open society in the world order survive and flourish in the competitions of peace. We believe that freedom and diversity are the best climate for human creativity and social progress. We reject all fatalistic philosophies of history and all theories of political and social predestination.

We doubt whether any nation has so absolute a grip on absolute truth that it is entitled to impose its idea of what is right on others. And we know that a world community of independent nations accepting a common frame of international order offers the best safeguard for the safety of our shores and the security of our people. Our commitment to the world of the Charter ex-

1. From *The New York Times,* October 24, 1962.

presses both our deepest philosophical traditions and the most realistic interpretation of our national interest.

Had we any other vision of the world, our opportunities for self-aggrandizement immediately after the war were unparalleled. In 1945 we were incomparably the greatest military power in the world.

Instead, our commitment, then as now, was to the world of the Charter—the creation of a community of freely cooperating independent states bound together by the United Nations. In the service of this commitment, and without waiting for the peace treaties, we dismantled the mightiest military force we had ever assembled.

History has not seen, I believe, a more complete and comprehensive demonstration of a great nation's hope for peace and amity.

I have often wondered what the world would be like today if the situation at the end of the war had been reversed—if the United States had been ravaged and shattered by war, and if the Soviet Union had emerged intact in exclusive possession of the atomic bomb and overwhelming military and economic might. Would it have followed the same path and devoted itself to realizing the world of the Charter?

To ask this question suggests the central paradox of the United Nations.

Has the Soviet Union ever really joined the United Nations? Or does its philosophy of history and its conception of the future run counter to the pluralistic concept of the Charter?

Against the idea of diversity, Communism asserts the idea of uniformity; against freedom, inevitability; against choice, compulsion; against democracy, dogma; against independence, ideology; against tolerance, conformity. Its faith is that the iron laws of history will require every nation to traverse the same predestined path to the same predestined conclusion. Given this faith in a monolith world, the very existence of diversity is a threat to the Communist future.

Soviet 'War' Against U.N.]

The ink was hardly dry on the Charter before Moscow began its war against the world of the United Nations. The very first meeting of the Security Council—and I was there—was called to hear a complaint by Iran that Soviet troops had failed to withdraw from the northern part of that country on the date on which they had agreed to leave.

This was only the beginning. In one event after another, on one stage after another—the rejection in the United Nations of the American plan for the internationalization of atomic energy, the rejection of the Marshall Plan, the blockade of Berlin and the invasion of South Korea—the Soviet Union assailed political independence, resisted the world of the Charter and tried to impose its design of a Communist future.

The record is clear: treaties, agreements, pledges and the morals of international relations were never an obstacle to the Soviet Union under Stalin. No one has said so more eloquently than Chairman Khrushchev.

With the death of Stalin in 1953, the world had a resurgence of hope. No one can question that Chairman Khrushchev has altered many things in the Soviet Union.

But there is one thing he has not altered—and that is the basic drive to abolish the world of the Charter, to destroy the hope of a pluralistic world order. He has not altered the basic drive to fulfill the prophecies of Marx and Lenin and make all the world Communist. And he has demonstrated his singleness of purpose in a succession of aggressive acts—the suppression of the East German uprisings in 1953 and the Hungarian revolution in 1956, in the series of manufactured crises and truculent demands that the allies get out of West Berlin, in the resumption of nuclear testing, in the explosion—defying a resolution of the General Assembly—of a 50-megaton bomb, in the continued stimulation of guerrilla and subversive warfare all over the globe.

U.S. Aims Explained]

Our response to the remorseless Soviet expansionism has taken many forms.

We have sought loyally to support the United Nations, to be faithful to the world of the Charter and to build an operating system that acts, and does not talk, for peace.

We have never refused to negotiate.

We have worked for general and complete disarmament under international supervision. We have tried earnestly to reach an agreement to end all nuclear testing.

We have assisted nations, both allied and unaligned, who have shown a will to maintain their national independence.

Together with our allies, we have installed certain bases overseas as a prudent precaution in response to the clear and persistent Soviet threats. The North Atlantic Treaty Organization without concealment or deceit placed intermediate-range ballistic missiles in the NATO area. The warheads of these missiles remain in the custody of the United States, and the decision for their use rests in the hands of the President of the United States of America in association with the governments involved.

I regret that people here at the United Nations seem to believe that the cold war is a private struggle between two great super-powers. It isn't a private struggle; it is a world civil war—a contest between the pluralistic world and the monolithic world— a contest between the world of the Charter and the world of Communist conformity. Every nation that is now independent and wants to remain independent is involved, whether they know it or not.

The foremost objection of the states of the Americas to the Castro regime is not because it is revolutionary, not because it is socialistic, not because it is dictatorial, not even because Dr. Castro has perverted a noble revolution in the interests of a squalid totalitarianism. It is because he has aided and abetted an invasion of this hemisphere—and an invasion at just the time when the hemisphere is making a new and unprecedented effort for economic progress and social reform.

The crucial fact is that Cuba has given the Soviet Union a bridgehead and staging area in this hemisphere—that it has invited an extra-continental, anti-democratic and expansionist power into the bosom of the American family—that it has made itself an accomplice in the Communist enterprise of world domination.

If Cuba has withdrawn from the American family of nations, it has been Dr. Castro's own act. If the present Cuban Government has turned its back on its own history, tradition, religion and culture, if it has chosen to cast its lot with the Communist empire, it must accept the consequences of its decision.

We now know that the Soviet Union, not content with Dr. Castro's oath of fealty, not content with the destruction of Cuban independence, not content with the extension of Soviet power into the Western Hemisphere, not content with a challenge to the inter-American system and the United Nations Charter, has decided to transform Cuba into a base for Communist aggression, into a base for putting all of the Americas under the nuclear gun and thereby intensify the Soviet diplomacy of blackmail in every part of the world.

If the United States and the other nations of the Western Hemisphere should accept this basic disturbance of the world's structure of power, we would invite a new surge of Communist aggression at every point along the frontier which divides the Communist world from the democratic world. If we do not stand firm here, our adversaries may think that we will stand firm nowhere—and we guarantee a heightening of the world civil war to new levels of intensity and danger.